CHILD CARE IN
BLACK AND WHITE

THE WORKING CLASS
IN AMERICAN HISTORY

Editorial Advisors
James R. Barrett
Alice Kessler-Harris
Nelson Lichtenstein
David Montgomery

CHILD CARE IN BLACK AND WHITE

Working Parents and the History of Orphanages

JESSIE B. RAMEY

UNIVERSITY OF ILLINOIS PRESS
Urbana, Chicago, and Springfield

Library of Congress Cataloging-in-Publication Data
Ramey, Jessie B.
Child care in black and white : working parents and the history
of orphanages / Jessie B. Ramey.
p. cm. — (The working class in American history)
Includes bibliographical references and index.
ISBN 978-0-252-03690-3 (hardback : alk. paper)
1. Orphanages—Pennsylvania—Pittsburgh—History.
2. Children—Institutional care—Pennsylvania—Pittsburgh—History.
3. Working poor—Pennsylvania—Pittsburgh—History.
4. Poor women—Pennsylvania—Pittsburgh—History.
5. Race discrimination—Pennsylvania—Pittsburgh—History.
6. Race relations—Pennsylvania—Pittsburgh—History. I. Title.
HV995.P6R36   2012
362.73'2—dc23   2011039810

For Caldwell and Ian.
In memory of Robert Ramey (1925–2009)
and Gertrude Geisler (1914–2009).

CONTENTS

LIST OF ILLUSTRATIONS

Figures

Tables

ACKNOWLEDGMENTS

In producing this study, I have accumulated many debts of gratitude and been reminded many times that writing history is a collaborative activity, no matter how many hours we spend alone with our computers. I wish to gratefully acknowledge Tera Hunter at Princeton University, and Steve Schlossman and Lisa Tetrault at Carnegie Mellon University, all scholars I admire and whose tremendous work has influenced my way of thinking. I am very grateful to Jean Ferguson Carr and the Women's Studies program at the University of Pittsburgh for the institutional support and affiliation as a Visiting Scholar during a crucial writing period. A New Faculty Fellows award from the American Council of Learned Societies, funded by The Andrew W. Mellon Foundation, assisted the final completion of the book.

Also at Carnegie Mellon I thank Caroline Ackerman, Jay Aronson, Paul Eiss, Kate Lynch, David Miller, Scott Sandage, Judith Schachter, John Soluri, and Joe Trotter. I especially thank Peter Stearns, now at George Mason University, for his inspiration early in my career and continuing encouragement. A number of other scholars have earned my everlasting appreciation for their engagement with this project: Kyle Ciani, Linda Gordon, Rob Hudson, Michael Katz, Alice Kessler-Harris, Nelson Lichtenstein, Kriste Lindenmeyer, and Lara Putnam. In addition, I extend my gratitude to Laurie Matheson and the staff at the University of Illinois Press.

Librarians are historians' favorite people, and this project could not have happened without the wonderful staff at Carnegie Mellon's Hunt Library as well as in the Pennsylvania Room at the Carnegie Library of Pittsburgh, and David Grinnell at the Library and Archives division of the Senator John Heinz History Center. I applaud the efforts of the board and staff at Three Rivers Youth, under the leadership of Executive Director Peggy Harris, for celebrating and preserving their own unique history. My enormous gratitude also goes to the board of directors and staff of the Mars Home for Youth, now under Executive Director Martin Harris, for the use of their invaluable collections. This project would not have been possible without their generosity in allowing me to occupy their boardroom for weeks at a time poring over documents, and in extending me full photocopier privileges.

A number of Carnegie Mellon colleagues have been special friends and mentors to me for two decades. The late, great Barbara Lazarus defined what it means to be a mentor and demonstrated an unfailing belief in my scholarly potential; working under her wing daily for eight years was the best education anyone could hope for. I have also been the lucky beneficiary of countless hours of warm guidance and insightful wisdom from Indira Nair and Stephanie Wallach, extraordinary women and role models all.

I thank Kate Chilton and Brian Robick, who read every word of the manuscript several times in its earliest drafts, and Becky Kluchin for her ongoing enthusiasm for this project and her cheerleading. A merry band of historians and friends has kept me laughing at our weekly STD (Salon of Thursday Dinners): Amy Crosson, Lara Putnam, John Soluri, Lisa Tetrault, John Zimmerman, and all the kids. Dear friends Victor Forberger and Stephanie Schauer helped during a critical week of editing. Fellow women's historians from Sarah Lawrence College have become an unbelievable source of sustaining friendship: Rihana Azam, Erin Gerber, Shelly Henderson, and Erica Poff. I also thank Priscilla Murolo and Lyde Sizer for assuring me that I could be both a mother and a scholar. I would not have been able to complete this journey without a host of incredible child care providers: Robin in New York, Martha ("Tata") in Pittsburgh, and all the amazing teachers and staff at the Carriage House Children's Center. A special thank you to terrific friend and Managing Director at the Carriage House, Sharon Amick.

I extend my biggest thanks of all to my family: Thank you for being there to celebrate the highs and console me during the lows. Most of all, thank you to my parents, Janis and Bob Ramey, for everything from child care and financial assistance to emergency electrical repairs and boundless love and support. I dedicate this work to the memories of my father, and of my grandmother, Gertrude Geisler, whose writing inspired me to take up history and led the way to this study. And to my children, Caldwell and Ian, who have grown up with stories of orphans and orphanages.

John Zimmerman deserves the final note of praise and gratitude. We've learned that there is no such thing as "balancing" family and work, but we've gotten pretty good at "juggling"; and the clown metaphor is probably more apt for our family, anyhow. Managing and enjoying this three-ring circus would not be possible without him.

CHILD CARE IN
BLACK AND WHITE

Constructing Orphans

> I don't know too much about [Mama's] early life except that her
> Mother . . . died in 1891 when Mama was five years old. I don't
> know why Grandpa . . . didn't keep the family together, but I
> suspect it was a matter of where he worked and people available
> to keep the children. . . . For a while they were all in a Methodist
> Orphanage on the North Side in Pittsburgh.
> —"Roberta Caldwell Snyder," in Gertrude Geisler's
>   unpublished book, "Getting to Know Grandma"

The idea for this book began with these words, written by my grandmother
about her own mother's childhood in an orphanage. In thinking about her
experience one day, it occurred to me that my great-grandmother was not
an orphan at all—her mother had died, but her father was living—and it
suddenly seemed strange to me that she and her siblings had been placed in
an institution for parentless children. But it turns out that the vast majority
of "orphans" in orphanages at the turn of the last century actually had one
or even two living parents, often struggling through a family and financial
crisis. Some historians have characterized the decision to institutionalize
children as a family survival strategy, which resonated with my great grandmother's story: the orphanage allowed her to stay together with her siblings
and eventually to be reunited with her father. But as I thought about this
story some more, it seemed to me that my great-great grandfather had been
using the orphanage as a form of child care. He had lost the mothering and
housekeeping labor his wife contributed to the family economy and was not
able to perform her work on top of his own wage-earning work.

This book reconceptualizes orphanages as child care, exploring the development of institutional child care from 1878 to 1929 through a comparison of the United Presbyterian Orphan's Home and the Home for Colored
Children. Founded in Pittsburgh by the same person, these "sister" agencies permit the first full-length comparative study of black and white child

care in the United States. I am particularly interested in the ways in which working families shaped the institutions through their use of them as child care: this study emphasizes the historical agency of parents and even the children themselves in that process. That is, it demonstrates the ways in which families were active participants in the history of institutional child care, making decisions and choices that affected the development of early social welfare. Working parents and their children continually negotiated and cooperated with orphanage managers, who also had to bargain with progressive reformers, staff members, and the broader community over the future of their organizations.

Indeed, these actors constantly negotiated over child care practice and policy, and the choices they made together ultimately rested on deeply held assumptions of gender, race, and class. For instance, who should be caring for children (mothers but not fathers?), which parents should perform wage labor and which were deserving of assistance (should white women work? should black women receive support?), would children work or go to school (should poor children attend nursery schools or high schools?), and what would they grow up to become (manual or skilled laborers? domestic workers or wives and mothers?). I argue that the development of institutional child care at the turn of the last century was premised upon and rife with gender, race, and class inequities. Further, I suggest these persistent ideologies had consequences for the evolution of social welfare and modern child care. Finally, this book raises questions about the role of child care itself in constructing and perpetuating these social inequalities.

In modern usage, the term "child care" brings to mind "day care," perhaps provided at centers where parents drop off their children each day while they are at work. But throughout this study, I use the term "child care" more broadly to mean assistance with the daily labor of caring for children; and specifically in the case of orphanages, parents' tactic of placing their children temporarily in institutions with the intention of retrieving them after a relatively short time. The comparison to modern day care is useful, however, as parents did not necessarily give up custody of their children and often maintained a degree of control over them while they were in the institutions. Some parents used orphanages interchangeably with day nurseries, a similar type of institutional care that developed at the same time but only operated during the day.[1] Yet, based on the number of institutions and comparative enrollment, working parents appear to have far preferred orphanage care to the day nurseries. In 1907, for instance, six thousand Pittsburgh children were in institutions compared to three thousand in day nurseries.[2] Indeed, while modern day care has multiple antecedents, orphanages arguably provided the most significant, and most highly utilized, precedent in the development of institutional child care.

Historians who have examined orphanages have typically focused on what the institutions reveal about class relations, largely overlooking their racial and gender dimensions. In the 1960s, historians began suggesting that middle-class charitable institutions were not strictly benevolent undertakings and that motivations of "social control" were at play: a conservative middle class built social institutions to control the teeming, urban working class and as insurance against revolution from below.[3] By the 1980s and '90s, the historiographic pendulum had swung again, with much of the social welfare literature preoccupied with countering the social control theory, or at least complicating it.[4] The orphanage literature followed suit.[5] As the century closed, most historians seemed to agree on a middle-of-the-road interpretation, acknowledging elements of both benevolence and social control on the part of the middle class but also stressing the agency of the working class in using institutions for their own purposes and shaping them to their own needs.[6]

In a parallel trend, historians began pushing back the timeline of social welfare in the United States, tracing the roots of 1930s New Deal and later policies to earlier efforts such as the mother's pension movement.[7] Women's historians in particular have demonstrated the critical role that women played in this development, with their focus on programs for mothers and children.[8] This historiography offered a key insight, illustrating the ways in which both gender and racial assumptions molded those programs and thus later social welfare policies as well. These historians argue that institution builders and progressive reformers did not challenge traditional gender roles—the primacy of motherhood for women and breadwinning for men—while creating programs that excluded many people of color from channels of support altogether.[9] This book builds on these observations, exposing the ways in which poor families used orphanages to meet their own child care needs, and through negotiation with the managers, shaped the institutional basis of the nascent welfare state.[10] Furthermore, it centers child care in the historiographic conversation about the long-term gender and racial implications of our social welfare system.

Child care itself has received scant attention from historians.[11] The literature has focused mainly on the day nursery, a substantially less popular child care option among poor families at the turn of the last century than the orphanage.[12] Meanwhile, the historiography of orphanages virtually ignores the African American experience, largely overlooking orphanages, built by either whites or blacks, intended for black children.[13] In addition, the issue of child care, both historically and in modern times, lies squarely at the intersection of gender and labor. Yet histories of labor often overlook the centrality of child care obligations in the lives of both women and men. Histories of family life, on the other hand, tend to focus on women's reproductive labor, failing to account for the child care responsibilities of fathers.[14]

Ironically, historians of child welfare have reinforced the idea that child care is solely a "women's issue," replicating the historical invisibility of fathers with child care responsibilities, by narrowly focusing on single women with children. Despite the large number of fathers, both white and black, using orphanages at the turn of the century, the historiography of child welfare has avoided serious attention to the care-giving responsibilities of men.[15] Furthermore, the scholarship on fatherhood is still in its infancy and has given almost no attention to working-class or African American fathers. This is not to suggest that a focus on women is misplaced, as they were indeed the primary child care providers, and even today they bear the disproportionate burden of child care responsibility. However, the historiographic construction and reconstruction of orphans as specifically fatherless children does more than merely overlook a group of men: it reproduces the assumption that child care is women's work.

This project mines new sources not previously available to scholars, through the privately held collections of the two orphanages at the center of the study. Both institutions—still extant and now serving troubled teens in Southwest Pennsylvania—preserved unusually comprehensive documents that reveal the intersection of families' child care needs with other central concerns we are more familiar with, such as wage labor and housing. I was the first scholar granted access to the archives of the Mars Home for Youth in Butler County, Pennsylvania (formerly the United Presbyterian Orphan's Home). Three Rivers Youth (formerly the Home for Colored Children) recently donated its records to the Historical Society of Western Pennsylvania, though the unprocessed collection remains closed to the public for the foreseeable future. The latter is a particularly significant collection, as there are so few extant records of similar institutions for African American children. The documents of these two institutions permit both rigorous quantitative and qualitative analysis, setting black and white child care for the first time in comparative context. They also provide new insight into the lives of working-class families struggling with the modernizing industrial economy and the ways in which marginalized populations used institutions for their own purposes.

Using original admissions and dismissal records, cross-referenced with notes kept by the managers, meeting minutes, and other sources, I created a relational database capturing over fifty variables for 1,597 children who lived at the two orphanages from 1878 to 1929. (See appendix A for a detailed discussion of the database and statistical methodology.) This kind of granular detail allowed me to recreate "case histories," tracing individuals over time, and in some instances, as they entered and left the institutions multiple times. The large, and unprecedented, size of this sample also yielded important statistical results, including a uniquely detailed portrait of working families and the specific ways in which they used the orphanages. For instance, multivariable analysis revealed the placement pattern of children in the orphanages by age, sex, and sibling cohort as well as by sex, race, and widowed status of the admitting parent. This quantitative investigation highlighted significant racial and gender differences in the way that poor families used the orphanages. Sources such as census records, social reformers' reports, and city directories support the statistical findings. In addition, the methodological insights of feminist and African American scholars have inspired my close reading of the evidence: looking for "gaps" and reading documents such as meeting minutes and personal correspondence "against the grain" expose the actions and voices of people often hidden because of their gender, race, or class.

Names and labels are powerful symbols, and the process of naming can itself be an exercise of power, an act of exposure. Throughout the study, I use the current cultural labels of "African American," "white," and "black" in my own analysis, recognizing that these are problematic constructions that only exist in relationship to each other. I have preserved other contemporary labels, such as "Negro" and "colored," when quoting primary sources. Likewise, I have maintained original spelling, grammar, and punctuation in all quotations, not only to avoid distracting correction marks, but also to preserve the speaker's "voice." Letting these historical actors speak for themselves, I reclaim many of these lost stories, especially those of the poor families who used the two orphanages to care for their children.

Yet these parents and children did not anticipate having the intimate details of their family lives ever made public, especially when they include sometimes painful or even confidential information such as desertion, unintended pregnancy, or adoption. Therefore, to protect anonymity, I have substituted names for all but a few of the orphanage clients, the only exceptions being Isabella Nelson Longmore and Nellie Grant Earley—both recognized and celebrated by the two institutions today in their founding stories and through named buildings and award programs—and James Caldwell, my own great-great grandfather, whose legacy and story I claim as part of my own. This project did not attempt to trace the lives of children after their stay in the orphanages, for reasons both legal and methodological: because of the sensitive nature of some of the records at one of the orphanages, including legally sealed adoption information, I agreed to keep identities confidential, which prevents any attempt to contact descendents. This type of genealogical digging also yields very scattered fruit, and while I frequently yearned to know "what happened to the children," a longitudinal study of orphans awaits future research. Instead, I am satisfied here to let the stories of orphanage families speak for themselves, narrating a tale of despair and hope: working parents struggled with the horrible reality of having to institutionalize their children, but ultimately, most succeeded in reuniting their families and brought their children home.

Turn-of-the-century Pittsburgh provides an ideal location for this study, as it embodied the intense, simultaneous processes of industrialization, urbanization, immigration, and migration that set the stage for child care crises in many families.[16] Historian Roy Lubove has suggested, "Pittsburgh is . . . a prime exhibit . . . illustrating the social and civic consequences" of these urban processes.[17] For instance, factories not only changed the nature of work and the workday, but also were dangerous places that killed and maimed, leaving families without a breadwinner. The crowding of workers in cities gave rise to tenement housing, abysmal sanitation, polluted water, and epidemics. And waves of immigration and migration dramatically increased the city's population, changing its racial and ethnic composition and isolating some families from extended networks of support. Pittsburgh's infamous reputation as "hell with the lid off"—a reference to the omnipresent smoke- and fire-belching factories—reflected both the city's typicality and distinctiveness: it possessed all the urban ills of a typical, industrial northern city, but in a concentration unlike most others. In choosing the city as the site of extensive investigation for the six-volume *Pittsburgh Survey*, turn-of-the-century social reformers recognized that it served as a veritable Petri dish for the problems they wished to address.[18] Indeed, many working families were just one mill accident or tuberculosis case away from a child care crisis.

The Steel City's preponderance of heavy industry created a somewhat unusual labor environment for women and children, which also had a direct impact on child care for struggling families. Because many factories hired only men, women and children could not find jobs as easily as in other cities.[19] While some poor families did depend on income from their children's labor, their options were curtailed. In fact, historian S. J. Kleinberg argues that in the late nineteenth century, mothers increasingly went out to work in place of their children as a family survival strategy. Concurrently, between

1880 and 1900, the percentage of six- to fourteen-year-olds attending school in Pittsburgh rose, including the children of widowed parents. These were the parents often thrust into financial crisis with the loss of a spouse who might have previously turned to their children's labor to supplement family income; but during this period, children's workforce participation went down, and Pittsburgh children stayed in school longer than in comparable urban centers.[20] The city's poor families turned less often to child labor, but the corresponding increase in maternal employment also created a child care crisis for many.

While Pittsburgh's economic base made it distinctive, its institutional child care response was fairly typical of other cities, both in terms of the number and type of institutions that were founded. The city may have actually been somewhat more generous to the poor than other towns, especially since elites could not promote wage labor as the sole solution to widows' financial troubles in an area with few jobs for women.[21] Yet, as in other cities at the time, poor parents could not count on direct assistance from government sources—mainly limited "outdoor relief" programs such as coal and food distribution—to sufficiently meet their needs, and turned instead to private charities. During the period of this study, at least fifty-two child-caring institutions operated in the city, excluding day nurseries, and most were founded by religious associations. This included a handful of reform schools and homes for children with special needs, or in the parlance of the day, institutions for "delinquent" and "defective" children. But the vast majority of homes served "dependent" children: those who had lost the protection and care of one or both parents. These homes mushroomed in the late nineteenth and early twentieth centuries, a crucial period of institution building that laid the groundwork for later development of social welfare policies.[22] Thus, both the turn-of-the-century period and the Pittsburgh location provide a highly relevant and representative setting for a study of child care.

Furthermore, Pittsburgh struggled in this period, like many other U.S. cities, to define the boundaries of public responsibility for children. It had one of the earlier juvenile courts in the country, founded in 1903 under state legislation intended to separate children from adult criminals. Yet the court heard an increasing number of dependency cases, and was sometimes criticized for acting as a poor relief agency when it directed children to institutions and foster placements. (In 1925, for instance, 44 percent of the cases heard before the Juvenile Court of Allegheny County, in which Pittsburgh resides, were for dependency and neglect.)[23] State law used the terms "dependent" and "delinquent" somewhat interchangeably, overlapping with definitions of "neglected" and "destitute" that reflected subjective assessments of parents' ability to take care of their children. Pennsylvania lawmakers increasingly grappled with clarifying these definitions, but also imposed purposefully broad categories that brought more children under the purview of the law.[24] Eventually, the legislature appointed a Children's Commission, which worked from 1923 to 1927, to compile laws relating to dependent children and recommend changes. While very few children in the two orphanages in this study arrived via the courts, and therefore most lacked the legal designation of "dependent," the institution managers maintained their own standards of dependency and rejected children they deemed delinquent or defective, or not destitute enough.

What's more, the orphanage managers applied the concept of dependency to parents as well as children, with key gender and racial implications. They assumed that women were naturally best suited to care for children and that men would be confined to a breadwinning role. The managers' adherence to traditional white, middle-class gender roles shored up the pillar of economic dependency for all white women, while refusing to exempt black women from the dual obligations of maternity and wage labor. Their ideas of economic dependency, intertwined with racial beliefs, became enshrined in later social welfare policy and had long-term repercussions on the development of U.S. child care. Perhaps most significantly, while other countries developed publicly funded child care in the twentieth century, the United States remained committed to the family wage ideal, with its embedded notion of women's economic dependency and men's participation in the workforce but not child care.

At the end of the nineteenth century, orphanage founders constructed the urban, industrial child care crisis as a problem of dependency. The crisis was very real for a great many families as the new wage economy wreaked havoc with their ability to care for their children. But the orphanage managers' "discovery" of the child care problem—their interpretation and response to it—was culturally constructed.[25] That is, these women reacted to emerging conditions in the city through the social lens of their time, with a historically specific understanding of labor and family relationships. They also responded in a specific historical moment, in the context of the great depression of the 1870s; in the midst of immigration, migration, urbanization, and industrialization; and influenced by religious trends such as the Social Gospel movement. Crucially, the managers' gender, racial, and class ideologies formed the basis of their construction of the child care crisis, having a powerful impact on the development of the two orphanages during their first half century.

Yet the orphanage managers were hardly alone. These women were constantly interacting with other groups—variously resisting, negotiating, cooperating, and collaborating—with working parents, children, progressive reformers, staff members, and the broader community. Although the managers generally maintained the balance of power, these deliberations shaped child care practice and policy, both within the two orphanages and across Pennsylvania. What's more, these groups often agreed on several key points at the foundation of institutional child care.

Together they constructed a turn-of-the-century child care crisis as a problem of dependent children, not working parents, of children deprived of male breadwinners, not mothers forced into wage labor nor struggling solo fathers. They constructed child care itself as charity, and not a right; as a private responsibility and not a public obligation; and they viewed orphanages as a temporary solution, not a permanent fix or fundamental social change. The managers, in particular, pitied the poor white women who had to take on wage work, yet they never exempted African American women from expectations of labor; they viewed black men as absent fathers; and they clung to a breadwinner model, even as evidence mounted that wages in the new industrial economy would often not support a family. We have inherited the consequences of this construction, which drew on the interdependent logic of gender, race, and class hierarchies. In turn, child care itself reinforced, and continues to reinforce, these social inequalities.

CHAPTER ONE

INSTITUTIONALIZING ORPHANS
The Founding and Managing Women

> In his essay on Self Reliance Emerson says, "An institution
> is the lengthened shadow of one man." If that be true the
> three institutions under the care of the United Presbyterian
> Women's Association are the lengthened shadow of Rev.
> James M. Fulton, D.D.
> —W. H. Vincent, "The United Presbyterian Women's Association
>   of North America, A Retrospect."

Nearly every historical account of the founding of the United Presbyterian Orphans Home begins by paying homage to Rev. James Fulton, the young pastor of the Fourth United Presbyterian Church of Allegheny. A dying widow appealed to Fulton to find homes for her five soon-to-be-orphaned children. Moved by their plight, Fulton called together the United Presbyterian women of Pittsburgh and Allegheny on October 9, 1878, launching the United Presbyterian Women's Association of North America (UPWANA), which immediately undertook the organization of an orphan's home. When Fulton died in 1896, the managers commissioned a portrait of the minister and hung it in the home. They prominently displayed the portrait in the orphanage and at anniversary celebrations, and the painting hangs today at the top of the grand staircase in the main building, welcoming visitors to the Mars Home for Youth.[1] In words and image, the organization consistently presented, and continues to present, Fulton as the "founding father" of both the women's association and its first project, the orphanage.

While Fulton was indeed a central figure in the founding of UPWANA and its United Presbyterian Orphan's Home (UPOH), he was by no means alone. Dozens of women attended that first association meeting and then set to work establishing the orphanage. The organization's official histories frequently reference the enormous efforts of these founding women, but they

Figure 1.1. The Rev. James M. Fulton near the time of his death in 1896 at the age of forty-six. *Source:* 18th Annual Report United Presbyterian Women's Association, UPWANA, MHY.

are invariably an anonymous bunch. By contrast, Fulton is almost always named and honored with a label, such as "The Man of Vision."[2] When he died in 1896, the UPWANA directors memorialized him, saying, "In his kind heart originated the thought of our United Presbyterian Women's Association," and he "inspired the women to do something" for orphaned children.[3]

Some evidence, however, suggests that the vision may not have been his alone. When founding manager Jessie White McNaugher died in 1907, her fellow managers looked up her record of service in order to write her obituary and discovered that "we had to go back to the conference she held with her pastor, Rev. J. M. Fulton, D.D. . . . when [he] was a member of her household. [T]he plans for . . . the work . . . were the product of their counsels."[4] Mother of nine children still at home in the late 1870s when Fulton was apparently living with her family, McNaugher certainly knew about the needs of children. As the woman who fomented plans for the orphanage in conversations with Fulton while he stayed in her own home, and as one of the four witnesses who appeared before state officials to sign the original charter, McNaugher might rightfully be considered a "founding mother" of UPOH. Indeed, if Fulton is the founding father, the orphanage has many founding mothers.

Similarly, founding stories often credit Rev. Fulton with inspiring another group of religious women, the Women's Christian Association (WCA), with starting the Home for Colored Children (HCC) in 1880. A newspaper reporter later summarized the tale, saying, "Rev. M. Fulton of the Fourth United Presbyterian Church, Northside, one dreary, rainy morning found a little Afro-American girl of 4 or 5 years of age wandering in the streets of Lower Allegheny." Fulton sought "admission, in vain, for this little outcast in the various institutions."[5] Yet it was the women of the WCA who took the girl in and ultimately launched the orphanage that would shelter her. What's more, Fulton's wife, Mary Fulton, became intimately involved with both the Home for Colored Children and the United Presbyterian Orphan's Home, serving on the board in both organizations. Later in the twentieth century, managers' use of historical memory in writing their founding stories served to dim the lights on women like Mary Fulton and Jessie White McNaugher.

Nevertheless, it was women who played the crucial role in founding and managing these "sister" orphanages, both apparently spawned by Rev. Fulton. Significantly, the women's religious and social motivations shaped the institutions as they developed during their first fifty years. Similarly, the managers' traditional gender ideology and understanding of dependency placed them within the volunteer tradition of nineteenth-century maternalism and also deeply influenced the ways in which they structured their organizations. Yet, these women also formed surprisingly early, if somewhat tentative, experiments in cross-class and interracial cooperation through their managing boards.

"My visits to the Home were numerous": A Demographic Profile of the Founding Managers

The HCC and UPOH managers are critical to understanding how the two institutions functioned and developed over their first half century. Because the women tended to serve lengthy terms on the boards—some for decades—and brought in similar colleagues to join them when seats opened, board composition changed very little over these years. The women who served as managers in the 1920s looked remarkably similar to the women who had founded the institutions fifty years earlier. Their management style—hands-on, labor intensive—also changed very little during this period. Like many women in the tradition of nineteenth-century benevolence, these managers were a hard-working, committed lot who typically dedicated a large portion of their adult lives to volunteering.[6] After a particularly busy month, one HCC board manager noted, "During the month my visits to the Home were numerous, on an average once every day, sometimes spending the day."[7] The orphanages demanded an enormous amount of attention that approximated full-time work for at least a few of the women: they were intimately involved in nearly every facet of the homes, from major financial planning and construction projects, down to deciding what kind of butter the children would eat and whether it would be spread on the bread for them or not.[8]

A song from the 1890s about life in UPOH reveals the role of the managing women in the day-to-day life of the orphanage as well as their view of their own work. Written from the children's supposed vantage point, one stanza humorously states, "Anxious Managers drop in merely to inquire / What in the world are we doing, we use too much fire!" The song pokes fun at the "anxious managers" who seem to do nothing but worry about the cost of running the orphanage. One can imagine the managers chuckling in recognition as the children would sing, "Gas bills are enormous, meat bills make them groan," but then nodding approvingly to the final verse, "Eighty little orphans on the road to fame / If they fail to reach it, who would be to blame? / Not the managers surely, for all the world you roam / You'll never find another like the U. P. Orphan's Home."[9] The song's tongue-in-cheek humor implies that the managers did spend considerable time worrying about institutional finances, but that they did more than merely "drop in to inquire" about things. Indeed, the managers receive the final credit for setting eighty children "on the road to fame," and the song suggests that they could not be blamed if the children failed, as they had established a world-class orphanage. From the managers' perspective, as revealed in the song, they had worked hard and done everything possible for the "little orphans."

Each managing board met at least monthly, sometimes more often when needed, and every member served on multiple committees. For instance, the admissions committee (called by any number of names over time at the organizations) was a powerful group that met with families, investigated their home situations, interviewed neighbors and clergy, collected the necessary application materials, and made recommendations to the full board for acceptance or rejection. In a given month, this committee typically handled dozens of applications and sometimes also acted as the placing committee, reviewing applications from potential foster families and investigating those homes as well. The managers also took turns being on the visiting committee, which supervised the daily operation of the orphanages. These women generally visited once or twice a week, though sometimes every day, and stayed anywhere from a few hours to the full day, taking inventory of supplies, handling disciplinary issues with the children and conflicts with the staff, prioritizing maintenance needs, supervising the kitchen, and sewing an endless stream of clothing. Through these two committees, and others, the managers wielded a great deal of authority, which, while not uncontested, allowed them to craft institutional policy and practice.

Founded by largely white middle-class and elite women, the HCC and UPOH managing boards also contained a somewhat surprising element of diversity. Both had a sizable minority of working-class members (18 percent and 27 percent, respectively), and the HCC included several African American women from its inception.[10] (See appendix B for complete biographical comparison of the two boards.) Though the boards remained largely white and middle and upper class, they represent early, if clearly hesitant, efforts at cross-class and interracial cooperation. To be sure, this relationship was lopsided, and the more numerous middle-class and elite women of the boards maintained the balance of power. Yet, the working-class and African American members were more than mere tokens, as they actively participated in board meetings, fund raising, and committee duties: their voices were loud and clear at the institutions, though generally in concert with the other women of the board. The presence of black and working-class women adds new texture to the historiography of child welfare, which has mainly portrayed institutions such as orphanages as one part genuine benevolence toward the poor and one part instrument of social control. The most recent orphanage scholarship has come to agreement somewhere in the middle: managers wanted to both help and control, lift up and reform, their poor clients.[11] Indeed, these appear to be the motives of both orphanage boards, including their African American and working-class members.

Even with their limited diversity, the HCC and UPOH boards shared many of the same demographic characteristics, permitting a composite portrait of the early managers to emerge. Eighty percent of the women were married, with the remaining 20 percent either widowed or single. Most were in their thirties and forties, with a median age of forty, and the majority had children still living at home, ranging in age from infancy through late twenties. Two-thirds of the UPOH and just over half of the HCC managers had live-in servants, no doubt assisting in the care of children and household duties, making their volunteer work possible. All were Protestant, and most of the managers at each orphanage were born in Pennsylvania or a handful of other northern states. With many of the managers serving for decades, this composite portrait sustained well into the twentieth century.

Figure 1.2. A typical orphanage manager, Agnes K. Duff served on the UPOH
board for over twenty years and was at
various times Vice President, Recording
Secretary, and the Chair of the Receiving
Committee. *Source:* 35th Annual Report
United Presbyterian Women's Association, UPWANA, MHY.

Both boards were largely middle class, though UPOH had more elites
with nearly half the women married to entrepreneurs, such as merchants,
dealers, and manufacturers. While fiscally upper class, these women tended
to come from the margins of the city's elite: very few, for instance, appear in
the social registers of the time. However, these elite women did bring social
connections to the boards of both orphanages, allowing each to quickly start
crucial endowments to help the institutions weather difficult financial times.
They also performed the regular, time-consuming, and sometimes labor-
intensive work of board management: an almost endless cycle of attending
meetings, serving on committees, hiring and supervising staff, working in
the orphanages, sewing, meeting with poor families, and raising money.
Substantially fewer of the HCC women came from entrepreneurial homes,
but a fifth were married to professionals such as salesmen, teachers, and
insurance agents. Both the HCC and UPOH boards boasted a significant
minority of minister's wives, roughly a fifth of the members.

Many of the women had adult children living at home who were working
in professions indicative of the family's middle-class status, such as clerks
in stores and railroad offices.[12] The employment of live-in domestic help by
well over half of the members of both boards serves as another marker of the
managers' largely middle- and elite-class status. A few of the working-class

managers also employed domestics, though live-in help was largely enjoyed by the middle-class and elite women of the boards. Domestic work such as cleaning, cooking, and washing was labor intensive and time consuming, and even working-class women often hired help as soon as family finances permitted, though their employees were generally part time (and thus far less likely to be living in their employers' homes where they would have appeared on the census).

Perhaps not surprisingly, those women hailing from the working class belonged to the upper echelons of that class, suggested by their husbands' (or fathers') employment in largely skilled labor. Over a quarter of the UPOH managers and 14 percent of the HCC managers were living in homes where the head-of-household performed skilled labor: these men were carpenters, coopers, and tinsmiths. Where the occupation of husbands and fathers provides a useful benchmark of "class" for the white women of the boards, severely curtailed employment opportunities for African Americans in this period means that "status" is often a more useful description of socioeconomic relationships.[13] Two of the three original African American members of the HCC board were married to men with relatively high-status occupations in the black community: a headwaiter and a porter.[14] Thus, while the boards included substantial minorities of working-class members, and in the case of the HCC, a smattering of African Americans, these women were not poor and did not necessarily reflect wholly the interests of the poor families the orphanages served. At best, the boards represent hesitant and incomplete cross-class and racial coalitions.

With many of the founding managers serving lengthy terms on the boards, turnover was slow and the boards remained quite consistent for their first half century. In addition, when openings did appear, the women frequently brought in their daughters and church colleagues—who also often happened to be neighbors—to join them in the their work. For instance, in this fifty-year period, at least fifteen mother–daughter pairs worked on the HCC board, and twenty-four pairs at UPOH. Where historian Elizabeth Rose found that some young women in Philadelphia treated their board service at day nurseries as a social obligation, shoring up their status as debutantes and lacking a true desire for the work, this did not appear to be the case at either the HCC or UPOH, where second-generation board members regularly attended meetings and served on time-consuming committees for many years.[15] While both institutions drew managers from citywide networks of affiliated churches, meaning members came from miles around, each maintained a sizable core of women from the heart of Allegheny City (later Pittsburgh's Northside). These trends provided continuity and stability for the boards, though it also prevented much expansion across class and racial lines. Not until the 1940s and '50s, under increasing demand from reformers and the black community, did the HCC board integrate more fully. By contrast, the UPOH board (now Mars Home for Youth) remains to this day remarkably similar to its origins, consisting entirely of women and with strong ties to the Presbyterian Church.

"The needs of the women and children appeal to us very strongly": Social and Religious Motivations

Religion and a commitment to help other women provided the essential common ground for these managers to work together.[16] They felt a keen connection to the struggling members of their own sex who arrived on their doorsteps in search of child care assistance. For instance, the UPOH managers noted that "as Women, the needs of the women and children appeal to us very strongly."[17] Religion also bound the women together. The managers all belonged to Protestant churches, though the HCC women were interdenominational while the UPOH women belonged solely to United Presbyterian congregations. Both boards, however, were formed in a similar fashion by recruiting members from a geographic range of churches, thus involving women from all over Pittsburgh and Allegheny. Both orphanages also operated under the auspices of separate Christian women's associations—UPOH under the United Presbyterian Women's Association (UPWANA) and the HCC under the Women's Christian Association (WCA). These associations served as umbrella organizations sponsoring a broad range of social service programs such as old age homes, maternity homes, and hospitals.[18]

By the end of the nineteenth century, Protestants involved in social reform increasingly subscribed to the ideology of the Social Gospel movement, which incorporated new insights from science and sociology, including Darwinian theory. Inspired by theologians such as Walter Rauschenbusch, the movement emphasized the interdependence of people at all levels of society and provided a religious rationale for tackling pressing social and political issues. Rauschenbusch was influenced by the writings of Congregationalist minister Charles Sheldon, who coined the phrase "What would Jesus do?" capturing the imperative to social action felt by many adherents. For evangelicals, their relationship with their god was not only personal but also communal, and mandated social activism.[19] A brief investigation of the two associations that founded the orphanages in this study reveals the ways in which the women's spiritual concerns were tightly woven with social concerns, and underscores the centrality of religion in women's reform work in this period.[20]

The older and more evangelical of the two associations, the WCA formed following an 1867 Christian convention in Pittsburgh hosted by the already established men's corollary group, the YMCA. Under the leadership of Mary Hogg Brunot, the women quickly raised $1,640 (worth $24,858 in 2009) and incorporated the following year, hoping "to rescue the depraved of their sex from vicious companionship and crime," and to "protect those not yet fallen from the dangers which surround the homeless and friendless."[21] In their constitution they explained that they were "actuated by desire to improve the moral, intellectual, and social condition of women and children in the city of Pittsburgh."[22] Concerned with the dire fate that could befall young, single women newly on their own looking for work in the industrial city, many of the WCA's programs addressed this population.[23] Their flagship effort, the Temporary Home for Destitute Women, responded to the plight of Civil War widows and young wage-seeking women then swelling the ranks of the urban poor. Remarkably, the WCA also founded an old age home, boarding house, industrial school, maternity home, depository, and employment bureau, all for women.[24] In addition, the association sponsored the Allegheny branch of the Women's Christian Temperance Union (WCTU), a national movement that generated enormous enthusiasm among those seeking to preserve more traditional gender roles within the family by restoring drunken husbands to productive breadwinning and reducing domestic violence.[25] In 1875, following another series of evangelistic meetings, the WCA founded the East Liberty YWCA in the east end of the city, which eventually split away, choosing to affiliate with the national association in 1906 and then merge with other local "Y" branches in 1925.[26] The WCA, meanwhile, remained independent from the local and national organizations, but might rightfully be considered the "mother" of Pittsburgh's YWCA movement as well as the Home for Colored Children, which it continued to support for decades.

In contrast to the WCA's interdenominational efforts, UPWANA drew its members solely from United Presbyterian churches and was committed to relief work more narrowly within the structure of the church. Though its programs were open to members of all faiths, it primarily served United Presbyterians and carefully noted even the distinction between United Presbyterians and other branches of the Presbyterian Church in its records. In 1880, this branch of Presbyterianism had only been in existence a little over twenty years, resulting from a consolidation of two major streams of the religion. Sometimes called the "split P's" for their long history of divisions and unions, the Presbyterian Church family tree in the late nineteenth century consisted of four main trunks and several additional branches. With its heavy concentration of Scottish and Scots Irish Presbyterians, Pittsburgh served as a significant hub of activity for several of these branches and continues to be the home of two different denominational seminaries. Collectively, Presbyterians controlled 40 percent of all religious establishments in Allegheny County in the latter half of the nineteenth century.[27]

Founded in October 1878 at the meeting called by Rev. Fulton, UPWANA initially focused on creating an orphanage as part of its mission to "improve the moral, intellectual and social condition of women and children"—the exact phrase used by the WCA to describe its work.[28] When the association decided in 1889 to open a separate hospital, at first on orphanage grounds and later expanded and moved to Wilkinsburg, just to the east of the city, it proposed it would be for "sick and disabled women and children."[29] Once it moved, the enlarged hospital did not carry out its original plan to restrict entry to women and children, though community demand for its obstetrical and gynecological services remained extremely high and a large part of its business. In 1892 UPWANA opened the last of its institutions, the Home for Aged People; all three are still in existence.[30]

Both the WCA and UPWANA emphasized religious practice in their orphanages, making prayer and Bible readings part of daily life for the children, and ensuring that foster homes contained "good Christian people." They also presented Bibles to children as they left the institutions, highlighting their belief that they were saving not just children's bodies, but their souls. UPWANA women viewed themselves as united in a national, even international movement aimed at "advanc[ing] the Kingdom of Christ."[31] The WCA, the more evangelical of the two, noted, "[A]bove all, the great aim of the Association is to win souls for Christ" and, "While charity and philanthropy enters largely into all our work, the salvation of immortal souls is the main object sought."[32]

But UPWANA was quite different from the WCA in that it relied heavily on a national network of donors, many of whom were relatively poor or working-class themselves. Ladies Aid Societies—church based groups that pooled resources and performed mission work—provided crucial support to UPWANA's three institutions.[33] Many of these societies were located in predominantly working-class towns and neighborhoods or rural areas, and they lacked deep financial resources. For instance, the society in Indianapolis, Indiana, sent UPOH a quilt, two comforters, nine small dolls, and twelve pincushions, explaining, "the offering is a small one, but we are a mission ourselves."[34] Similarly, women from the town of California, Michigan, sent several small articles and wrote, "Our society is small and some of [the members] are so poor that we had to get some things to make them a little comfortable this winter yet we decided to try and give what we could."[35] Many women gave in-kind donations of household items, especially hand-made goods resulting from their own labor, such as jams, canned produce, quilts, bedding, and clothes. As the Ladies Missionary Society from Sago, Ohio, explained, "Gifts of this kind which require time and *labor* more than *money* seem to suit our people better than to give all money."[36] The Beaver Falls (Beaver Co., Pennsylvania) Ladies Aid Society wrote, "We do not have much money but we make domestic articles etc. and would be glad to have our ladies interested and help what we could."[37] These Ladies Aid Societies allowed women to perform charitable work in a communal setting, participating in collaborative efforts such as piecing quilts at their regular meetings, which also served an important social function.[38]

While UPWANA, like the WCA, remained a largely white, middle-class and elite association, these working-class and rural societies were integral to its success. The association viewed these donors as partners in the work, reflecting another aspect of cross-class cooperation. The Ladies Aid Societies also turned a local effort into a national movement and provided their individual members with a sense of connection to a larger project. While the WCA was initially connected to national, and even international, efforts, it largely represented the work of local women acting within the city. The WCA of Pittsburgh and Allegheny had been closely affiliated with the International Conference, hosting the third meeting of that national organization in 1875, the first time it entertained foreign chapters and adopted the "International" name. But its fundraising was local, and by the turn of the century it had decided to isolate itself from the national "Y" movement entirely, as the national affiliates merged and enforced more of a uniform "brand."[39] The WCA's subsidiary orphanage, the HCC, did not even attempt to solicit individual donations, let alone from working-class donors, until the 1920s when it came under increasing pressure from progressive reformers to reach out to the black community.[40] Overall, however, the two associations were quite similar in their commitment to women and children and religiously based social action.

"Especially is woman fitted for and needed in this work": The Managers' Gender Ideology

The orphanage managers were particularly concerned with women and children because of their subordinate status as dependents. The notion of dependency itself underwent change in the industrial era, fracturing into three distinct components—social, political, and economic—with both gender and racial dimensions.[41] Where white men's wage labor increasingly came to define independence, liberating them from social and political subordination to other white men, the state of dependency was largely reserved for white women and people of color. As the socio-legal tradition of *coverture* remained largely in place, with women subject to male heads of households (literally "covered" by their authority), social and political dependency was both feminized and stigmatized. These forms of dependency were similarly racialized, deemed suitable for nonwhite men as well as all women. As women's social and political dependency took on a new meaning of deviance and shame, many middle-class women began to challenge its various manifestations: they agitated for suffrage, as well as divorce, property, and custody rights.[42] Yet the orphanage managers clung to the tenet of women's economic dependency, especially for white women with children. At the same time, the managers were reluctant to view African American women as economic dependents, which would have required their withdrawal from wage labor.

The managers' preoccupation with economic dependency formed the basis for the literal construction of orphanages as well as their rhetorical construction of the very notion of "orphans." They empathized with women, especially those left without the protection and provision of husbands and fathers. Even today, the common linguistic pairing of "widows and orphans" reflects their mutual dependency on the absent husband/father, while excluding the possibility of widowers with children. Rhetorically, to become a true—or "full"—orphan, reliant on the state or private institutions for help, the managers suggested a child needed to lose his or her father. The United Presbyterian Orphan's Home, for example, refused to admit children whose fathers were living but had abandoned them, saying, "As a rule we try to avoid such cases, as they are not orphans."[43] Although the managers gave great sympathy to the half-orphaned children of widowed women, often calling them simply "orphans," they would not extend that "orphan" status to children whose fathers were still living and, they felt, should be providing for them. Similarly, while the Home for Colored Children served a sizable proportion of children from families with both parents living, they spoke of their clientele as primarily without fathers. In looking back over two decades of their work, they noted, "Surely our God has been a father to these fatherless and destitute little ones."[44] This rhetorical construction of orphans as specifically fatherless children, while not literally true, emphasized their dependency and thus their sympathetic plight.

The managers' focus on dependency reflected a larger, national conversation that used gender to construct the orphan problem. This was quite evident at the influential 1909 White House Conference on the Care of Dependent

Children, convened by President Theodore Roosevelt. The conference, which had a far-reaching impact on child welfare in the country, concluded, "Children of worthy parents or deserving mothers should, as a rule, be kept with their parents at home."[45] Attendees, including two Pittsburgh delegates, considered how to keep children in the homes of poor parents "suffering from temporary misfortune, and . . . widows of worthy character and reasonable efficiency."[46] In the discussions, men appeared only as part of intact families "suffering from temporary misfortune." A 1919 conference of child welfare leaders meeting under the new U.S. Children's Bureau echoed this language, concluding, "Child welfare begins, then, with the preservation of the home. It is better to prevent an orphan than to care for one."[47] When the authors of a 1930 Pittsburgh Child Welfare Study quoted this passage, they were not worried about literally preventing children from losing both of their parents, but rather, preventing them from becoming dependent—generally through the loss of a father's support—and thus "orphans" in need of assistance.

Significantly, this gendered construction of orphans also intersected with a racial construction. Where UPOH would not serve children from homes when both parents were living and fathers were supposed to be supporting their families, the HCC was relatively unconcerned with the status of black fathers. The HCC managers accepted a far greater proportion of children from homes where both the mother and father were living, and when solo mothers arrived at the institution with their children, they rarely showed much interest in whether the fathers were alive and could support their families. Some of these seemingly "absent" fathers were still in residence with their families, while others were living elsewhere for work, had abandoned their wives and children, or had died. This apparent indifference toward black fathers reflected racial hierarchies of dependency: while many white reformers tried to enforce paternal responsibilities on African American men in this period in an effort to reduce the dependency of black women and children, the HCC managers did not seem overly concerned with black men at all. Instead, they assumed black women would work and were not, therefore, economic dependents. Thus, an "orphan" was a rhetorical construction based on notions of both race and gender.

With the managers' unwillingness to challenge the notion of economic dependency (at least for white women), it would be incorrect to label them "feminists," despite their concern for the needs of women and children. The word "feminism" itself did not come into popular usage until the second decade of the twentieth century.[48] In fact, in 1915, UPOH flatly refused to permit a discussion of women's political independence at their annual fundraising event: the managers noted, "Mrs. E. B. Mahood had asked that we give her a few minutes of our time Donation Day to present the cause of suffrage," but they promptly turned her down.[49] This was an extremely unusual request, and the only time that either orphanage board even remotely discussed "women's rights" during a meeting, at least as recorded in their minutes.

A better descriptor of the orphanage managers is "maternalist," a term coined by late twentieth-century historians and never used by the women themselves.[50] An outgrowth of nineteenth-century domestic ideology, maternalism legitimized women's—particularly middle-class white women's—efforts outside the home, especially in the arena of child welfare, which they claimed as their unique purview.[51] A speaker at the 1879 WCA conference epitomized this view when she explained, "Especially is woman fitted for and needed in this work [of child welfare]. Her love for children, her hope, patience and perseverance, all are needed. The Lord has given us talent for such work; let us not bury it."[52] While maternalism itself underwent change in the early twentieth century as a younger generation adopted progressivism, Pittsburgh's orphanage managers retained the older, more traditional ideology of volunteerism well into the twentieth century.

Where the "progressive" maternalists supported suffrage as well as women's right to choose a career (though not motherhood at the same time), and embraced scientific study and professionalism for women as well as men, the HCC and UPOH managers remained rooted in a nineteenth-century set of assumptions about women's proper sphere and their economic dependence on men.[53] Philosophically, the orphanages were similar to organizations such as the National Congress of Mothers (which became the PTA). These groups helped achieve mothers' pensions in the 1910s but never supported suffrage and were never interested in having the state aid working men or wage-earning women.[54] Mother's pensions, which paid single women with children presumably to stay home with them, provided government support to only a fraction of those in need and rarely offered enough to prevent women from having to also work for wages. Yet, the programs proved a significant antecedent to later public funding of social welfare.[55]

In one extremely unusual case, the UPOH managers petitioned their umbrella association and received permission to pay "Mrs. Handel five dollars a week for two months, to enable her to care for her child at home." They assigned one of the managers "to personally give the money each week and see that it is properly applied."[56] This was effectively a mother's pension—though privately funded and not coordinated with the state—yet it illustrates the organization's support for such arrangements, at least for white women and under careful supervision. Indeed, most of the managers

at both the HCC and UPOH were likely conservative in their gender beliefs, envisioning their work with women and children not as radical social
reform but as corrective measures in a city where some men had lost their
ability (though not their responsibility) to care for their dependent wives
and offspring and where these dependents were sometimes deprived of their
"natural" protector.

Significantly, many African American women who built social welfare
institutions in this period were not maternalists. For instance, the National
Association of Colored Women, founded in 1896, used the rhetoric of motherhood to justify their work but was more likely to support women's combined wage labor and family, as well as economic independence for women,
and did not idealize motherhood in the same way as did white maternalists.[57] Furthermore, maternalism grew out of white, middle-class women's
sense of social and economic vulnerabilities that led to their assumption of
a shared maternal experience, a bond that supposedly united women. While
all women did share certain social, physical, and political inequalities, the
logic of nineteenth-century maternalism was a distinctly white, middle-class
construct. By contrast, the African American community constructed its
own definition of gender that permitted women to transcend race, class,
and sex barriers, emphasizing both women's individual achievement and
their duty to give back to the community. Historian Stephanie Shaw calls
this "socially responsible individualism," distinguished from the more indi-
vidualistic Protestant work ethic of the white majority.[58] The black women
of the HCC board, then, may not have completely agreed with their white
peers on the issue of women's economic dependency but found common
cause in helping poor families in need of child care.

Perhaps not surprising given the preponderance of white women on the
HCC board, both orphanages constructed a public image of themselves
within the bounds of traditional white middle-class gender norms that did
not appear to challenge women's social and political subordination. In their
founding stories, the HCC and UPOH rarely gave credit to their charter
members for the initial inspiration for their institutions, citing instead other
sources such as the Rev. James Fulton, or changes in state laws. These external, male voices granted authority to the women to act, allowing them to appear proper while extending their domestic expertise beyond the confines of
the private sphere.[59] The rhetoric of maternalism allowed women to expand
their "natural" role as mothers, to become "mothers of all children," both
figuratively, and in the case of orphanage work, quite literally.[60] In speaking
about their work, the managing women almost invariably employed the
rhetoric of docile femininity, passivity, and submission. For instance, when

HCC charter member Eda McKee died, her coworkers wrote, "By nature retiring, her service was rendered quietly, but with a constant concern that evidenced a heart full of sympathy."[61] McKee was only twenty-eight years old and had three children under the age of five when she helped to found the HCC. She held several officer positions during her fifty-one-year tenure on the board. She may have indeed possessed a "retiring" and "quiet" personality, but McKee's memorial also presented a portrait of feminine virtues quite typical of these death notices.

The memorials also reveal the immense pride the women took in their own work, performing skilled jobs that were among the earliest to be professionalized in the new century, including accounting and social work functions.[62] The UPOH managers embraced a degree of professionalism for women, working with a new, salaried social worker from their sister agency at Columbia Hospital, who increasingly helped families find their way to the orphanage. Yet their affirmation of a departed colleague's efficiency and effectiveness reflected their belief in their own role as competent volunteers, rather than the emerging role of trained professionals. For example, Kitty G. Steele served as UPWANA treasurer for thirty-three years, a position that expanded dramatically as the association grew beyond the orphanage to include the old age home and hospital, which as a recipient of state funds required detailed public accounting.

Herself orphaned as a young teen, Steele taught public school until she married in 1880 and soon had a child; but the following year she was "glad to accept" the manager position "as the death of her baby had deepened her interest in little children." When Steele died in 1917, her colleagues eulogized her, boasting, "It is safe to say that at least two millions of dollars have passed through her capable hands. Our auditor . . . says he never found the slightest error in her books and that they were models of neatness." They remembered with obvious delight, "The deputy auditors of Pennsylvania hardly knew what to expect when they learned that the treasurer of Columbia Hospital was a woman, but after their first audit several of them remarked that few treasurer's books of Pennsylvania hospitals equaled hers."[63] In a break from custom, the managers paid tribute with a portrait of Steele in their annual report and went so far as to pay for her cemetery plot and "Scotch granite tombstone." Steele's coworkers clearly held her in high regard, but just as clearly, took great pride in her accomplishments as a skilled woman, albeit in the older mold of maternalist volunteer.

Perhaps most importantly, the managers' success in building distinctly female-controlled spaces, even under the mantle of maternalism, led ultimately to women's participation in the public sphere.[64] Their institutions

Figure 1.3. Kitty J. Steele, UPOH manager and UP-WANA treasurer. *Source:* 39th Annual Report United Presbyterian Women's Association, UPWANA, MHY.

operated at the intersection of public and private, allowing the managers to extend their moral and vocational authority regarding women and children's issues into the masculine realm of real estate purchase, investment and finance, and business management.[65] The HCC, in particular, functioned as a quasi-public institution, petitioning for, and receiving, state monies nearly every year beginning in 1885.[66] Both organizations served as a form of early social welfare in an era when government invested only a trifling amount in outdoor relief programs and long before the state assumed greater responsibility as a safety net under the New Deal. Like the women who founded other nineteenth-century benevolent institutions, the managers created a system dominated by women, from the associational directors to the orphanage managing boards and staffs.

While both orphanages had male advisory boards, they limited the role of these men. They sought their advice on certain legal and fiscal matters and used the men's names for publicity and as a veil of authority, but largely remained autonomous from them. For example, in an annual report, UPOH praised their advisory board, "without whose valuable services we would be like a vessel without a pilot." They claimed to seek their guidance on "every undertaking or transaction calling for the expenditure or raising of large amounts of money, or business requiring judicious advice." Yet, meeting minutes reveal the women were far more the pilots of their own ship, calling

rather infrequently upon their advisory board, and often merely seeking affirmation of conclusions they had already reached. Even more telling, UPOH
boasted its advisory board consisted of "men in the public eye, pursuing
different kinds of business and professions, differing in creed."[67] Although
the managers could quite easily have recruited knowledgeable men from
among their United Presbyterian congregations, they proved to be quite
savvy at board development. They selected instead prominent men, such as
the vegetable and condiment king H. J. Heinz, reflecting their interest in the
men's social and economic position within the city—using it to bolster the
orphanage's reputation in the community—as much as any actual advice
the men might have to offer.

The HCC also tapped its male advisory board only on occasion and used
it defensively when needed. For instance, in responding to criticism from
the Pittsburgh Child Welfare Study, the HCC managers reassured the investigators, "All proposed investments of the Endowment Fund are passed
upon by our Advisory Board."[68] They also listed the men's names in larger
type than those of the female managers on their letterhead, emphasizing the
advisory board's figurative, if not literal, importance to the governance of
the organization. While the HCC board remained all female for its first fifty
years, by midcentury it started to accept men among its ranks (whereas the
UPOH board consists solely of women even today).[69]

The HCC's gradual inclusion of male managers signaled not a retreat
of the female managers or a concession of power to men as much as the
group's eventual willingness to racially integrate more fully. By 1954 at
least 40 percent of the board was African American, including leaders such
as Louis Mason Jr., who, following his work with the HCC, served as the
first black president of Pittsburgh City Council.[70] Prominent members of the
black community had taken a keen interest in the HCC for decades—Dr.
Henry M. Garrett worked with the home in the 1910s, and Revs. B. F. and
Maddie Glasco began their long association in the 1920s—but slow board
turnover, and quite probably reluctance on the part of some white managers,
meant the process of inclusion moved glacially.[71] The managers' resistance
to this change, however, likely reflected concern over losing a distinctive
female dominion as much as losing white control of the institution. The
HCC managers, white and black, ultimately recognized that granting more
voice to the black community meant accepting that community's chosen
representatives, both male and female. For the African American women of
the board, this was not necessarily a zero-sum choice between allegiances,
of sex versus race, but a more holistic approach that had long typified their
reform work, combining their gender and racial interests.[72]

Though perhaps unintentionally, the actions of both the UPOH and HCC managers challenged women's—at least white middle-class women's—political and social dependency. They built female-controlled spaces, engaged in the public realm, embraced women's professionalism, and some even moved away from the strict use of their married names. Yet they left intact the assumption of economic dependency for white women and expectations of wage labor for black women. And they continued to exclude men from child care altogether. This was evident, for instance, in UPOH's promotion of the family wage ideal, with husbands as sole breadwinners, despite mounting evidence that the new industrial economy required the compensated labor of women and children to keep many families afloat.[73] They were particularly displeased when men failed in their duties as providers, whether through abandonment of their families or, occasionally, refusal to work. For example, Roger Turn, a carpenter from Allegheny, placed his two- and five-year-old sons in UPOH six months after his wife died, agreeing to pay ten dollars per month for their board and clothing. He made his payments for ten months, and then stopped. Nearly a year and half later, the managers packed the boys up and sent them to their father, noting with annoyance, "Mr Turn's sister paid the amount he owed $195.00 although we objected to her doing it as he was an able bodied man and should have done it."[74] The managers' objection was not to being paid as much as Turn's refusal to fulfill his role as wage earner for his family.

The managers' support for the family wage ideal for their white clients, and the underlying rationale of women's economic dependency, was also evident in the training they provided the children. For instance, when the Poor Board or parents occasionally bound their children to the institutions (who could, in turn, indenture the children to private homes), the precipitating legal agreement dictated the type of training each boy or girl was to receive. In one typical case, a father bound his daughter to UPOH "for a period of 12 years, one month and 28 days," during which time the orphanage agreed to "teach and instruct, or cause to be taught and instructed, the [girl] in sewing, knitting, housewifery."[75] Boys, on the other hand, were generally to be trained in "some useful trade or occupation."[76] The managers treated similarly those children in their care who were paid boarders (who comprised the vast majority of residents). After moving the orphanage to the country in 1929, UPOH noted, "The older boys are allowed to help with the farm work, and the older girls with the work in the house so it is conducted as much like a real home as possible."[77] These references to the skills they would naturally learn at "home" evoked the gendered basis of the family wage ideal, where boys would grow into productive citizens and family providers and girls would become mothers and homemakers, dependent on their husbands.

Yet many poor white women were forced to combine wage work and maternity, a situation the managers viewed as an unfortunate and, they hoped, temporary necessity. The UPOH managers assisted their clients in need of work, reporting one year, "5 mothers have been helped to secure positions."[78] Their short-lived sister organization, the Allegheny Day Nursery, which shared many of the same managers, gave "a woman and child a permit to remain over night in the nursery room. . . . The woman secured work next day, through the efforts of two of the managers."[79] This group also "decided to open an employment office" to assist their beneficiaries in finding jobs.[80] In addition, both the HCC and UPOH hired many widowed mothers to work in the orphanages. However, through their charitable work, the UPOH managers aimed to correct a grim situation for individual families, not endorse a new social norm challenging the ideal of a family wage.

Similarly, the HCC managers tried to help African American families in need without challenging social norms: in this case, leaving untouched expectations of wage labor for black women. In her study of New York's Colored Orphan Asylum, historian Leslie Harris argues that the white managers filled a dire need for child care, yet as they made it possible for black women to continue serving as live-in maids, they "reinforced the idea that keeping black families intact was less important than fulfilling white middle-class families' needs for domestic labor."[81] The HCC managers, too, seemed to believe that it was likely their girls were going to work as adults, even through marriage and motherhood. In 1924 the WCA's daughter organization, the YWCA, conducted a study of girls in the city, with an entire chapter devoted to "The American Negro Girl in Pittsburgh," which concluded, "[T]he custom of continuing work after marriage is more predominant among the negroes than it is among the whites. . . . In Pittsburgh today we find a large group of married negro women working as well as bringing up families." Although the report acknowledged, "This presses upon their shoulders a double burden . . .," it suggested the remedy lay solely with African Americans themselves, who needed to pursue "proper and better educational preparedness."[82] The HCC managers never endorsed the family wage ideal for their clients, as reflected in their lack of concern about the status of fathers: whether resident or absent, living or dead, the managers did not presume that black fathers were the sole supporters of their families.

Thus, the orphanage managers reinforced the links between charity and child care, between child care and mothering, and between mothering and racial expectations of labor. Their gender ideology, intertwined with racial and class logic, formed the basis of their construction of the orphan problem as well as their institutional response to it.

⌘ ⌘ ⌘

Just as the founding managers constructed the child care crisis through their understanding of dependency, so too did later managers construct their own histories of the organizations. Written years later in the twentieth century, their founding stories effectively erased women's agency from the conception of the institutions. For example, while the HCC and UPOH remember the Reverend James M. Fulton as instrumental to the founding of both orphanages, his wife, Mary Shafer Fulton, was equally, if not more, involved in the two institutions. Her story provides an instructive counterpoint to her more celebrated husband and is representative of the women who founded and managed the orphanages. Mary served as vice president of the HCC and president of UPWANA during the time when that association was directly in charge of UPOH. Yet ironically, memory of Mary's service to both organizations has been nearly lost in the shadow of her husband: in fact, UPWANA has written her out of its history altogether. Whether due to simple error or some other more purposeful reason now lost in the mists of time, an official history of the organization prepared in 1938 skipped over Mary Fulton in its listing of presidents, and all histories written since appear to have used this incomplete information.[83] Like her "sister" managers at both institutions, then, Mary's legacy as a founding mother has faded next to the memory of Rev. James Fulton.

Yet in many ways, Mary Fulton's biography illustrates the traditional maternalism of nineteenth-century board membership that persisted well into the twentieth. Mary was born in Deer Creek, Pennsylvania, north of Pittsburgh where her father, the Reverend Alexander Geary Shafer, was pastor in the United Presbyterian Church. He wrote a friend two weeks after her birth announcing his "grand daughter," calling her "quite a good child," and complaining good-naturedly of the "streams of ladies of all sizes to see the Babe."[84] When Mary was seventeen, her father was struck and killed by lightning, and her mother moved with her six children to New Wilmington, Pennsylvania, near Westminster College, where she "operated a boardinghouse at her large home." The family papers suggest Mary graduated from the college along with the rest of her siblings, including her older brother Judge John Douglas Shafer, who studied briefly to become a minister but then switched to law when their father died. He went on to become President Judge of the Court of Common Pleas in Allegheny County and helped found the law school at what is now the University of Pittsburgh.

Their mother wanted another son, Archibald, to attend the seminary, but he "ran away and apprenticed himself to a plumber," while the youngest son, Alexander, became a physician who died treating yellow-fever victims in Mexico.[85] Like many of the other orphanage managers then, Mary came from a solidly middle-class, professional family with strong ties to religion and community service.

And like 20 percent of the women on both boards, Mary was married to a member of the clergy. She fell in love with the young, up-and-coming minister, James McFaddand Fulton, who already had an appointment to his own church in Allegheny City. When UPOH began in 1878, James was only twenty-nine and Mary twenty-seven. Two years later, their first son, Charles Shafer Fulton, was born, and by the time he was a year old, Mary was already serving as vice president at the Home for Colored Children. By 1882, she was president of UPWANA, and she held one if not both posts through the birth of a second son, Alexander, in 1884. Like Mary, at least two other managers maintained ties to both orphanages in this period: Elizabeth Campbell served on the HCC board and was president of UPWANA for several years, while Elizabeth Young Patterson also served on the UPWANA board and was a major benefactor of the HCC, selling her home on Greenwood Avenue to the orphanage in 1882 without interest and then donating another fifteen hundred dollars to the building fund.[86] But unlike most of her fellow managers, Mary died quite young, before she could provide the decades of service to the institutions that were quite common to her peers. By 1885 Mary was gone, leaving behind two young children: the Ladies Missionary Society in Harshaville, Beaver County wrote, "Mrs. Fulton will be missed in many places, which she seemed to be peculiarly qualified to fill" and assured that her "husband and children will need and will have the warmest sympathy of the church." They added, "What a comfort that tho God removes the workmen the work goes on."[87] Indeed, the work did go on, with women very much like Mary Fulton at the helm.

Through the 1920s, both the HCC and UPOH boards remained filled with women, who were largely white, middle-class, Protestant, and married with children still living at home. These women took tentative first steps toward cross-class and interracial cooperation, but resisted any deeper ties that would have threatened their dominance. Grounded firmly in traditional nineteenth-century maternalism, the managers' interdependent ideologies of gender, race, and class shaped the development of institutional child care during the orphanages' first fifty years.

CHAPTER TWO

RAISING ORPHANS
The Child Care Dilemma of Families in Crisis

> Dr. Fulton, the young pastor of the Fourth United Presbyterian
> Church of Allegheny, was appealed to by a dying mother to try
> to find Christian homes for her five fatherless children soon to
> be left without relatives to care for them or money to sustain
> them. Dr. Fulton caught the vision of the church providing care
> for its needy children and called together the women of the
> United Presbyterian Churches of Pittsburgh and Allegheny in the
> Fourth Church Allegheny to consider the matter.
> —W. H. Vincent, "The United Presbyterian Women's Association
>   of North America, A Retrospect."

Born in Ireland in 1836, the ill-fated Isabella Nelson was living in Allegheny, Pennsylvania, with her mother and sister when she met her future
husband, James Longmore. The Nelsons had little money, and Isabella
and her younger sister, Ellen, both worked as dressmakers to support their
mother, Catherine. In 1861, at the age of twenty-five, Isabella married James
and almost immediately became pregnant with their first son, who was
born the following year. The Longmores had four children—ages seven,
four, three, and an infant—when James died in 1869, leaving Isabella to
support her family by keeping a store, a common occupation for widows
who often could keep their children with them as they worked.[1] James
may also have left her a little nest egg, as she reported personal property
shortly after his death totaling $1,500 (worth $21,923 in 2007), possibly
reflecting the value of the merchandise in her store. Longmore's neighbors
were solidly working-class families: the men worked as carpenters, bridge
builders, railroad men, and police officers, while the women kept house.
Some of the older daughters worked, making dresses and boxes. In these
working-class neighborhoods it was not unusual for multiple families to
economize by living together, which may be why Longmore shared her

home with another woman, Lizzie Gardner, a forty-year-old Irish immigrant who kept house, and ten-year-old Susan Herren. Gardner may also have helped provide child care for Longmore's children, making it possible for her to work longer hours in the store.[2]

Regardless of whatever child care arrangements she had made previously, by the time she realized she was dying, just seven and half years after her husband, Longmore had no one to permanently care for her children, now aged fifteen, twelve, eleven, and eight. If her mother and sister were still alive, they were either unable or unwilling, or Longmore thought them unsuitable to take the children. Longmore also could not find willing or suitable friends and neighbors, and instead turned to the Rev. James Fulton for help. Fulton may have indeed helped Longmore locate "Christian homes" for the children, but there is no evidence they ever lived in the United Presbyterian Orphan's Home (UPOH).[3] In fact, Fulton did not even convene the women of the church to contemplate an orphanage until October of 1878, more than a year and a half after Longmore's death, and the institution did not accept its first children until the end of December that year, nearly two full years after the Longmore children became orphans. Yet, the Longmore story and name have become an integral part of UPOH's identity: the tale of the "dying mother" and her "fatherless children" is often repeated, a Bible reportedly belonging to Isabella Longmore is prominently displayed in the institution's board room, and the organization recently opened Longmore Academy, an on-site school for the troubled teens served today by the orphanage's descendent, the Mars Home for Youth.[4]

Although the Longmore children were likely never residents of the facility, this founding story resonates with larger truths about "orphaned" children and their families in the late nineteenth century. "Orphans" generally had at least one living parent and, while institutional rhetoric often constructed them as homeless waifs, most residents had active, involved parents who were integral to the very founding and functioning of the orphanages. It was Isabella Longmore's own plaintive cry for help that launched UPOH, and other parents' consistent demand for child care services that kept them in business. Yet parents sometimes withdrew their demand—as happened at UPOH's sister organization, the Allegheny Day Nursery—leaving those organizations that did not suit them and refusing to engage those that did not meet their needs. Parents at both UPOH and the Home for Colored Children (HCC) participated in the larger community dialogue about child care, complicating the construction of the child care crisis as a problem of dependent children without regard to the needs of their working parents.

Poor families' own demands helped shape the institutional landscape of child welfare in turn-of-the-century Pittsburgh, as they made choices based on religious preferences as well as location and reputation. Significantly, racial prejudice limited African American families' choices and led the black community to found its own child care institutions in this period. A demographic analysis of these families who chose orphanage care for their children reveals the often multiple, overlapping crises they faced—from the loss of a spouse to disrupted support networks and inadequate housing. As parents attempted to combine wage labor and child care responsibilities, they used orphanages as a strategy for family survival.

"Where they may be properly cared for": The Institutional Landscape of Pittsburgh Child Care

In 1878 when the United Presbyterian Orphans' Home opened, poor families had limited options if they needed institutional help with child care. For those who needed or preferred residential care, there were only eighteen institutions in the Pittsburgh region (including a few in adjacent counties) that would accept children, and most restricted admission on the basis of religion, age, gender, disability, or race, further narrowing the options.[5] Of course, most families facing some sort of crisis cobbled together care through relatives, friends, and neighbors, leaning on financial resources from religious associations, beneficiary societies, and the meager "outdoor" government relief programs that were available. In 1907, for instance, 9,269 children lived in families that received outdoor relief from the city or county (usually in the form of food, coal, or shoes), while 6,000 children lived in institutions.[6] Pittsburgh's public relief was relatively small, since elites preferred to keep their taxes low and to contribute to charity on their own terms, yet private organizations were generally not up to the task of dealing with the immensity of need and the unpredictable swings in the steel business.[7]

Many parents relied on schools to provide a few hours of supervision while they worked. Public schools were available for both white and black children as early as 1837 in the twin cities of Pittsburgh and Allegheny (which was annexed in 1907), though the schools were segregated until 1875 in Pittsburgh and 1880 in Allegheny.[8] Other families turned to day nurseries.[9] However, far more parents appear to have preferred orphanage care to day nurseries: one turn-of-the-century study, for instance, counted twice as many Pittsburgh children in institutions than day nurseries, and a 1929–30 study found only thirteen day nurseries operating in the city, serving a total of only 285 children.[10] In 1890 several UPOH managers founded the Allegheny Day Nursery, but they were forced to close it just two years later for lack of demand. They blamed competition from a neighboring day

Figure 2.1. Allegheny County Home (Almshouse) at Woodville. Original captions: *(top)* "These little boys played in this men's community room, ate with them, and slept in the open ward with paralytic and otherwise disabled men." *(bottom)* "With a toilet installed alongside the beds, this was used as both sleeping room and children's play-room." *Source:* Slingerland, *Child Welfare Work in Pennsylvania* (1915), p. 56.

nursery as well as the "the poor of the city" who needed to be "educat
know that we are a help to them."[11] While the number of day nurseri
Pittsburgh undoubtedly mushroomed around the turn of the century as
did nationally in this period, poor families continued to strongly favor
"help" they could receive at orphanages. In this way, parents' own choi
of institutions to care for their children helped to shape the very optic
that were available, creating demand for some services while shutteri
others with their tepid response.

Of those organizations that cared for children, publicly funded institu
tions were the fewest in number and probably least desirable, yet provide
essential services for the most desperate families. For a time, the state operated a Soldier's Orphan Home in Pittsburgh for the orphaned children of
Civil War soldiers. The cities of Allegheny and Pittsburgh also each had an
almshouse, as did Allegheny County, housing orphans, half-orphans, and
destitute parents with their children in large congregate settings. Reformers
lamented that these "poor houses" exposed young children to morally bank-
rupt adults, the sick and insane (see figure 2.1). Critics viewed the county
home at Woodville as a particularly wretched place, expressing concerns
about sanitary conditions, such as the proximity of toilets to beds, and worrying that children spent all their time in common areas, eating, sleeping,
and playing with "suspect" adults.

Families undoubtedly considered almshouses as a last resort, yet social
investigators' own photographs illustrate some of the very reasons poor
people may have chosen to use them: until the Home for Colored Children
opened in 1880, they were the only institutions that would accept African
American children; they cared for infants who were turned away from nearly
all privately managed facilities; they allowed parents to remain with their
children; and, compared to the overcrowded tenement conditions in many
neighborhoods, the almshouses at least had indoor plumbing and large
windows to let in light and air. In 1883 Pennsylvania passed its landmark
Children's Law, commonly known as the "Sixty-Day Law," as it limited the
stay in a public almshouse for "normal" children between the ages of two
and sixteen to sixty days.[12] Decades later, however, poorhouse directors
admitted they were still keeping children in these institutions much longer,
reflecting continuing demand for such assistance, and possibly, poor parents'
own preferences.[13]

Yet public almshouses accounted for only a small fraction of those families
seeking assistance. Far more parents and children received help through
private, largely religiously based institutions. For instance, by 1878 two
private maternity homes accepted unwed mothers and their babies, though

they did not provide continuing care for children born in their homes.[14] A small number of respectably widowed mothers could find housing assistance for themselves and their children through the Allegheny Widow's Home Association of Pittsburgh. At least one resident preferred to use orphanage care, however: Mary Morrison lived in the Widow's Home but went "out to work" as a general housekeeper to pay $1.25 a week for two years to board her seven-year-old daughter, Mattie, at UPOH.[15] Several organizations served "delinquent" or "defective" children, but "dependent" children accounted for the largest proportion of institutionalized children, and parents overwhelmingly chose orphanages for their care.[16] At the time of the HCC and UPOH's founding, nine orphanages operated in the Pittsburgh area: the Catholic church ran three, including the massive St. Paul's Orphan Asylum with a capacity of over a thousand children, and the Lutheran, Protestant Episcopal, and Reformed Church each maintained one.[17] A final three institutions were "nonsectarian," though generally Protestant, including the city's oldest orphanage, the Protestant Orphan Asylum (established 1832).[18]

Some orphanages had gender or racial restrictions, limiting families' options. In the Pittsburgh region, almost without exception, child welfare organizations served both boys and girls, though as time went on, a handful of institutions restricted admission to one sex or the other, generally focusing on older children and "delinquent," rather than "dependent," teens. Through the period of this study, six institutions in the Pittsburgh region opened to care solely for boys and five for girls. Race served as a far more restrictive barrier: at the time of the founding of the HCC, only the public almshouses would accept black children. Statewide, only two private orphanages, both in Philadelphia, served African American families.[19] By 1890 Pennsylvania had four dedicated black orphanages—among the highest number of any state in the nation—yet there were only twenty-seven in the entire country. In 1923 the Keystone State still had only eight African American orphanages.[20]

A few "white" orphanages that did not have specific racial restrictions occasionally accepted African American children, but the number was generally very small, and some that advertised an open policy may never have admitted a black child. For instance, while UPOH reported in 1915 to the Russell Sage Foundation for a study on child welfare agencies that it had no color restrictions, there is no evidence it ever accepted black children. In fact, two years earlier, UPWANA (UPOH's parent organization) received an inquiry on behalf of a widowed, United Presbyterian father, "asking if we admit colored children," setting off a flurry of discussion. After reviewing his request for help, the board of directors referred the matter "to the

Orphan's Home board for further investigation," which then sent the issue back to the UPWANA directors. Two months later, UPWANA sent a letter to the managers "stating that an application for the admission of a colored child had never been received hence no precedent had been established."[21] Clearly unsure of how to act, the UPOH managers looked for precedent and, finding none, chose to continue a de-facto whites-only policy despite an official stance that they had no color restrictions.

Through the first two decades of the new century, dozens of orphanages opened in Southwest Pennsylvania, but the choices remained very limited for African American families. Nineteenth-century orphanages followed the same growth pattern as other institutions such as hospitals, which were fairly common by the Civil War, and experienced rapid expansion at the end of the century. Both the HCC and UPOH were founded in the post–Civil War period during a period of national reform aimed at getting children out of almshouses and providing more customized care for various populations, such as homes for crippled children, and deaf and blind institutions. While Pittsburgh had orphanages as early as 1832 with the founding of the Protestant Orphan Asylum, it followed the national trend with the bulk of its child care institutions emerging around the turn of the twentieth century (see figure 2.2). In this sense, the HCC and UPOH were somewhat early responders on the scene, particularly in the case of institutional care for African American children. By the 1920s, only four other institutions had

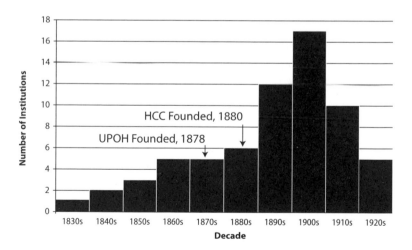

Figure 2.2. Founding Decade of Pittsburgh Region Child Care Institutions. Source: Analysis of 72 Southwest Pennsylvania child welfare institutions active from 1878 to 1929.

opened to serve black families: the short-lived Allegheny Institute of Avery College (1908 to 1917) and Fairfax Baby Home (1910 to the early 1920s) and the slightly longer-lived Coleman Industrial Home for Colored Boys (1908 to the 1940s) and the Davis Home for Colored Children, run by the Colored Women's Relief Association (1908 to the 1950s). The latter two were founded and managed by African Americans, a more common trend from the 1890s onward.[22]

Parents chose from available institutions based on a combination of factors, including religion, location, and reputation. For some, especially immigrants, Catholics, and Jews, religiously affiliated orphanages could serve as a bulwark against unwanted cultural influences from the Protestant mainstream and preserve ethnic traditions.[23] (Although some historians have argued that Jewish orphanages actually caused children to lose touch with their cultural heritage, especially as older, settled generations tried to acculturate recent immigrants through the institutions.)[24] There is no indication that any Jewish families applied to either UPOH or the HCC, although a few Catholic families did send their children to UPOH and, even more rarely, to the HCC, despite anti-Catholic sentiments at both institutions and the relatively small pool of black Catholics in Pittsburgh. A single church, St. Benedict's, served all African American Catholics in the entire city.[25] Most African Americans belonged to Baptist and AME churches, with roughly twenty-eight black religious institutions in Pittsburgh by the early 1900s, half located in the Hill District, near the city's core, alone, though upper-class blacks were disproportionately attracted to Congregational, Episcopalian, and Presbyterian churches.[26] UPOH served United Presbyterian families first and foremost, and often had so many children that it had to stop accepting others, but most years it served children from a range of denominations. In one typical year, for instance, 35 percent of the children came from Protestant homes (other than United Presbyterians), 5 percent from Catholic homes, and 23 percent from families with no church relations at all.[27]

Some parents may have deceived the managers about their religious affiliation to gain admission. For example, shortly after admitting Elizabeth, James, and Tricia Roth—only the second family of children taken into the orphanage—UPOH managers discovered "the mother had represented herself to be a United Presbyterian, but upon learning they were Catholics ... dismissed [the children] to their Aunt."[28] At the HCC, the managers decided to "admit two Catholic children into the Home if the Mother will pay one dollar per week for Boarding," but warned, "the children will have to come under the [Protestant] teachings of the Home."[29] The vast majority of HCC and UPOH children hailed from Protestant homes.

Parents frequently chose these two orphanages specifically because of those Protestant teachings—or at least they claimed to. Audrey Winebiddle, a mother of two, wrote to the UPOH managers using strong anti-Catholic rhetoric: she begged for assistance so "the Roman Catholics dont get my little children from me." She said she feared her neighbors were trying to convert them, and wrote, "i would rather some one would come with the new[s] and tell me that the undertaker was coming to streach [stretch] me for my coffin before i will give my consent to have them Roman Catholic," and concluded, "Roman Catholics is a class of people I can not bare to hear the name mention."[30] Whether Winebiddle strongly felt this way or hoped to appeal to what she thought were the managers' shared sentiments—or both—she clearly used an anti-Catholic narrative in her bid for sympathy. While surely not all UPOH and HCC families agreed with her comments, many parents sought out orphanage care where their children would be raised in familiar religious surroundings. Annette Douglas, a widowed mother of three, specified in her last will and testament, written shortly before her death, "I, further, desire and request that my said executor place my three children . . . in some good church home, preferably a Presbyterian Home, where they may be properly cared for and educated."[31] Religion also provided an important network, connecting parents in need of services with the institutions, as evidenced by the common involvement of clergy acting on behalf of families to admit children to the orphanages.

Location and reputation also played a role in parents' choice of institutions. Both UPOH and the HCC pulled families from a wide geographic range in southwestern Pennsylvania (and occasionally even beyond). But most parents lived in the city within relatively easy traveling distance of the orphanages, making it possible to call on their children on visiting days. For instance, UPOH managers noted that Mrs. Morris "[i]s a Lutheran but wants her child in our home so as to be convenient."[32] For poor parents who relied on public transportation or their own feet, "convenience" could make the difference between seeing one's children once each week or not at all. When it moved out from the urban center of Allegheny to its Termon Avenue location in 1893, the HCC became somewhat more remote, especially as migration after the turn of the century began to concentrate the African American population in a series of neighborhoods across the river, near Pittsburgh's central business district.[33] UPOH's move in 1929 to a country estate in neighboring Butler County made it extremely remote for urban parents. Yet both orphanages remained quite popular, suggesting that families were satisfied with the location of the institutions, or were at least willing to travel the extra distance to get there.

Parents sometimes cited the reputation of the orphanages in petitioning them for admission, though these statements may also have been partially designed to appeal to the vanity of the managers sitting on the receiving committees. For instance, John Mann, a widowed coal miner described by the UPOH managers as "a respectable man but without education," told the managers he wished to place his four children as he was "anxious his children should have a good education and home training."[34] The UPOH managers boasted they were "frequently told by applicants in no way connected with the United Presbyterian Church, that they came to us because our Home has been so highly recommended."[35] Some parents may also have chosen UPOH for access to its medical facilities: "Mrs. Aspen wishes to place a little child in the Home who can get treatment at the Hospital."[36] UPWANA opened a hospital in a separate building behind UPOH in 1889 to serve orphanage children, and then in 1906 built the much larger Columbia Hospital in Wilkinsburg, in the East End just outside city limits, providing some assurance to parents that their children would receive professional medical care.

While it was poorer than UPOH, the HCC boasted far better facilities than the two other orphanages serving African American children, no doubt boosting its reputation among potential clients. A 1915 report, for instance, commended the HCC for its building, which provided "very good quarters for its inmates," and noted its toilet facilities, large dining room, airy dormitories, and hospital room. By contrast, the Coleman and Davis homes were described in harsh detail and characterized as "extremely dilapidated," "vermin-ridden," "filthy" and "totally inadequate."[37] While these observations also reflected the racialized opinions of white social investigators viewing black-managed institutions, photographs of the orphanages suggest the reasons parents may have preferred the HCC, with its spacious building and parklike setting, away from the urban core (see figure 2.3). Though it meant sending their children to a white-managed institution farther from their own homes, African American families' strong demand for child care services through the HCC helped sustain the orphanage through a period of rapid change in the 1920s and '30s.

"To earn their daily bread":
The Conflict of Wage Labor and Parenting

Despite our Charles Dickens–influenced cultural memory of orphanages as grim repositories of parentless children, most "orphans" at the end of the nineteenth century actually had one, if not two, living parents. Popular

Figure 2.3. Original captions: "Shack dignified by name of 'Industrial Training School.' It is a feature of the Coleman Industrial Home for Colored Boys."
(top) "The physical equipment." (HCC, *bottom*). *Source:* Abraham Oseroff,
Report of the Allegheny County Committee (1915), pp. 38, 46.

literature such as Dickens's *Oliver Twist* has done much to promote the lingering image of fully orphaned street children and institutional managers themselves frequently employed a melodramatic narrative of desperate children in need of rescue. This narrative effectively erased parents or vilified them as abusive and neglectful, focusing on their moral failings rather than the underlying causes of poverty.[38] Often repeated in the institutions' public documents such as annual reports, this storyline created a dramatic pretense for the orphanages' mission that undoubtedly appealed to both the managers' understanding of their work as well as the heartstrings of potential donors. For instance, UPOH described the very first child it admitted, a two-year-old boy named Christopher Wright, "who was rescued . . . from a wretched home, where he contracted disease and lingered with us but a short time."[39] The parents are implied here, yet invisible, as they are accused of causing little Christopher's death by providing such a "miserable and wretched," germ-ridden environment. While some parents were most certainly guilty of such accusations—and much worse—most families of orphanage children were themselves victims of circumstances beyond their control. Chiefly, the new industrial wage economy made it extraordinarily difficult for some parents to simultaneously earn an income and take care of a household. For these families, orphanages served as a survival strategy.

Only a small fraction of children in either the HCC or UPOH were actually orphans, sometimes called "full orphans" or "true orphans" (see figure 2.4). Like their institutionalized counterparts around the country, the vast majority of children had one or both parents living.[40] While it officially did not accept children from families with two living parents, UPOH did occasionally make exceptions in particularly sympathetic cases, yielding a small 5 percent of the total orphanage population.[41] By contrast, HCC more often accepted children from two-parent households, for a total of 23 percent of its admissions, though it characterized some of these children as abandoned, leaving them effectively orphaned: "Sometimes we are forced to take children whose parents are living but who have deserted or neglected them—this ought not to be." The managers complained, "The parents are the natural protectors of the child and they should not seek to put that responsibility on others."[42] UPOH managers shared these sentiments but drew a harder line when it came to the many two-parent families applying for admission. In other words, the smaller percentage of UPOH children from two-parent families should not be construed to mean that African Americans were somehow more likely to institutionalize their children when both parents were still alive: both orphanages received a steady stream of applications from two-parent families. Indeed, by 1911 UPOH was receiving "so many cases of children having two parents and very needy," they considered petitioning UPWANA to allow them to start "new work" in this area.[43]

By far, the largest class of children served was the "half orphan," or those with just one living parent. The HCC followed a pattern typical of other orphanages in the period, with over half (53 percent) of the children claiming a solo mother. UPOH children were more evenly split, with 42 percent claiming a solo mother and 41 percent a solo father. As a category of analysis used throughout this study, "solo" parents include those whose spouses are dead, incompetent, deserted, separated, or divorced, as well as a very small number of those who were never married. The term "solo," in other words, is intentionally broader than "single," which as a modern label implies simply marital status and does not capture the full range of parents' experiences. Overall, then, between 88 and 94 percent of all the children in this study had at least one living, solo parent, usually struggling through a financial or family crisis, from the loss of a spouse to the lack of support networks or adequate housing.

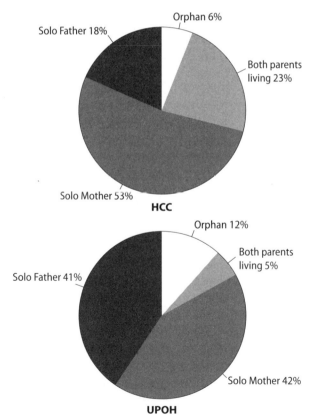

Figure 2.4. HCC and UPOH "Orphan" Status of Children, 1878–1929. *Source:* Analysis of HCC and UPOH admissions logs and children's case histories.

The vast majority of white families were solidly working class: they were working and getting by until a crisis, or series of crises, made caring for their children impossible. For instance, mill accidents made Pittsburgh a particularly dangerous place for working-class men, accounting for many half-orphaned children.[44] In the midst of the economic depression of the 1890s, UPOH managers saw a spike in truly needy cases and implicitly acknowledged that, until that point, the typical white orphanage client had *not* been impoverished: "We have provided for more really destitute children whose friends were utterly unable to contribute even a trifle toward their support, than we have for many years past."[45] Occupational data collected by UPOH suggests that many of these white orphanage clients may have been working class—working hard to make ends meet, perhaps, but not necessarily destitute—at least while the fathers were able breadwinners.[46] Since the women frequently had not worked before the loss of a husband necessitated their labor—and were then relegated to mostly domestic positions—the men's occupations provide a better indicator of the families' class status before the onset of the child care crisis. Over two-thirds of the men (68 percent) were employed in semiskilled and skilled labor (such as a steamfitter, bricklayer, and carpenter) or white-collar positions (such as a statistician, newspaper reporter, and insurance salesman) (see table 2.1). When wives lost their husbands' financial contributions, or when husbands lost their wives' domestic labor, these families slipped into poverty and became dependent on the orphanages for child care assistance.

By contrast, under the legacy of slavery and racism, African American men were largely concentrated in unskilled, and often more dangerous, occupations at the bottom of the urban economy. In 1900, for instance, 88 percent of all African American men in Pittsburgh performed unskilled or semiskilled labor.[47] A decade later, black men constituted only 3 percent of workers in the booming steel industry, while most remained in general labor and personal and domestic service.[48] As more jobs opened up in the

Table 2.1. Occupational Status of UPOH Parents

	Mothers		Fathers	
	N	Percent	N	Percent
Manual labor	78	74	38	32
Semi-skilled and skilled labor	20	19	66	55
White collar labor	8	8	16	13
Total	106	100	120	100

Source: Statistical analysis of UPOH admission logs and children's case histories.
Note: Total percentage may exceed 100 due to rounding.

factories, a few African American men moved into skilled positions, but managers placed most newcomers in "the most difficult, low-paying and dirty categories of industrial labor[,] . . . characterized by disproportionate exposure to debilitating heat, deadly fumes, and disabling and serious injuries."[49] These men met with more accidents, suffering more severe injuries and death than their white counterparts, and experienced disproportionate stretches of unemployment.[50] While the black middle class expanded slowly during this period and some African American men gained a foothold in business and entrepreneurial pursuits, economic security was more tenuous for most black families.

Solo mothers, both black and white, could find themselves in particularly dire circumstances without a family breadwinner, scrambling to find wage work in Pittsburgh's heavily industrial economy, which favored men's employment.[51] The UPOH mothers for whom there is occupational data most commonly did "housework," accounting for 58 percent of all working women in this sample.[52] (In the language of the period, a married woman who did not work for wages was "keeping house," later called a "housewife," distinguishing her from one who performed "housework" for wages.) This reflected the larger pattern for Pittsburgh women, who worked in domestic services in greater proportion than did women in other Midwestern industrial cities during this period. Pittsburgh's overall labor force participation rate for women was similar to that in other industrial cities, but it was a difficult city in which to find wage work as a married woman: the few occupations that allowed women, such as the public schools and electrical manufacturing, excluded married women, forcing those who needed wages into domestic services.[53] By contrast, in Philadelphia, only a quarter of the poor mothers who sent their children to day nurseries during the first three decades of the twentieth century worked in domestic service, while 59 percent worked in factories.[54] What's more, many of the UPOH women were not working when their husbands were alive or still resident with the family, as evidenced by the number of mothers who negotiated board payments for their children dependent upon their finding employment. For instance, one mother agreed to "pay $1.50 per week for both [her children] as soon as employed."[55]

Employment options for Pittsburgh's African American women—who more often combined wage work and maternity—were even more restricted, with most channeled into domestic service.[56] Live-in domestic positions for both white and black women frequently barred mothers from keeping their children with them, making such jobs highly undesirable for many widows. Furthermore, black women outnumbered black men in Pittsburgh nearly ten-to-one through the 1910s, and a "greater proportion of African American women had sole support of young children than did native- or foreign-born white women."[57] Not surprisingly, then, African American widows had the highest level of workforce participation: in 1890, for example, 80 percent of African American widows aged twenty to forty-four (those most likely to have young children still at home) were working.[58]

The preponderance of domestic positions also made it difficult for family members to assist in times of crisis: for instance, when Susan James's husband deserted the family, and she became ill and had to go to the hospital, she sent four-year-old Hannah to stay with an aunt, who worked as a domestic on the North Side. The aunt's employer "allowed the child to remain in her home for [a] week" and then approached the HCC, asking them to take the girl "until such time as her mother can again take charge of her." The managers "admitted her as a charity case," and James recovered enough to retrieve Hannah two weeks later.[59] Though the managers characterized the employer's actions as "kindly" in permitting Hannah to stay for a week, a longer-term arrangement was clearly not acceptable to her. The aunt's live-in position meant that she was dependent on the "kindness" of her employer in order to help her sister-in-law by caring for her niece. With limited employment options, solo mothers were in a precarious position and could easily tip into poverty.

The loss of a spouse, generally through death, desertion, or sickness, was frequently the key precipitating event leading to children's institutionalization. Many parents, like Mary Harold, discovered that they could not successfully combine wage labor with child care responsibilities: "she could not keep house and support her family so was obliged to place these boys in the Home for a short time."[60] When her husband deserted, Eleanor Gardener found she could take "the younger [son, four-year-old Alan] . . . with her when she goes out to work" as a seamstress, "but found it impossible to give [her] two girls the training and care they required." She placed the girls in UPOH, and within a few months sent Alan to join his sisters.[61] The UPOH managers acknowledged this difficulty faced by solo mothers when they accepted their children: "The mothers could not leave their little ones alone day after day while they went out to earn their daily bread."[62] Men, too, faced a crisis with the loss of a spouse, which also meant the loss of wives' crucial domestic labor. When John Kohler's wife died, he was "left with two small children." The managers noted that his sister took his little girl, but he "is a night watchman and has no one to care for Christopher."[63] Likewise, after they accepted the two Harrison boys, the managers learned "the father is grieving so for them that an aunt has consented to keep house for him, so he can have his boys."[64] For both women and men, then, losing a spouse—and their accompanying wages or domestic labor—was frequently the key trigger leading to children's institutionalization.

Yet both women and men generally resisted immediate placement of their children in the orphanages following the death of a spouse. Stanley West, for instance, "struggled to keep his family together for a year and then was compelled to place . . . three [of his five children] in the Home as no suitable person could be found to take care of them."[65] African American women waited the longest, holding out for an average of three years before turning to orphanage care, while white men had the shortest elapsed time, averaging one year and four months (see table 2.2).[66] This data lends some support to reformer Florence Lattimore's 1914 observation that "[t]he colored people of Pittsburgh did not seek institutional care for their children to any great extent except in cases of illness." Following her social investigation for the famed *Pittsburgh Survey*, Lattimore concluded, "They usually had strong home ties and were willing to adopt a lower standard of living than the white population before giving up their children."[67] They also had fewer institutional choices than white families and were essentially *forced* to "adopt a lower standard of living" due to economic barriers that prevented the majority of black families from achieving financial security. Regardless, both black women and men waited longer to institutionalize their children than their white counterparts.

Men, both black and white, chose to institutionalize their children more quickly than did women. In fact, widowers who placed their children in these orphanages were most likely to do so within the first year after the mother's death. Women also placed a substantial number of children within the first year after the death of their husbands, but they were even more likely to wait until the second year before institutionalizing their children. Widowers' shorter delay in placing children suggests that spousal death created more of an immediate crisis for men and that women may have employed other resources—such as networks of friends and family—to cobble together care before turning to the orphanages for assistance.

Table 2.2. Average Elapsed Time From Death of Spouse to Admission of Child

	HCC			UPOH		
	Average number of days	Yr - Mo - Day	N	Average number of days	Yr - Mo - Day	N
Widows	1095	3 - 0 - 0	118	796	2 - 2 - 6	115
Widowers	634	1 - 8 - 29	68	496	1 - 4 - 11	162

Source: Statistical analysis of HCC and UPOH admission logs and children's case histories.

A spouse did not necessarily have to die to generate a crisis for families: men and women were often left solo parenting through sickness, desertion, and divorce. For instance, when his wife fell "very ill with tuberculosis," Wallace Farmer sent his two girls, Bertha, aged ten, and Rose, aged five, to UPOH. The managers noted, "The children are admitted temporarily on account of having both parents." Farmer retrieved his children six months later, but the following year he was forced to send them back as his wife had died. The girls spent another thirteen months in the orphanage before he was able to take them home again.[68] Illness compelled a healthy spouse to take on the responsibilities of solo parenting but could also wreak havoc on a family's finances. Lilly Brighton placed her twelve-year-old son, Caleb, in UPOH but was "unable at present to pay for him . . . having debts pressing her now contracted during her husbands sickness."[69] Sometimes a parent struggled with mental illness, leaving a spouse to raise children alone. For instance, Jonah Harley placed five of his six children, aged four to nine, in the HCC when his wife was declared "insane" and sent to the City Farm. The youngest, Fannie, was only eighteen months old when her siblings went to the orphanage, and her father presumably made other arrangements for her, though he later placed her there, too, when she turned three.[70] In 1906 UPWANA, the parent agency of UPOH, clarified their policy on this issue, declaring, "The Orphans Home Board is authorized in the cases of children having both parents living with one or both insane, to admit them at their discretion."[71]

Desertion created even larger problems for the remaining spouse, who was left to cope with solo parenting but also did not qualify for some assistance. For instance, UPOH stated: "We are obliged to refuse many applications made, because the parents have been deserted, husband by wife, or wife by husband." The managers explained, "As a rule we try to avoid such cases, as they are not orphans; but occasionally the case is so sad—and the children are really worse than orphans—that we yield."[72] In New York during this period, anti-desertion reformers actually made wives participate in tracking down their missing husbands before they could receive aid. But that assistance was often far less than they needed for survival, and reformers were generally engaged in a largely symbolic effort to teach immigrants the American value of the single family breadwinner, reinforcing women's dependency on their husbands while trying to alleviate their dependency on the state.[73] Neither UPOH nor the HCC ever made women actively hunt down their runaway husbands, though the managers were keen to avoid providing assistance when an able-bodied spouse was around.

Iris Gallatin's struggle to raise her children after her husband abandoned them was typical. The children's "father having disappeared several months ago and the family . . . find[ing] no trace of him," Iris took the children to live with her father in rural Pennsylvania, "but they being very poor the mother must work constantly." She placed her three children, ages four, six, and eight, in UPOH, and "secured work in a hotel." Later, "the father returned so the children . . . were dismissed . . . to their mother."[74] Elizabeth Knauer's husband "had to flee the country because he infringed on a postal patent and left for parts unknown," forcing her to institutionalize their two children and look for work.[75] Occasionally, wives deserted their husbands, too, as the UPOH managers had observed, but the burden of abandonment fell disproportionately on women.

Divorce and separation could also leave women struggling to raise children alone. For instance, Philomene Barston placed her six-year-old daughter in UPOH, explaining that "she has a legal divorce from her husband whom she was compelled to leave."[76] However, divorce was extremely rare as it was difficult to obtain and socially stigmatizing; only eight cases in the entire dataset involved divorce or formal separation. Because mothers often did not retain custody of their children, women frequently viewed it as an option of last resort.[77] In addition, UPOH managers tended to be less sympathetic to divorce than desertion.[78] For example, they "Found that the parents of . . . two children . . . were divorced and did not receive them."[79] They also gave little sympathy to couples who mutually agreed to separate. For instance, in one month alone, UPOH recorded that "[t]hree applications for admission of children whose parents were separate were refused."[80] For some men, and more rarely women, it was easier to simply abandon their families. Desertion also left the door open for a possible return at a later date. For instance, Mable Moody's "husband deserted and refuse[d] to do anything for wife or children." She sent her two young daughters, ages one and three, to UPOH, but seven months later "removed them . . . believing she could now care for them at home—her husband having returned to her."[81] Though it did not guarantee admission, claiming desertion, rather than admitting to a consensual separation, often proved a better strategy for solo parents and did not carry the moral stain of divorce.

UPOH also strictly enforced its prohibition on the admission of "illegitimate" children, though unmarried women continued to apply. One mother sought "admission of an illegitimate child" and was turned away, only to reapply again two years later to be "refused on the ground that it does not come under our rules."[82] A letter from W. W. Grier, proprietor of the Dexter Spring Company who wrote on behalf of an unmarried mother and her child, reveals just how difficult it could be for such women: Miss Grant was living with her brother, who was "kind enough to give her a home without charge, but the sister-in-law [would] *not* let the baby be brought to her home." When the infant was just two weeks old, Grant sent her baby to "a farmer's wife who takes care of it" for three dollars a week. That amounted to 80 percent of her fifteen-dollar monthly salary, and she was having "quite a struggle."[83] Despite Grier's intervention, and an offer from the sister-in-law to pay boarding at the orphanage, there is no record that UPOH accepted this child.

In the UPOH sample, there was only one documented case of a child of an unmarried mother: Mollie Blaine placed her daughter, Lucy, in the orphanage, and a few months later met widower James Everhart, who had recently admitted his two children, Caleb and Polly. In what turned out to be either an orphanage love story or a marriage of convenience, or a bit of both, Blaine and Everhart were married shortly after that and retrieved all three children.[84] UPOH managers may have agreed with progressive reformer William H. Slingerland, who criticized child-helping agencies in Pennsylvania for accepting the children of unmarried mothers: "A ready acceptance of an illegitimate child . . . has too often left the door wide open for the carefreed mother to pass out to a life of degrading immorality."[85] The HCC accepted just three children of unmarried mothers during this fifty-year period, clearly marking them as "illegitimate" in the registration book. These were exceptional cases at both orphanages in which the managers likely felt swayed by pitiful circumstances, but nevertheless did not reflect a general openness to supporting the children of unmarried parents.

Faced with the challenge of combining wage work with child care, many solo parents relied on support networks of relatives and friends to avoid orphanage care for their children. However, massive immigration and migration in this period, especially among working-class people seeking jobs in the city's booming industrial sector, disrupted those networks for some families, leaving their children more vulnerable to institutionalization. During the 1880 to 1930 period, between half and two-thirds of the city's residents were foreign born or children of immigrants.[86] After the turn of the century, UPOH noted an increasing number of applications from immigrant families. In 1903 it reported that "the stranger within our gates is not neglected . . . as time and again we have opened our doors to receive those who speak in (to us) unknown tongue."[87] By 1912 the orphanage had added a new line on its application form asking for "parents' nationality," reflecting the growing number of immigrants in the city and possibly a heightened anxiety over immigration issues. Yet only 26 percent of parents after 1912 were foreign born, and nearly all hailed from Western European countries (rather than the Eastern and Southern Europeans who so troubled the white middle class).[88] This held true across the city, as other orphanages served mostly American-born families with Pittsburgh-born children.[89] Thus, despite immense immigration that fundamentally changed the face of Pittsburgh's working class—and no doubt contributed to a child care crisis in some families—UPOH continued to largely serve the children of U.S.-born parents.

Migration could be equally disruptive to support networks, and anti-migrant state welfare policies amplified the effect for needy families. While the bulk of UPOH parents and nearly all HCC parents were American born, some of these families may have been recent arrivals to Pittsburgh and lacked the deep networks of relatives and friends to fall back on in times of crisis. Through chain migration, most migrants, black and white, arrived in the city with some local contacts, whether family or friends, though these networks may not have always been sufficient for parents struggling in crisis.[90] The UPOH managers did not routinely collect information on migrant status, although they did record place of birth for each child: the vast majority of children were born in Pittsburgh or southwestern Pennsylvania, suggesting that most of these white families, at any rate, had been in the region at least a few years before seeking the aid of the orphanage.

By contrast, massive migration of Southern blacks in this period meant that a large proportion of families had recently arrived.[91] The African American population of Pittsburgh shot from 6,136 in 1880 (3.9 percent of the population) to 54,983 in 1930 (8.2 percent of the population).[92] The HCC managers recorded the birthplace of parents from the inception of the orphanage, permitting a fairly detailed analysis of the migration pattern of those African American families who used orphanage care for their children. Just under a quarter of the HCC parents were born in Pennsylvania (13 percent in Pittsburgh itself), with the vast majority having migrated to the state (see appendix C). A full half of the parents hailed from the upper South, with Virginia contributing by far the largest proportion of migrants (35.9 percent from that state alone). This pattern reflected earlier migration trends: by 1850 most African Americans in Pittsburgh had moved from others areas of the state, but around a quarter moved from Virginia and Maryland.[93] In 1913, when Pennsylvania instituted its Mothers' Assistance program in an effort to support widows with young children at home, the state specifically excluded recent migrants: applicants had to have resided in the county in which they applied for three continuous years in order to receive benefits.[94] This effectively prevented a large number of both immigrant and migrant women from receiving state aid, forcing desperate widows to seek assistance from private institutions, including orphanages.

In addition to the challenges of solo parenting and disrupted support networks, inadequate housing often played a role in families' decisions to institutionalize children. Social reformers in 1907 concluded that Pittsburgh's housing conditions, while similar to other industrial cities, were "inimical to public health and to private decency." Open sewage vaults and "omnipresent" privy sheds dumped human waste into the streets, which were further "fouled by bad drainage and piles of rubbish" and led directly to public water supplies. Overcrowded tenements "perch[ed] on the hillsides, swarming with men, women, and children—entire families living in one room and accommodating 'boarders' in a corner." Investigators found families crammed into windowless basements, and many residents had to haul water from a common pump up several flights of stairs. The city's steep slopes, clay soil, and wet climate contributed to housing woes: many structures were built into the hillsides, providing little natural light or air, while the soil and weather made nearly every underground room persistently damp. "An enveloping cloud of smoke and dust . . . [made] housekeeping a travesty in many neighborhoods."[95]

Under these conditions, working-class families struggled to find adequate, affordable housing. UPOH took in two children one year who "came from one of the most wretched homes in this city, part of the house being two stories below the ground."[96] Many parents turned to the orphanages when they lost their housing. John Jennings, a widowed grocer from Pittsburgh's West End, "had a housekeeper until his home was destroyed by fire and the housekeeper could no longer care for them."[97] Jennings returned for his three children six months later. Similarly, the managers noted that "Richard's mother having no home would like to have him placed" in UPOH. She returned for her son two months later, presumably after she found suitable lodging.[98] Louisa Charles, "a widow and obliged to wash or do general housework," placed her two children in the orphanage, telling the managers she "will want them when she is able to rent a little home for them."[99] Sometimes that home was truly "little," no more than a single room, as the parents themselves acknowledged: Margaret Shaw asked "to place her three boys in the Home for a short time" while she was hospitalized, promising that "as soon as she comes out . . . she will get a room and take them herself."[100] Other times, parents like James Harding found lodging in boarding houses, as the HCC managers noted, "The two little Harding girls Susan and Clarice were taken home by their Father to the house where he was boarding."[101] Parents' struggle to find adequate housing often exacerbated other factors such as widowhood and could lead to the institutionalization of children.

"Only until he gets work": Orphanage Care as Family Survival Strategy

Just as the vast majority of orphanage children had at least one living parent, the vast majority of those parents used the institutions as a short-term strategy for family survival. Rather than abandoning their parenting responsibilities, most viewed institutionalization as a temporary necessity and fully expected to claim their children after a time. Parents and managers, however, may have had different interpretations of "temporary." At UPOH, managers made a distinction between "temporary" and "regular" admissions, reserving the former for unusual circumstances such as when both parents were living but one was ill, or a deserting spouse could not be located. In these cases, the managers occasionally accepted children, making a special note in the admissions log, such as when Fred Seldon placed his son: "This child is received temporarily as the mother is in the hospital and will be removed when other arrangements can be made."[102] Yet most parents expected their children would be staying in the orphanages only temporarily, until they were back on their feet, earning an income, had obtained housing, or the children themselves were a bit older and required less care. James Schneider, a widowed basket maker, placed his three children in the orphanage "only until he gets work."[103] Parents tended to draw the line between "temporary" and "permanent" placement, intending to retrieve their children rather than give them up to the institutions for indenturing or adopting.

The overlapping crises often facing working families were frequently complex, requiring months, and sometimes years, to address before children could be retrieved. The mean length of stay for HCC and UPOH children matched the national average of one to four years, with important racial distinctions.[104] African American children remained in the orphanage roughly two years and four months, nearly a full year longer than their white counterparts, at one year, five months.[105] While black parents waited longer after losing a spouse to institutionalize children, once they were in the orphanage, the longer length of stay suggests these families faced even greater obstacles to achieving the stability needed to retrieve their children. In addition, while the mean length of stay rose over time for both white and black children, it climbed more steeply for African Americans (see figure 2.5).[106] As the spike in children's tenure during the terrible depression of the 1890s suggests, external factors such as the economy could play an exaggerated role in black families' ability to retrieve children. Furthermore, this data complicates historian Timothy Hacsi's finding that the average length of stay dropped over time in the nation's orphanages.[107]

Parents were strategic in their efforts to reclaim children, generally keeping them in the institutions just long enough to find employment, housing, or, occasionally, a new spouse, and then achieve some stability. While both orphanages maintained an average length of stay of more than one or two years, a substantial proportion of children returned to their parents within the first year (see figure 2.6). Dismissals at both orphanages peaked at around a year and continued to fall thereafter. Within two to three years, most children had left the orphanage; those that stayed for several years or more were often full orphans for whom the institutions had complete custody. Though a year or more of separation from parents certainly could not have felt "short" to a child, very few children were actually "raised" in the orphanages.

While parents placed and retrieved their children throughout the year as individual child care crises waxed and waned, some parents deliberately kept their children at the orphanages through the end of the academic year, suggesting that they viewed the institutions almost as a form of boarding school.[108] For example, Mrs. Dearborn asked the UPOH managers "if she takes her children out for the summer can she return them again in September."[109] In this instance, they refused, but UPOH parents frequently took their children for a month or more in the summer when the managers

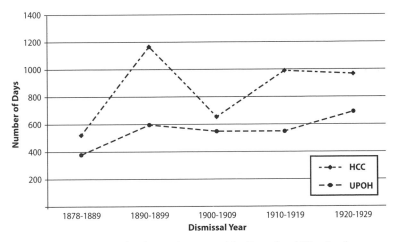

Figure 2.5. Mean Length of Stay, Aggregated by Decade of Dismissal.
Source: Analysis of HCC and UPOH admission and dismissal data.

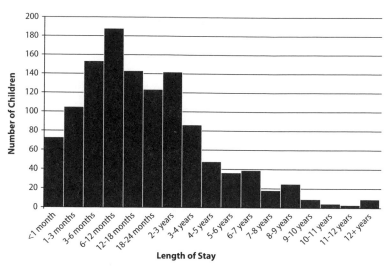

Figure 2.6. Number of HCC and UPOH Children by Length of Stay. *Source:* Analysis of HCC and UPOH admission and dismissal data.

closed the home, sending all remaining children to temporary foster homes. In 1891, for example, they noted that nearly half the sixty children in the orphanage "went to the homes of relatives who, while unable to care for them all the year, were glad to have them with them for a few weeks."[110] For several decades, the orphanages recruited volunteer families to host children in their homes each summer, often in the country. This practice was reminiscent of older child care systems, such as apprenticeships, that removed children to other homes, sometimes in distant locations, as with the infamous orphan trains that shipped New York City street children to the West.[111] Both HCC and UPOH parents resisted formal indentures or foster placements, but some appear to have tolerated these summer arrangements, perhaps because they had no other choice, with limited ability to care for their own children. But parents may have also acquiesced since these were temporary, short-term placements and had the advantage of removing the children from the stifling city for a few weeks during the hottest part of the summer.

As summer approached, UPOH declined new applications and recommended that parents apply again in the fall, no doubt a maddening situation for families in a crisis with pressing child care needs. One mother negotiated for the admission of her son in May, the managers agreeing to accept him "until the Home closes" if she would "provide for him during the summer."[112] Parents also negotiated to have their children kept past the home's age limit so they could complete their studies uninterrupted. For instance, UPOH managers noted, "Martha Penny was 12 yrs old Oct. 4th and her mother asks we keep her another year." They agreed she could stay "until the close of school in June."[113] UPOH children attended public school and received the same education they might otherwise have received at home, assuming their parents could afford to spare their labor while they studied. In contrast, the HCC educated children within the orphanage until the second decade of the new century, functioning more literally as a boarding school. Pittsburgh had desegregated its schools in 1880 when it disbanded its single African American school and distributed black children throughout the ward schools; the following year, Pennsylvania overturned an 1854 segregation ruling, effectively integrating schools throughout the state in law, if not in practice.[114] Thus, the HCC could have sent the children out to the local public school, but chose instead to keep them within the confines of the orphanage, largely because the managers felt they were providing a superior education. (For further discussion of schooling within the HCC, see chapter 6.)

Summer could present a special challenge for parents who relied on the public schools to provide child care. Fanny George, a widow who found work as a clerk, made arrangements in April to send her children to the orphanage, "when school closes," evidently able to balance work and child care until summer arrived, and perhaps not wanting to disrupt their studies at their current school.[115] Bernard Felling, a widowed father of three, told the managers he was "in distress over our action in dismissing his children at the end of the school term and says he has no way of caring for them." They relented and allowed the children to remain "for the present."[116] Similarly, the managers agreed when "Mrs. Roland, a widow on the North Side, [applied] for the admission of her boy for the summer, in order to keep him of[f] the streets."[117] Seasonal employment, especially for men, could also exacerbate summertime child care needs. Wallace Taft, a farm laborer working in Montgomery County, Ohio, wrote to the managers asking for winter employment, "as i will [be] out of work when we get our corn gathered. . . . i must have some thing to do or i will not be able to pay for my boys this winter as it takes all of my wages in the summer to pay for them."[118] Other unskilled labor positions, such as those in construction and road building, that were dependent on warmer weather also coincided with the summer months when children were out of school.

In addition to negotiating the timing of their children's stays, parents strategically placed their children in the orphanages and retrieved them on the basis of the child's age. Solo parents with very young children frequently requested assistance only to be turned away as both orphanages had a minimum age limit of two.[119] UPOH very rarely broke its own policy and admitted younger children, whereas the HCC was slightly more flexible in accepting infants. Although babies and toddlers had a much higher mortality rate in institutions and required additional staffing, parents maintained a high demand for this service, and both orphanages repeatedly expressed their desire over the years to increase their capacity to handle the very youngest children.[120] To fulfill their infant child care needs, parents may have utilized multiple institutions at once. For instance, in Philadelphia, historian Elizabeth Rose found that some families placed younger children in day nurseries and older children in orphanages; in one day nursery she examined, 15 percent of the children's siblings were in another institution.[121]

Throughout the period of this study, the median age of admission at both orphanages remained at six.[122] However, as figure 2.7 illustrates, the distribution of children's ages was consistently high from the ages of two (the age at which the orphanages officially began admitting children) to eight. Both UPOH and HCC tended to refuse children after the age of ten or eleven, and generally dismissed them after age twelve, so the steep decline in admission ages from ten on is not surprising; however, the somewhat smaller proportion of nine-year-olds admitted suggests that some parents were choosing to keep these slightly older children at home rather than place them in institutions.

Dismissal data further supports this observation, as the median age of children at dismissal remained at nine, with the distribution of dismissal

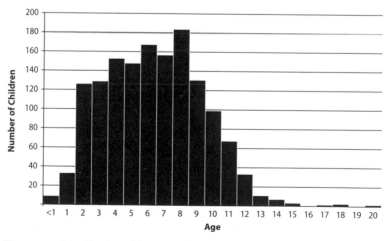

Figure 2.7. Distribution of Ages at Admission, HCC and UPOH. *Source:* Analysis of HCC and UPOH admissions data.

ages spiking at eight, nine, and ten, and falling off sharply at eleven (see figure 2.8).[123] If parents were simply waiting until their children "aged out" of the orphanages and were dismissed by the managers, we would expect to see a higher proportion of eleven- and twelve-year-olds being dismissed. Instead, the larger number of eight- to ten-year-olds suggests that parents were making active choices about retrieving their children at these slightly younger ages, well before they aged out. In sum, parents generated high demand for the care of children in infancy through the early school years, while placing fewer nine- and ten-year-olds and, at the same time, retrieving more children in this same age range than any other. These older children were more likely to be able to care for themselves (and younger siblings) for longer stretches of time, and could also assist with housekeeping duties.

Some parents may even have depended on the labor of those children for family survival. James Harding, for instance, took his two girls "to the house where he was boarding to assist the family." His ten-year-old daughter, Clarice, "cried bitterly on leaving," perhaps unhappy about the work arrangement her father had made for her.[124] While the managers preferred to see children remain in school through their early teen years, many poor families could not afford the "luxury" of extended schooling, and sent children to work to supplement family income. For example, managers worried when they learned that "Henrietta Carlisle who was dismissed . . . is not attending school," but decided the case fell outside their jurisdiction now that the girl was no longer in their care.[125] African American children in the city

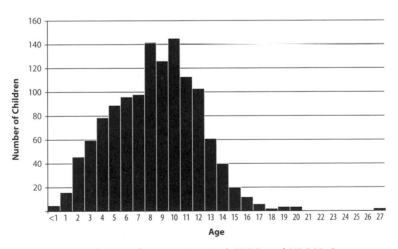

Figure 2.8. Distribution of Ages at Dismissal, HCC, and UPOH. *Source:* Analysis of HCC and UPOH dismissal data.

were somewhat less likely to work for wages than were white working-class children, and when they did contribute their wages to the family income, they were more likely to do so for specific things, like the education of a sibling.[126] Pittsburgh actually boasted higher school attendance rates than similar cities, with half-orphans attending school in increasing numbers over time. This was due in part to the heavy industrial economy that, relative to other cities, did not provide as many opportunities for children's wage labor: steel mills, for instance, did not hire many children. In fact, during this turn-of-the-century period, Pittsburgh families increasingly replaced child employment with mothers' employment as a survival strategy.[127]

Parents also strategically placed their children in the orphanages by sex and sibling status. On average, throughout the period of study, boys out-numbered girls 56 to 44 percent, though at times the populations were as lopsided as two to one. The HCC noted in reviewing its own admissions records, "A strange fact being that nearly always there are twice as many boys as girls."[128] In 1909 UPOH was even forced to turn down "[a]pplications for admission of seven boys . . . on account of having so many boys."[129] At the HCC, the gender balance eventually evened out in the late 1920s, with girls finally overtaking boys in 1928 for the first time, creating the "need of re-arranging dormitories."[130] The tendency to place boys while keeping girls at home (or retrieving them sooner than their brothers) likely reflected a strategy of using older daughters to care for younger siblings as well as for household duties. For example, James Caldwell placed four of his children in the orphanage and then "having established a home at McKees Rocks in charge of his eldest daughter Susie removed Mamie," the youngest child.[131] There was also a high demand for girls to work as indentured servants, and potential employers frequently wrote to the orphanages looking for young workers. The UPOH managers noticed that "[m]any homes seem to open for our little girls, indeed we cannot supply that demand, but few ask for boys."[132] This was a national trend, as most institutions found it easier to place out girls than boys.[133] The higher demand for girls to serve as in-dentured labor also meant that parents were likely able to make their own private arrangements for their girls' labor, resulting in reduced need for their institutionalization. On the flip side, Pittsburgh's heavy industrial economy provided comparatively fewer job opportunities for boys, meaning parents may have had increased need of institutional child care for their sons.

The higher ratio of boys to girls in both orphanages also illustrates par-ents' strategy of institutionalizing some, but not all, of their children. Both African American and white families placed a large number of individual children without any siblings, with singletons making up well over half the population (58 percent) at the HCC (see table 2.3).[134] While UPOH was home to a substantial number of singletons (42 percent), parents placed the majority of children in that institution along with at least one brother or sister. The white sibling groups also tended to be slightly larger. Smaller black family size, at least after the turn of the century when the typical Pittsburgh family had fewer than two children, may partially explain this apparent racial difference in placement patterns.[135] Parents often kept infants at home, though sometimes this was not by choice, as the orphanages would not usually take children until they were two. Occasionally, the managers would help parents find homes for underage babies or recommend other institutions, but families appear to have preferred keeping siblings—or at least some siblings—together, if they were to be institutionalized. Many times, parents would have younger children join their siblings after they came of age. Parents particularly resisted allowing their children to be placed out in indentured homes, quite possibly because those arrangements nearly always divided siblings. Even as the indenture system evolved during this turn-of-the-century period into foster care, the host families continued to have high expectations of children's labor, and often visited or wrote to the orphanages looking for children who would fulfill specific work needs. Foster families rarely requested or received more than one child. (For a discussion of the evolving foster care system, see chapter 3.)

The vast majority of families used the orphanages as an interim survival strategy, requiring assistance only one time to regain enough stability to reclaim children. However, a small proportion of children—6 percent overall—had multiple stays in the institutions, suggesting that for at least some of these families, long-term stability was harder to achieve. For example, Maggie Carson retrieved her two boys from the orphanage after just a month, "having found a home for the eldest [Elliot] and she had

Table 2.3. Frequency of Sibling Group Size

Number of siblings	HCC		UPOH	
	Number of families	Percent of total	Number of families	Percent of total
1	358	58	121	42
2	163	26	81	28
3	76	12	55	19
4	17	3	24	8
5	3	<1	8	3
6	2	<1	1	<1
Total	619	100	290	100

Source: Analysis of UPOH and HCC admission records, *n*=1597 children.

arranged to keep Peter." But two months later, she was forced to return them to the home as she "had been disappointed in finding a home for them and they were in a very destitute condition." A short time later, she took Elliot home again, only to find once more that she could not keep him. When she tried to readmit Elliot, the managers "told her we could not do so and that she must come and take Peter, which she did."[136] Families that required additional stays for their children were often the most destitute, or struggling with overlapping crises, sometimes resulting in the intervention of other child welfare agencies. Widower James Bailey, a reporter with the *Pittsburg Post*, retrieved his three children after eighteen months in the orphanage, "as he had provided a home for them." But "the children were returned . . . by the agent of the Humane Society as they were found alone and without food in a house in the East End and the father being under arrest for forgery."[137] Children with multiple stays returned to their families only slightly more than half the time following second, and subsequent, admissions, suggesting that this cohort represented some of the most fragile families, having the most difficulty with child care.[138]

African American families were far less likely to use orphanage care more than once, but when they did so, their children remained in the institution longer. The proportion of UPOH children with multiple stays (10 percent) was nearly three times as great as that of HCC children (3.5 percent).[139] This discrepancy may partially reflect the fact that UPOH more frequently placed out children, and those returning from foster homes and indentures were recorded as an additional admission. Of all the children at both orphanages who had multiple stays, the great majority (80 percent) stayed just twice, and nearly all of those with three or more stays were white.[140] White children with multiple stays remained in the orphanage roughly the same amount of time as their UPOH peers on their first stay. For African American children who stayed more than once, though, the length of time in the orphanage during their first stay averaged seven months longer than their HCC peers.[141] Similarly, on subsequent stays (second stay and beyond), black children averaged nearly twice as many days in the orphanage as white children.[142] These figures again illustrate the comparative struggle of African American families to regain stability when faced with a child care crisis. Still, in the larger scheme of things, the vast majority of families, black and white, regained sufficient security such that their children stayed only once in the orphanage.

In a handful of cases, parents literally used orphanage care as day care, an uncommon strategy for this period, but one that reflected families' varied child care needs. The earliest recorded instance of this arrangement occurred in 1886 at UPOH, which accepted Haddie Putnam's three children, noting, "They are day boarders only." This case was all the more unusual as Putnam's husband was still alive (and UPOH rarely accepted children with two living parents), though the managers recorded no additional information about him, suggesting that he had likely abandoned his family. Furthermore, Putnam was a Methodist, so the orphanage would not have felt obliged for reasons of religious affiliation to accommodate a special request. Unlike most deserted wives seeking help with their children, she was a white-collar laborer, working as a stenographer at J. P. Witherow, a mining engineering company across the river in downtown Pittsburgh. Putnam lived at the "head of Arch St.," just four blocks away from UPOH, and was likely able to drop her children off at the orphanage each morning before walking or catching the streetcar into work, and then pick them up each evening. If the children ate their supper at the orphanage, Putnam would have saved the labor-intensive work of meal preparation and was likely able to stretch her stenographer's wages just far enough to cover housing, ready-made clothing, food for the weekends, and other household necessities.[143]

Few women were as fortunate as Putnam, however: even if the orphanages had been willing to accept day boarders, most solo women seeking child care performed domestic labor, earning minimal wages and leaving insufficient time to perform their own household labor required to feed, clothe, and shelter children on those wages. This reason alone helps to explain the lack of enthusiasm for day nurseries and preference for full-time orphanage care among Pittsburgh's working class. However, at least one other parent during this period used UPOH as a daycare facility: when Cameron Wallace requested space for his two boys, the managers admitted them, noting, "the older one will stay with him at night." A year later, the arrangement held, and the managers observed, "Mr. Wallace has been taking one of his boys at night and the other Sabbath afternoon." They decided to "make exception" for Wallace that "he be allowed to take his boys Sabbath afternoons."[144] In a few rare cases, then, orphanages literally served as day care, whereas most parents turned to them for full-time care, albeit as a short-term strategy for family survival.

❊   ❊   ❊

In 1952 John Longmore Thompson presented his grandmother's bible to the United Presbyterian Orphan's Home; it now bears an inscription: "This Bible belonged to Mrs. Isabella Nelson Longmore, the mother of the five children, whose appeal to Dr. Fulton opened up this vast vista of service in our denomination."[145] Although the Longmore children never resided at the orphanage, this statement reveals a fundamental truth: desperate parents in need of care for their children created the demand that justified the founding of such institutions. It was their direct requests and pleas for assistance that ignited the largely middle-class movement of benevolent women committed to help. As UPOH managers themselves acknowledged, their mission was to "rescue" the poor, "whose beseeching cries day and night are sounding in our ears."[146] Furthermore, those cries belonged to parents, not to orphaned or abandoned children, despite institutions' rhetorical tendency to represent their clients as young waifs, alone in the world. Over time, both organizations began to emphasize founding stories centered around innocent, orphaned children that downplayed the direct involvement of parents: at UPOH, it was the Longmore children, and at the HCC, it was a little four-year-old girl named Nellie Grant, discovered wandering by herself in the rain.

In fact, the vast majority of HCC and UPOH children had at least one living parent, such as Robert Highland, the father of four boys, the very first residents to arrive at the Home for Colored Children in August 1880.[147] Most of these parents were working class, though they had tipped into poverty after struggling through one or more crises, often including the loss of a spouse through death, sickness, or desertion. Immigration and migration patterns cut families off from stable networks of support, and inadequate housing exacerbated problems for many. For these parents, orphanages offered a temporary solution to the conflicting demands of wage labor and child raising. Furthermore, parents used orphanage care for family survival, strategically placing and retrieving children by age, sex, and sibling status.

For families facing a child care crisis, there were few institutional alternatives, particularly in the 1870s when both the HCC and UPOH were organized, and especially for African Americans. While their pleas for help called attention to the critical needs of the poor—indeed, launching institutions such as UPOH itself—parents also shaped institutional offerings through their demand for services. This was most clearly demonstrated in the lackluster enthusiasm parents gave to a day nursery operated by a group of UPOH managers for a short time in the 1890s: the women who managed the Allegheny Day Nursery were disappointed to learn that they could not get parents to send their children there, while demand remained high at the orphanage, with some families even turning to that institution as an early form of day care.

Poor parents were thus important participants in a larger community dialogue about child care, yet they did not fundamentally change the basis of the conversation, which continued to focus on the needs of dependent children and not working parents. They were unable to challenge the underlying constructions of race, class, and gender that wrought the orphanage system at the end of the nineteenth century. For example, African Americans could not directly protest racial segregation through their use of the HCC. And poor parents, black and white, used orphanages to solve their personal child care crises but were unable to mount a broader attack on the new industrial economy and its inherent and inequitable class structure that was so often responsible for families' situations. Rather, what they *were* able to do was to shape the orphanages to their own purposes, as the next chapter explores, using the institutions as a form of child care.

CHAPTER THREE

BOARDING ORPHANS
Working Parents' Use of
Orphanages as Child Care

> In looking back over the years since the opening of the Orphan's
> Home, we can see a long line of children, numbering into the
> thousands, going on, and on. All of these children have tarried
> with us for a while and received the protection and care and
> Christian training that loving hands and kind hearts alone can
> give. . . . Beside this line, we see another line of good and faithful
> women, who have given of their best to comfort and cheer these
> little ones, who, in some way, have lost the support of their
> natural protectors.
> —50th Annual Report United Presbyterian
>   Women's Association, 1928

In their fiftieth anniversary report, the United Presbyterian Orphan's Home
proudly reflected on the thousands of children they had helped and pictured
them stretching back in time in a long procession next to a line of dedicated
orphanage managers. Parents are not only missing from this imagined scene
but are literally portrayed as absent from their children's lives, the "little
ones" having "lost the support of their natural protectors." What's more, the
"protection and care and Christian training" required by children came not
from their own families but from the "loving hands and kind hearts" of the
managers, acting as substitute mothers to provide "comfort and cheer." In
their self-representations, the Home for Colored Children often painted an
even more dismal picture of parents, pointing to not only their absence but
their alleged abuse and neglect of children. For instance, managers described
the institution as "A Home for those who are orphans, friendless, destitute,
neglected, or ill treated." They emphasized that they were authorized by
their founding charter "[t]o bind out all children committed to its charge

where maintenance is unprovided for by their parents or guardians."[1] Yet, as the previous chapter argued, most HCC and UPOH children had at least one living parent, and while a few were undoubtedly victims of abuse and neglect, the vast majority hailed from families struggling through crises to combine wage labor and child rearing. Indeed, the vast majority also had parents providing "maintenance" through board payments, and only a fraction were ever bound out through formal indentures.

Beneath the surface of orphanage rhetoric and managers' historical memory, parents were very much present and played a crucial role in the institutions. Parents initiated the admissions and dismissal processes, negotiating terms with the managers, and asserted control during their children's stay. They viewed their children's institutionalization as a temporary necessity and often a service for which they were paying, a deliberate parenting choice and not an abandonment of their parenting responsibilities. Families, including the children themselves, also helped to mold the nascent foster care system as it evolved in this period from formal indenture practices coordinated by the orphanages. While they were not always successful in getting what they wanted, families used the orphanages for their own purposes as a form of child care.

"I will pay you every cent and work hard": Parents in the Admission and Negotiation Process

From their very first contact with the orphanages during the admissions process through their final decision to retrieve children, parents remained active in their children's care. While managers liked to think of themselves as "child rescuers," saving innocent children from the ravages of poverty—and by extension, saving them from their own poor parents—client families viewed their use of orphanage care quite differently. The UPWANA (UPOH's umbrella association) characterized its orphanage work as a "Life Saving Station . . . to rescue the endangered lives stranded by poverty and misfortune" and "a noble Christian endeavor to assist helpless humanity."[2] The WCA (HCC's umbrella association) spoke of their work as "one of rescue, reconstruction and upbuilding."[3] Their rhetoric effectively erased parents, as the managers both literally and figuratively separated children from their families. While the orphanages' public rhetoric disguised the presence of parents, this was more a matter of emphasis than conscious attempt to perpetuate an illusion: the managers chose to emphasize the plight of poor children over that of their struggling parents. In part, this reflected their deep ambivalence about women's wage work, but it also promoted their own role as surrogate mothers and their institutions as foster homes. Yet far more often than not, parents were the ones making active choices in their children's lives: seeking assistance, choosing an institution, negotiating with managers over the specifics of their children's care, and employing a variety of strategies aimed at family survival.

Not only did most UPOH and HCC children have at least one living parent, but the vast majority of them were also placed in the institutions by one or both of their parents. At UPOH more than three-quarters (77 percent) of the children had parents who took the initiative in placing them (see figure 3.1).[4] The figures for HCC are slightly less telling at first glance, because the managers only recorded who placed a child in the orphanage 14 percent of the time. They would note information on one or both parents but often did not indicate who actually placed the child unless it was not a relative—such as a charitable organization or the courts—suggesting that these were special, or more unusual circumstances. Yet these partial records are still revealing: even when the managers did not specify the placing party, many records imply the direct involvement of parents in the admission process, as they contain information on parents' place of birth and other details likely only known to those parents. Over half of those HCC children without placement data had at least one living parent noted in the admission register, and it is reasonable to assume that at least *some* of these children were placed in the orphanage by a living parent.[5] Furthermore, the HCC documents suggest substantial involvement of parents in placing their children. At both the HCC and UPOH, then, parents were highly active in initiating the placement of their children.

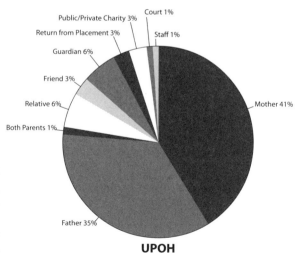

Figure 3.1. UPOH Admissions by Placing Party, 1878–1929. *Source:* UPOH admissions registers and case histories.

Court 1%
Public/Private Charity 3%
Staff 1%
Return from Placement 3%
Guardian 6%
Friend 3%
Mother 41%
Relative 6%
Both Parents 1%
Father 35%

UPOH

Even when parents were not the placing party of record, evidence suggests they may have had some involvement with the admissions process. For instance, while most children coming from another charitable organization appear to have been orphaned or abandoned, a few had parents who actively participated in their transfer to the orphanage. Wallace Taft, a widowed farm laborer from Ohio, was forced to place his children in the local county home, "where they would have been kept if Mr Taft would have consented to give them up to them to find [indentured] homes for them, but this he would not do." Instead, Taft transferred his three boys to UPOH, where he paid ten dollars out of his sixteen-dollar monthly wage to board them.[6]

Similarly, some of the court placements may well have involved parents using the new juvenile system (founded in Pittsburgh in 1903) to regulate their children's behavior. Parents around the country were also beginning to use the courts to make claims on the state for a variety of assistance.[7] For example, in Philadelphia in 1922, parents themselves brought 59 percent of the dependency petitions filed before the juvenile court in an apparent effort to obtain financial help.[8] Even when parents did not initiate contact with the juvenile courts, they sometimes remained involved with their children's care at the orphanages. For instance, the HCC noted, "The Juvenile Court wishes the Home to care for three children—the 'man will pay.'"[9] Of course, these payments were not always voluntary: Pennsylvania's 1903 child welfare act allowed the courts to place children in an institution and order the child's parents to contribute to their support.[10] While some parents whose children came to the orphanages through the courts or other charitable organizations were no doubt guilty of the abuse and neglect they were often accused of, others played an active role in negotiating those systems to find care for their children and remained at least somewhat involved, to the extent that they were paying board.

Board payments, in fact, were a significant point of negotiation with the managers. Some parents even insisted that they were paying a fee for a service. Nearly all parents paid something for their children's care: the HCC bylaws required board payments for every child, and more than half of the UPOH admission records specifically named a boarding fee.[11] Furthermore, most of those without a recorded fee were likely paying one, as actual charity cases were generally noted in the board minutes as exceptions to the rule and were not admitted all that frequently. The managers, however, tended to view all children as charitable cases, and their families as needy assistance-seekers, rather than paying clients. In an address to the WCA, Mrs. Swartz, President of the Children's Industrial Home Association of Harrisburg, spoke for many of her peers when she explained she was against the giving of outright charity, since it "ultimately does more harm than good . . . because it fosters a spirit of dependence upon the labor of others." This, she felt, was "incompatible with self-respect, self-reliance and self-exertion, and tends to cultivate all those arts of lying, hypocrisy and deception." Swartz warned: "Supply the physical needs of this class without a return of labor, and you remove all stimulus to useful exertion."[12] In a separate address some years later, the Rev. David S. Kennedy reminded the WCA women, "Our duty is to help" the poor, but he concluded "with a caution, lest our labors should encourage charity-getting, or a disposition to depend on us."[13] Board payments were one way to demand "a return of labor" and prevent the "evils" of "idleness" and dependency.

Yet the poor parents who used the orphanages for child care were rarely idle, and by their own accounts often worked extremely hard to make their payments. While some acknowledged that they were accepting charity in using the orphanages, others insisted they were not, viewing their financial contributions as a payment for services rendered. For instance, Luella Dade placed her son in UPOH and took her newborn to Chicago, where she wrote to the managers, "I have weaned my baby and will soon be able to work. . . . I will pay you every cent and work hard to get [the board money]."[14] At the HCC, managers noted that Sarah Dennis "was causing a great deal of trouble in the Home—objecting to her children working as their board is paid."[15] Dennis represented her children as paid boarders who ought to be free of work obligations, rather than recipients of aid, while the managers portrayed her objections as causing trouble. When Nancy Madison took her children out of the orphanage, she "decided to keep them out and asked to have her money refunded." Madison viewed the board fee as a literal payment for service, which her children had not yet received, and the managers agreed, voting to "charge her for one week which would be $2.00 and return her the remainder $6.00."[16]

Similarly, when UPOH threatened to report J. A. Dunham to the "prison board" for delinquent board fees, he responded angrily, "I have not refused to pay the bill . . . but will pay it just as soon as i can make arrangements to meet it." He reminded them, "I have paid . . . over a thousand dollars cash myself for the very poor boarding of my children and my friends and relatives contributing many hundreds of dollars in different ways to the support of same."[17] By criticizing his children's care as "very poor," Dunham implied that this was an economic transaction in which he had purchased a service, entitling him to quality child care. Furthermore, he suggested he was a good customer, having paid "over a thousand dollars" and that his friends and family had also given to the orphanage as generous donors.

Though he agreed to pay the "small amount" he owed, Dunham appears to have viewed his board bill as a fee-for-service, representing his family as dissatisfied clients rather than needy mendicants.

Parents' board fees, in fact, represented a significant portion of orphanage revenue streams. A 1907 report of all institutionalized children in Pittsburgh indicated that families' board payments roughly equaled public subsidies from the state and county combined.[18] In the HCC's early years, before it built an interest-yielding endowment, board fees provided a quarter of the organization's entire income.[19] Many years at UPOH, board fees were the single largest source of revenue: in 1891, for instance, those fees brought in three times as much as the next largest source of income, an annual fundraiser.[20] In addition, while both orphanages received significant in-kind contributions from donors (such as bedding, clothing, and food), board fees continued to provide a crucial source of monthly *cash* income that allowed the organizations to pay their bills. Over time, the managers actually shifted an increasing proportion of the financial responsibility onto families: for example, the average UPOH boarding fee of $1 per week in the 1880s rose to $2.50 in the 1920s, well beyond the rate of inflation that would have kept the fees closer to $1.80. Despite their view of board payments as a means to prevent idleness and dependency among the poor, managers also understood the importance of those fees to the financial security of their organizations. They spent an enormous amount of time tracking down those who fell into arrears, sometimes sending dunning notices to large groups of parents in an attempt to retrieve back payments and other times turning cases over to their lawyers for collection.

Board fees were a site of constant negotiation between parents and managers, over their meanings (regulation of the poor vs. income stream and payment for service) as well as the amount and payment schedules. At UPOH a large space on the application form labeled "Conditions under which child entered" allowed parents and the admitting manager to literally negotiate the terms under which a child would be accepted into the institution, including how much the parents would pay, what clothing they would provide, and other details. While desperate parents eager to secure a spot for their children did not have as much power in that negotiation as the managers, they frequently pleaded their cases with the admissions committee, asking for reduced fees or to be allowed to pay more later when they got work. Catherine Meharry represents a typical case: an Irish-born widow who immigrated to the city with her young son, Douglas, she told the admitting manager she "does housework and cannot get a place to live with the child." They came to an agreement that Meharry would "pay according to her ability, not less than 50 cts per wk, not more than 75 cts."[21] Meharry stuck to this arrangement for five years, retrieving Douglas when he was eight years old. Similarly, Nola Stern negotiated a deal one January with the managers in which they would keep her three daughters "without compensation until April . . . [when she] thinks she will be able to pay a small amount for their board."[22] Good to her word, Stern paid $1.50 a week starting in April until she retrieved her girls the following January. During the admissions process, parents also negotiated payment schedules, agreeing to weekly or monthly payments.

Once their children were accepted, parents continued the negotiation over boarding fees, frequently requesting reductions, grace periods, and debt forgiveness when faced with periodic unemployment, illness, or injury that interfered with their ability to meet their board bills. For instance, the HCC managers granted Mr. Bowman, a widowed pastor with two girls, "eight dollars boarding for his children with the privilege of paying what he can until he gets work."[23] Working-class people in Pittsburgh averaged two months out of work each year, with African American workers facing longer and more frequent bouts of unemployment.[24] Parents used multiple strategies to deal with their board bills when they got behind, from making outright requests of the managers, to sending only partial payments or no payments at all.

Some parents went missing, making it impossible for managers to track them down, or denied they owed any money. When managers realized Mrs. Lavalley had "paid very little" for her three children, they decided her "children be returned at once to her when she can be found."[25] A week later they were still looking for her. Managers went all the way to Cleveland, Ohio, to find George Mason, a widowed insurance agent who had his two children in UPOH for two years, "to see . . . about his account which is still unpaid," but he "claims he does not owe us anything."[26] Others declined to pay rate increases: already $45 in arrears, "Mr. Arnold refused to pay the advanced rate of boarding and was requested to take his son Benjamin with him, which he did."[27] During a severe economic downturn in 1908, the UPOH managers noted, "A number of the parents who have been feeling the hard times have been unable to pay their childrens boarding but hope to soon," and decided "that these parents who have been faithful in the past and who are of duty now will be excused for a time."[28] They did the same thing again in 1915, reflecting a willingness to excuse fees for parents who were unable to pay but willing to lay bare the sad circumstances of their families' finances.

In making their requests for leniency, working parents adroitly adopted a sympathetic narrative designed to appeal to the managers' charitable instincts and quickly learned the "rules" of negotiation. For instance, the UPOH managers noted, "Mrs. Yarrow writes all about her troubles and promises to pay all she owes by April 1st." They agreed to "keep her child until that time and if she does not pay all she owes the child be dismissed to her."[29] Parents did not necessarily have to stretch the truth to demonstrate their neediness—though some undoubtedly did—but rarely failed to emphasize their innocence as victims of circumstances beyond their control. They wrote about being hospitalized, out of work, and "disappointed in business."[30] This narrative contested managers' tendency to blame the poor for their own poverty by reframing the issue of board fees in terms of economic and social conditions. Parents' letters and requests to the managers emphasized the structural causes of poverty that brought families to the institution's doorstep, rather than moral failure.

Parents' frequent inability, or unwillingness, to meet their board bills also spawned new policies at both orphanages threatening dismissal of children whose families owed more than a month or two of fees. For example, in June 1898 UPOH decided that "hereafter we will only keep children 1 month after the board bill is due," then their governing agency, UPWANA, revised the policy in 1903, saying that "when a party is two months in arrears their children will be dismissed at once." By 1917 they had rewritten this rule to apply to any parent who owed more than twenty dollars.[31] The HCC also threatened to dismiss children, but the only policy they passed in this period was an authorization "to send notices to any that are one month in arrears."[32] Often managers would threaten to send children home to their parents, who would then respond with a sympathetic request for leniency, to which the managers relented. Sometimes the orphanages tried to keep children, refusing to release them if their parents would not pay their bills. For instance, UPOH noted, "Mr. Reinhardt is in arrears, says he is going to take the children out. . . . If [he] comes and pays in full he be allowed to take his children and if he pays part and promises to pay later we hold the children."[33] Threatening to hold children hostage could be an ineffective strategy, however, as parents could retrieve their children fairly easily, even against the board's wishes. Three-year-old HCC resident Garrett Walsh, for example, was "taken away secretly at nite by his mother . . . and grandmother."[34]

Exasperated managers occasionally tracked parents down through their employers in an attempt to collect board. When Mr. Hanson "paid very little" for his children, UPOH managers wrote to his pastor, who replied, "the man is a drunkard." They also wrote to his employer, who spoke to him and then responded, "stating the man has promised to meet his obligation and if he does not to advise him."[35] Similarly, HCC managers contacted "the firm of West and Wilson, by whom Mr Crawford is employed," and they wrote back "saying that they would hold the sum of five dollars every two weeks from his wages until he has paid for the keeping of his children providing he still remains in their employ."[36] Parents actively negotiated their board payments, but they were never on equal footing in this cat-and-mouse game.

Clothing represented another area in which parents contested costs and meanings. Keeping children in clean, mended clothing occupied a tremendous amount of the managers' time and attention. Board members at both orphanages spent countless days cutting out and sewing new clothes, sometimes acquiring fabric and sending it out to church circles and other benevolent women's associations for assistance. Ladies Aid Societies all over the United States sent finished work to UPOH, and both orphanages received generous contributions of sewn pieces from the Needlework Guilds of Pittsburgh and Allegheny as well as numerous other organizations. After several churches donated sewing services, UPOH noted, "[even] with all the help we receive from sewing societies and individuals the amount of work still depending on our Matron and her assistants is appalling, to say nothing of the weekly mending."[37] The institutions experimented with ready-made clothing as early as the 1890s but largely stuck to less expensive handmade clothing through the 1920s, even though it usually meant keeping a seamstress on staff. To reduce labor costs, the orphanages often required older girls to assist with the nearly constant chore of mending. They also experimented with sending clothing out to commercial laundries, though they generally chose to employ laundresses as a cheaper alternative. UPOH eventually purchased an "Apex Institutional" washing machine in 1924 for $250 (worth $3,160 in 2010), which still required considerable labor to run.[38] With both laundresses and seamstresses on staff, clothing constituted a significant investment of time, energy, and financial resources for the orphanages.

Not surprisingly, managers were eager to have parents supply their own children's clothing, yet many were unable to do so and used the admissions process to negotiate the issue. Inability to supply clothing was not simply a reflection of a parent's finances, but of time and skills as well: few working-class families could afford the cash necessary for ready-made clothes, yet widows forced into wage labor would have very few hours remaining for the time-consuming tasks of purchasing materials and sewing, while widowers would likely have few of the skills (or time) to make their children's clothing. Some parents negotiated reduced boarding rates for their children in return for supplying some or all of the clothing. Once they provided clothing, parents were careful to be sure they got it back: after Mr. Samuel's children were dismissed, he wrote UPOH twice "asking for his children's clothing."[39] Many other parents agreed to a boarding fee that included orphanage-supplied clothing—another indication of the way in which parents interpreted boarding as a fee-for-service.

Either way, clothing could mean very different things to parents and managers. For parents, supplying their children's clothes provided a way to stay involved in the minutiae of their daily lives while physically cut off from them for all but a couple hours each week. For instance, the HCC managers noted, "Mrs Madison was visiting her boy and had brought him some clothing."[40] Geraldine Monroe sent a post office order for $1.50 to UPOH and requested, "If Norman needs shoes please pay for them out of this and keep the ballance for boarding," adding, "as soon as I can will send more money."[41] In this instance, Monroe prioritized proper clothing for her child above board payments. Parents could also use clothing as a barometer of care and a way of maintaining some control over their children's orphanage experience. After "Mrs. Enola . . . called and asked that warmer clothing be put on her children," UPOH passed a motion "to put enough clothing on the children to keep them warm, especially the Enola children."[42] Clothing could also allow parents to control how their children looked, providing them with a sense of identity.[43]

Managers, too, were interested in using clothing to give children a sense of unique identity amid growing notions of individualism and anti-institutionalism in the period. While neither the HCC nor UPOH ever dressed their children in uniforms, many orphanages continued that practice well into the twentieth century, much to the consternation of reformers.[44] In 1894 UPWANA president Elizabeth Campbell attended the General Committee of Our Young People's Institute held in Philadelphia and addressed a crowded church: "When describing the daily life of our Orphan's Home children telling how uniformity in dress was avoided and how they went as other children to Public School to Church and Sabbath School, she was loudly applauded."[45] As early as 1902 the HCC required that "each child must have its clothes marked with their own name," but nearly thirty years later the managers were still responding to accusations that their children lacked a sense of individual identity.[46] In a defensive letter to the Pittsburgh Child Welfare Study, the HCC emphasized, "Each child has his or her own wardrobe and is provided with play, school, and Sunday clothes. These garments are all marked with owner's name and kept in individual lockers."[47]

For both managers and parents, clothing served as a physical marker of individual identity.

Yet the managers also imbued clothing with a different meaning, using it to indicate children's transformed state, from "neglected" to "saved," from working-class origins to reflections of middle-class values. Popular representations of orphans in this time nearly always focused on their shabby, dirty clothes and shoeless feet as indicators of their neglect, though in fact, reformers sometimes manipulated images to heighten their effect. For example, London institution manager Thomas Barnardo staged his well-known photographs of "orphans," purposefully ripping their clothing to heighten their appearance of neglect.[48] A scathing 1915 report on dependent children in Pennsylvania featured a highly critical photo of the HCC basement playroom, with a shoeless boy sitting at an empty table (see figure 5.1). Day nurseries in the period also focused on clothing, often performing a ritual cleansing and redressing of children each morning, physically marking them as charitable cases with matching aprons.[49] Orphanage managers similarly viewed themselves as rescuing neglected children through the act of dressing them. Thus, for instance, the HCC managers reported visiting the home where they "found the Matron . . . busy mending the large quantity of children clothes . . . and could but feel it was largely a work of faith and love for the neglected ones."[50] UPOH described one little girl as "not considered a very promising looking child." However, "[a] clean dress, a bright ribbon on her hair, and she was quickly transformed, and had a school record above 90 per cent and two promotions in six months."[51] To the managers, the proper, "clean" clothing and "bright" accessories, literally transformed this girl into a high-achieving student.

Managers wished to have the children's clothing metaphorically erase their working-class origins, promoting instead a sense of middle-class values. UPOH explained to its largely middle-class readership, "Sending them out to the public school means they must be dressed as you or I would dress our boy or girl," and "we like to have our children look neat and well cared for when they go to school, church, and Sabbath School."[52] Statements such as these implied that the working class dressed differently, not "as you or I would," and appeared neither "neat" nor "well cared for." After taking the children on an outing to the Pittsburgh Exposition, the UPOH managers proudly crowed, "The girls with their white dresses, the boys with their white waists, together with their good conduct, attracted much attention."[53] Wearing clean white outfits in the notoriously filthy Steel City offered a sure sign of status, as such clothing required significant resources of time and money to keep them that way.

Along similar lines, HCC manager Julia Blair "made a plea for the boys to have their suspenders covered," and "after much discussion" they decided that all boys over the age of eight "be made to wear little jackets."[54] While working-class men labored in their shirtsleeves, exposing their suspenders, proper middle-class attire called for jackets. To illustrate, in its official seal, the Western Pennsylvania Humane Society, a "child rescue" organization that placed children at both the HCC and UPOH, used the imagery of suspenders and shirtsleeves to reference the coarseness of a man willing to beat children: the image showed children literally shielded by a woman, much like the managers who rescued orphans (see figure 3.2). Ironically, orphanage managers did not expect to literally transform their young wards into middle-class subjects—much of their care and training in fact focused on creating productive future workers—but rather, they used clothing to mark children's salvation from neglect and adherence to what they viewed as middle-class values of discipline and hard work.

In addition to negotiating the terms of admission for their children, including board payments and clothing arrangements, parents bargained with the managers during the dismissal process. Though the orphanages maintained the upper hand in this negotiation, parents were sometimes successful in resisting efforts to dismiss their children as they reached the age limit or for disciplinary reasons. For instance, UPOH noted, "Molly Atkins is now 12 years old but her father has no place to put her," and they decided that "she is allowed to remain in the Home until her sister Mabel is 12 when

Figure 3.2. The seal of the Western Pennsylvania Humane Society for the Prevention of Cruelty to Children. *Source:* Humane Society letterhead, letter from James L. Craven to UPOH, September 14, 1883,UPOH, MHY.

they can go together."[55] Similarly, while disciplinary problems could lead to children's rapid dismissal, parents often pleaded with the managers to keep children and give them a second chance. When the HCC wrote "to Mr. McCrary telling him of his son's having set fire at 3 different times to [the] building . . . he wrote back asking to please give him another chance, he having neither place nor means to care for him." They decided to "keep the [three] McCrary children and give them the food they need to keep them until Oct[ober]."[56] At UPOH, when "Stephen Moore stole a cake after Donation day," the managers "notified" his father, who responded saying "he cannot take him as he has no place for him."[57] The managers relented and agreed Stephen could stay.

In their negotiations with the orphanages, from the admissions through the dismissal process, parents became quite adept at navigating the unwritten rules of charity seeking. For instance, managers expected parents to support themselves and their children, but once a widow found wage work or a widower received a raise, they could face an increase in their boarding fees, undoubtedly leading some to hide income. UPOH managers discovered that "Mrs. Rogers is working now, making $20.00 per month," and decided to "notify [her] that she is to pay $10.00 per month for her children hereafter."[58] If a parent made too much money, he or she risked the children's dismissal altogether: the managers decided, "the Headley children be dismissed to their father as we have helped him over his troublous times and he is now able to care for them."[59] There were consequences if parents did not learn to accurately read the charitable landscape.[60] For instance, a prospective applicant had to pay attention to clothing to avoid appearing too well off: Mrs. Kane's two children had been accepted at UPOH, but when she brought them in, the managers noted she "[w]as well dressed and from all appearances the committee did not think she ought to be placing her children in a Home," and dismissed them.[61] Sometimes managers accused parents of outright fraud: UPOH accepted two children into the Home, "but finding Mrs. Conner was not what she should be they were dismissed. . . . [T]hey were placed here under false pretenses."[62] Similarly, UPOH investigated "[t]he case of Mrs. Saunders who has five children in the Home . . . and found the woman has misrepresented things." They promptly dismissed the children as they felt they were "relieving a mother of her duty."[63]

Parents sometimes deceived orphanage investigators about their true marital status. Widows and widowers might conceal a new marriage if they were not yet financially prepared to retrieve their children. It could also take some time to find adequate housing in the booming city before reuniting a family. For instance, when the HCC received a letter informing them that a widowed father had remarried, they decided to "send the letter to Mr Washington . . . and if he is married and has a home for his children to see they are returned to [him]."[64] Similarly, Mr. Davis admitted to UPOH managers that he had remarried, but explained he had "not gotten a home yet and ask[ed] that we keep his children awhile."[65] They refused and dismissed the children. While some parents undoubtedly made selfish choices and "worked the system" to keep their children longer than absolutely necessary, there is no evidence that this was common practice: for some, employing tactics of deception was simply a way to get what they needed from these charities for their families.

Unmarried mothers might assert that they had been deserted to cover up "illegitimate" children.[66] Furthermore, "desertion" and "separation" could be ambiguous categories, and parents sometimes colluded to obtain social services for the remaining, custodial parent by claiming abandonment.[67] For example, Mr. Johnson told the managers his wife had deserted the family when he placed his three children in the HCC, but the following month the managers reported the "mother was afterwards found to be living," and they dismissed the children. Johnson's employer "interceded on their behalf and asked" the managers to "reconsider [their] actions," but they refused, stating the "parents were living and able" but, in their opinion, simply "not willing to take care of" the children.[68] While it is possible that Johnson's wife had actually abandoned the family, the fact that the managers acted so swiftly when they discovered her "to be living"—he never claimed she was dead—but "not willing" to support the children, suggests that they suspected fraud. When poor parents lied about their economic circumstances or abandonment, they portrayed themselves as "deserving" and claimed the right to relief.

Parents' willingness to deceive, or at least managers' belief that parents practiced deception with regularity, led to an intrusive policy of investigation. For instance, one month HCC managers empowered their receiving committee to admit "several worthy cases . . . if after investigation they found matters to be as stated in application."[69] Their statement implies a degree of suspicion even of seemingly "worthy" cases, suggesting that all applications had to be verified. The members of the powerful receiving committee often visited applicants in their homes, taking note of the surroundings and seeking clues about the family's financial condition. When a widow applied to readmit her children to UPOH a second time, the committee visited her home and reported back to the board: "Think Mrs. Hastings in very comfortable circumstances with enough to provide for her children, do not recommend their coming back."[70] Families invited orphanage managers into their homes and petitioned them for aid but could not always maintain control over their relationship with them: parents did not always succeed in getting their children placed, especially if they had not learned the unwritten rules of charity seeking.[71]

Lacking the upper hand in this relationship, parents employed the tools they had, sometimes resorting to deception and fraud, which ultimately led to more intrusive investigative practices on the part of the orphanages. This dialectic of cooperation and conflict between parents and managers stemmed in part from their different views of the institutions and the problem they were meant to address. To the managers, the orphanages' mission was to serve abandoned, abused, neglected, and destitute children: their focus was on the children, not the needs of parents, and they treated all poor parents with a measure of suspicion. The managers were not aiming to address the underlying structural issues of poverty brought on by the ravages of the industrial economy; for instance, they did not try to tackle the sticky problem of women's labor or inadequate wages, and instead remained loyal to the breadwinner ideal, assuming that married parents would be able to support their children. Yet for poor parents facing overlapping crises, often precipitated by the loss of a spouse, the orphanages were addressing a child care emergency. Parents generally cooperated with the managers in order to get the resources they needed for their families, but also effectively negotiated with them.

"I dream of them almost every night": Parental Involvement in Children's Lives

Once families had placed their children in the orphanages, they frequently remained quite involved in their lives. Through letters and visits, parents supervised the care of their children, overseeing such things as their clothing, medical care, and discipline. Parents communicated with the managers and their children through letters on a regular basis, as evidenced by the voluminous references to them in the manager's meeting minutes. While most institutions did not keep records of this type, historian Judith Dulberger discovered an astounding cache of correspondence between parents and the superintendent of the Albany Orphan Asylum from the end of the nineteenth century. In her analysis of those letters, she found that working-class parents were just as sentimental about their children as middle-class families, and emphasized supposedly "middle-class" values such as delaying gratification, a focus on education, obedience, and self-sufficiency.[72]

This was apparent at the Pittsburgh orphanages, too, where families often inquired about children's needs and sent specific instructions for their care.

For instance, managers received a "[l]etter from the Grandmother of Bella Stewart asking if she were in need of anything," and "[a] letter from Mrs. Oakley says she would like Marvin to spend a few weeks in the Boy Scout Camp."[73] Mrs. Warner wrote to "request that her boys hair be cut instead of clipped and she will pay the cost."[74] Through this contact, and ultimately through the dismissal procedure itself, families resisted managers' complete control of their children.

Occasionally, parents wrote quite angry letters, but they had to tread a fine line in their interactions with the orphanages. Nancy Madison complained to UPOH, "stating among other things her children had learned bad language while in the Home."[75] However, when Sarah Dennis wrote "accusing [the matron] with beating" her children, the HCC managers responded, "As Mrs Dennis threatens to take her children out it was decided that she be told to do so."[76] Parents wrote to their children, too, and requested that their children write back to them. In one instance, UPOH managers used a mother's effort to regularly communicate with her daughter as evidence of her whereabouts and dismissed all her children as she owed back board: "Willa Rush hears about once a week from her mother who is still living in Bulger [a town about twenty-five miles west of the city]." They decided that "Mrs. Rush's children be sent to her at once for the reason she is in arrear $46.00 twice the amount we usually allow."[77] Even for families living in the city much closer to the orphanages, writing letters remained the most common way for families to stay in touch with their children and take charge of their care.

However, parents were regular visitors at the institutions as well. Visits provided an important emotional connection for parents and children, particularly for those forced to go long periods without seeing each other. Wallace Taft, a farm laborer working in Ohio, wrote the managers, saying, "i am coming out to see the boys in 2 or 3 weeks. . . . tell them that i am coming to see them and . . . i dream of them almost every night."[78] This father clearly maintained close emotional bonds with his children and hoped to move closer to the orphanage so that he could have more regular contact. Yet, even if Taft managed to find employment near the institution, he would have been limited to a narrow window of visiting time each week. Both the HCC and UPOH generally permitted visits only one or two days each week, which could make it difficult for working parents.

Their frequent requests for exceptions to this rule forced managers to experiment with different schedules to accommodate parents' needs.[79] For example, the HCC granted Mary Stuart "special permission to visit on day requested."[80] In 1913 UPOH decided, "Owing to the inconvenience for some of the parents and friends in being restricted to Saturday afternoons for visiting, it was decided to have two visiting days a week instead of one."[81] But managers often denied parents' special requests. For instance, when her children were placed out temporarily in country homes for the summer, Mrs. Reichland "wanted them brought in to meet her . . . but was refused."[82] They also refused when Mr. Baum "asked that the children be allowed to sit with him in Church."[83] By 1929 both orphanages had relaxed their visiting rules somewhat, permitting parents to come Monday through Saturday, though Sundays were still prohibited. After its move to Butler County that year, UPOH also began allowing parents to stay overnight and for meals during their visits, provided they pay.[84] Pressure also mounted on the orphanages from reformers who urged more liberal visitation policies. In 1930 the HCC responded defensively to the authors of the Pittsburgh Child Welfare Study, who had made a number of criticisms of the home: "All parents, relatives, and friends of the children are welcomed at any time before 7:30 P.M. on all days of the week, with the exception of Sunday."

Sunday visiting hours became a particular point of negotiation between managers, who wished to keep the children focused on observing the Sabbath, and parents, for whom the day was often one of the few times they had available to see their children. For instance, Mrs. Wrigley wrote to UPOH "in regard to her children, asks to be allowed to see them on Sunday as she is employed during the week."[85] Similarly, the HCC decided the "Board will allow Mrs Sampson to visit her child on Sunday because she is not able to come to the Home during the week."[86] UPOH acknowledged, "We find that many would like to visit on Sabbath, but our rule in this regard has been rigidly enforced."[87] The HCC experimented with allowing Sunday visiting, but then received "[c]omplaints of Sabbath Day visiting," presumably from the staff and board managers who had to accommodate parents during visiting hours, and decided to "dispense with" it.[88] Some parents persisted, however. Maggie Livingston repeatedly appeared on Sundays, even when asked not to, and even when the city had posted quarantine notices on the home (both orphanages were frequently under quarantine for a variety of diseases, including measles, mumps, flu, and diphtheria). The HCC managers noted, "Mrs. Livingston still annoying matron by Sabbath visits," and two years later, unrepentant, they told her "to come and get her children since she would respect neither rules of the Board [nor] of City Quarantine."[89] Parents' determination to see their children and repeated requests for changes to the visiting schedule reflected their desire to stay involved with their children's lives inside the orphanages.

Visits themselves were sometimes sites of conflict with managers and staff at the two orphanages. Some parents brought food and treats, which could cause trouble if there were leftovers. Managers told Mr. Waldron "not to bring eatables for his children more than they can eat in his presence." But he complained about the policy, writing "that he has been prohibited to bring anything to his children to eat."[90] Parents continued to break this rule, and the managers instructed the "[m]atron to inforce the rules about . . . bringing fruit" and also limited "friends visiting [to] once a week," suggesting they had been pushing this boundary as well and visiting more often.[91] Mrs. Sampson complained to the HCC managers "that Mrs Fitzhugh [the matron] had ordered her from the Home." But Fitzhugh reported "that Mrs Sampson was violating rules every time she visited Her child and when spoken to about it was very impertinent."[92] Parents had to tread carefully with their behavior and complaints, however, as managers could threaten to dismiss children. For example, UPOH resolved, "If a parent coming into our Home acts disrespectful to a manager or employee they be notified . . . and their children dismissed."[93] A month later, they acted on their new policy, dismissing the Jones boys "to their father on account of his disrespectful talk to our Sec[retary]."[94] They also threatened Daniel Tarrington with his children's dismissal, warning him "he must not come to the Home intoxicated."[95] That same month, the managers wrote to "Mr. Chaney stating we regret having heard he visited his child at [a foster home] taking with him whiskey and treating the hired help."[96] Parents challenged official visiting schedules, rules, and expectations of conduct, but did not have equal power in their negotiations with managers who held the ultimate card in dismissing children at a time when families most needed child care.

In much the same way, UPOH families negotiated with the orphanage to take their children for home visits, but often did not get the results they had hoped. For example, "Mr. Wright wanted to take his little girl for the weekend and her birthday," but the managers refused to bend their rules.[97] Similarly, they refused when Mrs. McFinn asked "if her children would be allowed to go out to visit their brother."[98] Nevertheless, parents persisted. After UPOH ruled that no children would be permitted to leave until summer vacation started, "a number of parents" wrote anyway, "wanting to take their children out."[99] At times the orphanage appeared more flexible in responding to parents' requests for home visits. In 1903 it "granted [children] leave of absence once a month if desired by their friends," though it warned "that the child will be dismissed if not returned at the time stated," suggesting that families had been stretching the time limit on these visits.[100] One month the managers also voted to allow "[t]he children . . . to go to the school picnic with their parents."[101] At other times, UPOH tightened its policy, declaring, for instance, that "children be not allowed to go out for [Christmas] vacation only on urgent request of parents," and "we do not allow children to go out to spend the night on Sabbath or Decoration Day."[102] Yet even the tightening of these rules indicates that UPOH parents, at any rate, had been successful in gaining overnight visits and vacations with their children. Though African American parents actively visited their children in the HCC, the absence in the records of similar requests for home visits suggests that even infrequent overnight stays were more difficult for these families to manage. The preponderance of black women employed in domestic labor, for instance, would have made an overnight stay nearly impossible for many. Until after World War I, a full 90 percent of African American women working for wages in Pittsburgh were employed as domestics, and those with live-in positions would likely have been barred from hosting their children.[103]

Visits with their children, both in the orphanages and in their own homes, allowed parents to remain involved in their care, supervising, among other things, their health and medical treatment. For example, an HCC board manager visited the orphanage and "[f]ound Mrs Morgan . . . the mother of little Jimmy [who was] sick with rheumatism" at the home when she arrived. The mother was there the next day, too, and went "to get a room ready for herself." A few weeks later, the board visitor reported Jimmy was doing better and "[h]is mother expects to take him home today."[104] Parents monitored their children's health and intervened when they felt additional treatment was necessary. The HCC managers remarked, "Little James Moore was not well and was taken by his father to the Suburban Hospital where he was operated upon for tubercular peritonitis." When James died a few days later, Mr. Moore "took charge of everything and paid all the funeral expenses."[105] Even if they could not be there in person, through correspondence, families instructed managers to attend to their children's health needs. For instance, UPOH received a "letter from the aunt of Emma Saville stating Emma's eyes needed attention."[106]

Children's bodies could literally become contested sites when managers and parents occasionally disagreed over proper medical treatment. Parents generally cooperated with managers in health matters—usually agreeing to have their children vaccinated, for instance—yet managers held the upper hand, as they could threaten to deny admission to or dismiss a child if families did not oblige. For instance, Mr. Cornwall told the managers during the admissions process that "he does not want his child vaccinated," but they replied that "unless his child [was] vaccinated and all rules complied with his child [would] be refused."[107] Similarly, UPOH managers discussed "the Baldwin child whose father refused to have it treated at the Hospital" and decided to dismiss her. Mr. Baldwin "came and paid his bill and took all the children," suggesting he was dissatisfied with their handling of his daughter's care and preferred to take all of his children home, rather than leave them at the orphanage.[108] Following the Baldwin incident, the UPOH managers decided "that the same action [dismissal] be taken in similar cases."[109] This left some parents with no alternative other than to retrieve their children if they disagreed with the managers' assessment of medical "needs," including apparently elective surgery. For example, UPOH noted, "Mr. Monroe has taken his three children today as he does not approve of having their tonsils removed."[110] Occasionally parents tried to remove their sick children, only to be refused: Maggie Walsh "asked for permission several times to remove [her son, Robert] but due to the fact that he had pneumonia [the doctor] objected to the child being removed." After Robert died in the home, Walsh and her mother sneaked into the HCC and removed her other son, Garrett, "from the home secretly sometime between 7:30–8:10 P.M."[111]

At other times, families were somewhat more successful in their negotiations, and over time, the orphanages slowly acknowledged parents' rights to control their children's bodies. For example, the HCC managers noted, "Mrs. Underhill refuses to have her child who is suffering from hernia operated," but they did not dismiss the child, and Underhill retrieved both of her children eight months later.[112] In 1914 UPOH had eye and throat doctors examine all the children and decided to "consult the parents" of any "children needing attention after examination."[113] They also decided "to notify the parents or guardians in case of operations and get their consent."[114] Around the same time, UPOH added a second, longer form to its admission process asking: "Do you consent to Hospital care and surgical operation to save life in case you cannot be communicated with? Do you consent to child taking swimming lessons under supervision?" By obtaining consent, managers formally acknowledged parents' right to make decisions about their children's healthcare.

The issue of consent resurfaced at both orphanages in the 1920s with the introduction of the new "Schick test" for diphtheria, a deadly childhood disease, and an associated live "anti-toxin" treatment. After the HCC appointed a committee "to investigate the inoculation for diphtheria," a manager "suggested getting parents' consent."[115] Similarly, the UPOH infirmary committee expressed some concern to the board "in regard to the toxin anti-toxin treatment being used on our children." They decided to get the advice of the home's physicians and added, "also the approval of the parents be secured."[116] There were frequent outbreaks of diphtheria across the United States in the 1920s, and children were the primary victims, with mortality rates as high as 20 percent.[117] The managers viewed healthcare as well within their purview, yet their tacit acknowledgement of parental rights implied in consent procedures represented a small victory for families in their ongoing negotiation with the orphanages. In addition, it reflects how parents' persistent involvement with their children's healthcare helped to shape institutional practice and policy, in this case by adding parental consent forms to the admission process.

Parents' decision to retrieve their children represented perhaps the ultimate point of involvement (or reinvolvement) in their lives at the orphanages. Just as families placed the vast majority of children in the institutions, so too did they retrieve most children: 80 percent of dismissed HCC children and 69 percent of UPOH children went home to parents or relatives (see figure 3.3).[118] While the managers spoke of "dismissing" or "releasing" children, these terms make the orphanages the active agents while rendering parents nearly invisible, when in many cases it was parents who actively initiated the

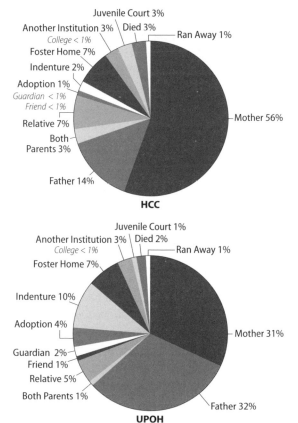

Figure 3.3. HCC and UPOH Dismissal by Retrieving Party, 1878–1929. *Source:* Case records compiled from children's registers, narrative histories, and meeting minutes.

process. The more common phrase "receiving party" acknowledges parents' role in the dismissal process, but in a passive manner, whereas "retrieving party" helps to more accurately categorize the various groups who took custody of children following their institutional stays. Although the orphanages occasionally initiated the dismissal process—sending children back to their parents for disciplinary reasons, when they aged out, or if families got too far in arrears on their board payments—more often, parents asked to have their children returned.

The formal dismissal process could be lengthy, with many days or even weeks elapsing between a parent's request and a board meeting when managers would approve the release of a child. Some families, reluctant to wait or unwilling to go through the formal dismissal process, simply took their children. For instance, UPOH managers noted, "Martha Gilmore was taken out by her grandfather without approval," and "Mr. Perry removed his two boys rather unexpectedly."[119] Retrieving a child could literally become a contest of wills, as in the case of three-year-old Jenny Conner, who had only been in the HCC a few weeks when her grandmother took her "away without a permit, the matron being absent [two employees] forbade her taking Jenny, but she walked away with her nevertheless."[120] The matron reported this to the managers as an "abduction," but for some families, retrieving their children against the wishes of the orphanages reflected their continued involvement with their children's lives and insistence on their own custodial rights.

Indeed, retrieving their offspring became a final assertion of control for some parents, intent on exercising authority over their children's lives and bodies. At UPOH, for instance, families contested hair-cutting policies, objecting particularly to having girls' hair shorn. Although the orphanage had a standing rule that "the children's hair be cut short when they come in and kept short," the managers intermittently strengthened and relaxed this policy in an ongoing contest with parents.[121] During one crackdown, managers decided to "notify parents of children having long hair that the hair will have to be cut by March 1st" and threatened to dismiss any children of families who did not comply.[122] Cassie Donaldson's father protested, as she had just turned twelve and was on the verge of leaving the home: "Her father does not want her hair cut if she has to be dismissed."[123] While managers may have preferred shorter hair for health and practical reasons, closely cropped hair, especially on girls, marked children as institutional inmates, and parents were no doubt anxious to avoid having them stigmatized. When their protests failed, parents resorted to removing their children from the orphanage. Following the renewed hair policy, UPOH noted that "a number [of children] left on account of the hair cutting."[124] A few years later, the managers passed a similar resolution, ordering, "The children's hair be cut irrespective of the parents wishes, except Eliza's who is only in temporarily."[125] Their decision acknowledged that parents held an entirely different opinion on the matter, but challenged their authority to control their children's bodies. Yet families responded again, by exerting what control they did have left in the situation, and the managers noted, "Five little girls left on account of the hair cutting."[126]

Some families also reacted to the news in 1929 that UPOH planned to relocate to Mars, Pennsylvania, by retrieving their children. The new orphanage, located in a rural area twenty-five miles north of the city and in another county, offered spacious grounds and amenities such as a swimming pool, but required considerable effort, time, and cost for parents to reach. A full seven months before the move, "Mrs. Dearborn [took] her children out and placed them in the Curtis Home as she heard we were going to the country."[127] Mr. Morgano also "took his two girls out," as he "did not want them to go to the country."[128] After a year of trying the new arrangement, Mr. Gordon wrote to the managers, saying he "[t]hinks he will take the children out where he can see them."[129] Though these were the exceptions rather than the rule, for at least some families, the greater physical separation from their children was more than they could bear, and they chose instead to remove them from the orphanage.

Even when children were dismissed to other institutions or the courts, rather than their families, parents were still sometimes involved in the process. Like Mrs. Dearborn, who did not want her children going to UPOH's new Butler County location and chose instead to send them to the Curtis Home, some parents actively transferred their children to other institutions. For instance, the managers dismissed the Smallman children "to their mother" because she had "broken the rule of the managers by taking her children to another home in the city without the consent of the Receiving Com[mittee] or Executive Com[mittee]."[130] Occasionally, when children neared the age limit, parents made arrangements to send them to boarding schools. For example, Mrs. Webber asked the managers "that her two boys be dismissed Tuesday to go to Girard College," a large boarding school near Philadelphia for orphaned and half-orphaned boys.[131]

Parents also used the new juvenile court system to retrieve their children. UPOH managers noted, "Mrs. Van Obling came with an order from the court to take her child."[132] While it is possible Van Obling obtained a court order to force reluctant managers to release her child, it is far more likely that her child had entered the orphanage through the juvenile court system in the first place, which then necessitated a judge's permission to remove the child. In this case, at least, it was the parent who appeared in person at the orphanage with the document in hand. The balance of power rested with the courts, however, and parents did not always get their children back. When the widowed Roberta Butler remarried and approached the court for permission to retrieve her daughter, the HCC managers noted: "Mary Butler . . . likes her new [foster] home and although her mother has remarried and wants the child, the Juvenile Court do not approve of any change nor that the child be returned to the mother."[133] Yet overall, these dismissals accounted for only a small proportion of children: 3 percent of HCC and UPOH children went to other institutions, less than 1 percent went to boarding schools (colleges), while another 3 percent of HCC and 1 percent of UPOH children were dismissed to the juvenile court. The larger point is that, like Roberta Butler, many parents actively pursued the dismissal of their children, whether through the courts, to other institutions, or simply back to their own homes. Indeed, parents remained involved in their children's lives inside the orphanages, overseeing their care through letters and visits, right up to the point of reunification.

"I will sign no papers":
Parents and Children in the Emerging Foster Care System

In 1880, as the two orphanages were getting started, a gradual shift in the nation's system of indenturing, or placing out, poor children was already underway, resulting ultimately in our modern foster care system. Parents, and to a limited extent children themselves, helped to shape this transition as they used the indenture process for their own purposes. Imported to the colonies from England, Elizabethan Poor Laws had established strict rules of responsibility for the poor, permitting local governments to place dependent children from the age of seven up into apprenticeships or indentureships.[134] Some institutions blurred the line between indentures and adoptions, such as the New York Children's Aid Society and its infamous "orphan trains," which, beginning in the 1850s, "rescued" poor children from the streets and shipped them to families in the West.[135] The rationale of placing out children in private homes borrowed notions of guardianship from the old English Common Law, with a heavy emphasis on Christian charity, and the "adoptions" that took place were often more of a social contract than a legal contract.[136]

In Pittsburgh, the Directors of the Poor also indentured dependent children to orphanages, which could in turn place them out in private homes. Both the

HCC and UPOH placed out children, either binding them out with formal indenture agreements or simply sending them to private homes where they were often expected to perform some labor in return for their keep. Formal indentures required a legal contract, signed by the indenturing family and usually an orphanage manager, in which labor expectations and terms of release were explicitly spelled out. Girls were generally bound until the age of eighteen and boys until twenty-one, and then released with a specified sum of money and change of clothes.

Since parents at these institutions did not give up custody, the managers could only place out children with their parents' permission or after families failed to provide financial support for a designated period of time.[137] The HCC charter authorized the orphanage "to indenture and provide suitable homes for all children committed to its care, when maintenance is not provided for by parents or guardians."[138] William Wilson, attorney for UPOH, offered his legal opinion to the board on this point: "[W]henever your home has supported a child for at least one year, and both its parents have neglected for that space of time to make any contribution towards its support, the court will permit of its adoption with your consent, and without requiring the consent of the neglecting parents." Furthermore, he suggested that this power could be used to threaten parents who were delinquent in their board payments: "It is my opinion that if your Board brings to the attention of neglecting parents the power which you have to obtain the adoption of the child without their consent, it will be an inducement to the parents to provide for the support of such child."[139]

Yet even when adoptions were confirmed in the courts with all parties signing documents, they were not always permanent, and some children found themselves returned to the orphanages.[140] Significantly, all of these arrangements, whether legal or social contract, indenture or adoption, were in a tradition of child care that responded to adults' needs—of lineage or labor—rather than children's needs.[141] But by the end of the nineteenth century, a new doctrine of the "best interests of the child" emerged, as Americans increasingly viewed childhood as a distinct phase of life that should be protected from too much work, and became alarmed at the extreme conditions of child labor in many U.S. cities.[142] Reformers worked for child labor laws and promoted the superior homelike qualities of temporary "foster" placements over the labor obligations of indentures. At the same time, child care institutions increasingly differentiated between adoption and these foster placements, the former now a legal procedure that transferred guardianship, whereas the latter transferred the child, while guardianship remained with an organization, such as an orphanage.[143]

By 1900 most orphanages around the country that had been indenturing children shifted to the use of foster homes.[144]

Yet, despite the declining acceptance of indentured labor, which Pennsylvania did not outlaw until 1927, both the HCC and UPOH continued placing children in formal indentures well into the twentieth century.[145] While the practice involved expectations of children's labor for the host family, in their official rhetoric the orphanages emphasized the emotional bonds of both children and foster parents. However, as orphanages around . the nation discovered, the promise of these emotional ties alone was not enough to secure sufficient numbers of "free" foster homes, and by the turn of the century some institutions turned to "paid," or subsidized, foster care in which families received a fee for taking in a child. By 1923 in Pennsylvania, the number of children in paid foster homes nearly matched the number in free homes (14 percent vs. 16 percent of dependent children being cared for outside their own homes).[146] Ten years later, with the rate of children in foster care at an all-time high, nearly a third were in paid boarding homes and only 9 percent were in free foster homes.[147] UPOH experimented briefly with paid boarding homes as early as 1902, but both orphanages largely frustrated reformers' efforts to de-institutionalize the bulk of their children. In Pennsylvania, reformers were particularly critical of Pittsburgh, and the western part of the state more generally, for lagging behind Philadelphia and the east. "A striking feature of the situation," lamented one report, "is the tendency in the Pittsburgh district to emphasize institutional care rather than the more modern and more effective system of placing out normal children in family homes."[148] Reformers characterized the orphanages as stubbornly resisting modernization, yet families also resisted this change.

Parents were extremely unwilling to permit the orphanages to indenture their children or place them up for adoption. Overall, just 12 percent of HCC and UPOH children were ever placed out in private homes, formally indentured, or adopted, with adoptions being by far the least common outcome (see table 3.1).[149] The UPOH managers acknowledged, "Many inquiries come to us for children to adopt," but noted, "Very few children under our care are for adoption."[150] Perhaps not surprisingly, a far greater proportion of those children placed out or adopted were full orphans compared to the general orphanage population: without parents to protest the placements, it was much easier for the institutions to make these arrangements.[151] For instance, when the Directors of the Poor arranged to formally indenture four siblings to UPOH (whom they had already been housing for over a year), so it could in turn place the children in private homes, the clerk of the poor board wanted to know "if anything has been paid for their maintenance

Table 3.1. HCC & UPOH Placements, Indentures, and Adoptions, 1878–1929

	HCC		UPOH	
	N	Percent dismissals	N	Percent dismissals
Placed out	55	7	32	5
Formally indentured	15	2	52	9
Adopted	8	1	22	4
Total	78	10	106	18

Source: Admissions and dismissal records, meeting minutes

within the past year." He warned, "Their parents are both living and may cause trouble unless we act in compliance with the law."[152] Demand for indentured children remained high through the first two decades of the new century, but managers lamented, "We regret that we have been unable to respond to opportunities of this kind. . . . Commonly the difficulty has been that a surviving parent was unwilling to permit such a transfer."[153]

As formal indentures and the placing out system transformed into foster placements in this period, parents may have found new reasons to resist such arrangements, wary that foster families might disrupt emotional ties with their children with the increased emphasis on affection rather than labor and training.[154] Parents likely preferred keeping their children in the institutions that they had selected, within reach where they could visit and maintain some control over their lives, and where siblings could remain together (since placements almost always split up family groups rather than keeping them together). For instance, when the UPOH managers began making plans to send all the children to country homes for the summer, the widow Bertha Stevens asked "if [her son] Peter could stay in the Home during vacation as she does not care to have him go too far away from her."[155] Stevens lived in the East End of Pittsburgh, several miles from the orphanage, but visiting her son in the country would have been much more difficult. In this case, however, the managers refused to make an exception, reflecting the limits on parents' power once they placed their children under an orphanage's control.

A rare surviving piece of parent correspondence illustrates perfectly the emotional bonds families maintained with their children and their strong resistance to giving them up. A few months after Luella Dade placed her six-year-old son, Henry, in UPOH, and took her newborn with her to Chicago, the managers wrote to her saying that the Humane Society had accused her of abusing Henry and wished her to give up guardianship of him. Dade wrote back, distraught and furious, saying, "I received your hard and cruel letter . . . and it would be impossible to try to convey to you how much misery it has caused me." She accused them of trying "to rob me of my child all I have in the world to live for," and suggested they were not acting like the Christians they "claim[ed] to be . . . you propose to try to save souls, do you know the step you are taking if you succeed would be the surest way you could send me to distruction." Dade called the Humane agents "vile," "wicked wretches," "worse than liers" willing to "perjare their souls," and retorted, "I think it would be a very inhumain instead of humain society that would canive to take him from me."

She denied their accusations, explaining, "To be sure I was almost driven crazy by grief sickness and trouble and was impatient and cross," and countered, "It was understood between you and I that it would be some time before I could pay anything on his board." Dade insisted she would "work hard" for the money she owed, "but I will sign no papers. I have weaned my baby and will soon be able to work for him and I will not give him up." She appealed to the managers as women, saying, "If you ever was a mother you must know how impossible for me to consent to your propositions." She concluded frantically that she was "nearly wild thinking of my boy. It will kill me to loose him please consiter my feelings and write me by return mail that he is still with you . . . I will not rest a minut untill I hear from you."[156] Dade's determined opposition to relinquishing guardianship of her son apparently succeeded in swaying the managers, as Henry remained at the orphanage another twenty months before joining his mother in Chicago.[157]

African American parents may have resisted the placing out or adoption of their children even more vehemently than white parents. The rate of both formal indentures and adoptions at the HCC was about a quarter of that for white children (see table 3.1). Some of this disparity—in the adoption rate, in particular—could be attributed to racist assumptions among white child-welfare workers, both volunteer managers and, increasingly, professional social workers, about the black community's ability and interest in taking care of "its own" children. As the role of the family shifted over the nineteenth century from performing an economic function to primarily an emotional and psychological one, the new emphasis on a "companionate family" meant that many childless couples wanted babies. But white attitudes about single African American mothers and the black community itself resulted in what historian Dianne Creagh calls the "pervasive neglect of black dependent children by the adoption community." As late as 1951, African American children accounted for only 4 percent of all U.S. adoptions.[158]

The significantly lower rate of indentureship at the HCC also points to the influence of strong parental opposition, especially since the demand for indentured children remained high into the first part of the twentieth century. The HCC managers were not particular about race when it came to placing out the children in their care and were happy to fill indenture requests from white families. In fact, at one point the UPOH managers even received a request from the HCC board "that we keep a list of the persons asking for children and send it to them, as they think this will aid them in securing homes for their children."[159] In the wake of Reconstruction and the flagrant abuse of imposed apprenticeships throughout the South—in which white landowners had newly freed-children bound to them, often without the parents' knowledge or against their wishes, and sometimes through the use or threatened use of violence—African American parents had reason to be deeply suspicious of the binding out process.[160] With 69 percent of HCC parents hailing from the South, most would have been all too familiar with the struggle many families endured to retrieve their children from forced apprenticeships (see appendix C). Historian Leslie Harris has performed the only other analysis of orphanage indenture data for African American children, though in an earlier period, and concludes, "Many parents approved of the indenturing process but still kept an eye out for their children." Her data, from 1837 to 1863, indicate that 28 percent of the New York Colored Orphan Asylum children were indentured—four times as many as the HCC children—suggesting that the post-Reconstruction context is critical to understanding parents' resistance to the arrangement.[161]

Though the HCC managers occasionally placed children with black families, parents were still quite reluctant to let their children go. For instance, when the managers intimated to one father that he ought to allow them to place out his daughter, as he owed board money, he replied that he "will not allow her to be taken and promises to pay the board."[162] The resistance of HCC parents to the practice of indentures may well have hastened the system's demise: in 1912, the managers did away with the "indenture" column in their register book and began recording "present address and home" for children placed in private homes, signaling a shift toward a more modern model of foster care. The transition was gradual, however, as the HCC still expected children placed in private homes as late as the 1920s to perform labor; yet it now required "proper wages for work done," and limited working hours to after the "close of attendance at day school."[163]

When families did permit the binding out of their children, they often exerted agency over those placements. Their authority was severely curtailed by the foster system, but many parents nevertheless attempted to assert what control they could. Some parents, for instance, requested specific locations for their children's indenture. Sonja Alanson gave her daughter, Margaret, to another woman "to raise but on account of poor health [the woman] had to give her up." Alanson then asked UPOH "to get her a good home some place in the country if possible," as she was herself "living in the country 4 miles from Mt Washington doing general housework."[164] Other parents went so far as to keep tabs on their children in their new homes. For example, one foster family returned a boy they had indentured because of his mother's unwelcomed involvement, noting that "the main fault we had was this George's mother claimed that the home could not find her boy ever." This parent expected the orphanage to keep track of her son so that she would know where he was. The foster parents explained that "we were down and seen the boys mother about it and it seems as though she would cause trouble with us we thought best to return the boy."[165]

Similarly, Mrs. Vandergrift told the managers she was "not satisfied with the home where her baby is." But rather than investigate, the managers replied that "the baby is to be dismissed at once as she is not satisfied." Vandergrift voiced concerns about the quality of her son John's foster home, but lost child care altogether as a result. The following month she "left $12.00 for the Baby's board," and the managers voted to send a committee to investigate the home, "as the mother complains of its treatment." Within a few weeks, John had died from pneumonia, and two months later the committee still had not visited the foster home. Mrs. Vandergrift "called and demanded an explanation in the United Presbyterian [the church newspaper]," and the managers appointed another "committee of three . . . to prepare an answer to Mrs. Vandergrift and return it before leaving [the board meeting]." Vandergrift's persistence forced the managers to act, though when they did visit the foster home, they reported they "were very well satisfied with all they saw and felt sure the baby had been well care for."[166] While most parents did not get as involved in their children's indentures as George's mother or Mrs. Vandergrift, these examples illustrate families' efforts to use the emerging foster care system for their own child care needs. Although the orphanages maintained the balance of power in the relationship—going so far as to dismiss children if parents complained—families used the resources available to them, including demanding public explanations, to enforce a level of care.

While they had even less power than their parents, children themselves could sometimes exercise influence over their placements, beginning with decisions about their adoptions and indentures. For example, UPOH noted that "Mr. and Mrs. Lytle are ready and willing to adopt William who does not want to be adopted, but they think he can be persuaded that it is for his best."[167] On the other hand, children sometimes did not wish to leave their placements: HCC reported, "The time of Annie Johnson indenture papers have expired. She prefers to remain with the family."[168] An orphan, and the oldest of six siblings who were all indentured or adopted out by the HCC, Johnson had lived with her indentured family for four years and opted to stay there rather than strike out on her own at the age of eighteen.

Many indenturing families returned children before their contracts expired, concluding that they were not receiving the labor they expected or deciding that it was simply too difficult to raise a foster child, especially if the child was sullen, morose, or acted out in any way. The breach of indenture contracts prompted frequent complaints from the UPOH managers, but at least one child tried to persuade the family to let her stay: Lydia Wharton's indenturing parents complained, "She has become uncontrollable and wont mind any thing that we say to her whatever and will have the last word in any advece that we give her." They explained, "[W]e would have sent her back to the home when the three months [trial period] was up but she would cry and promise to do better if we wouldent send her back and difernt times she wold promise the same." Wharton's pleas apparently persuaded them to keep her for four years, until the family insisted the orphanage take her back, saying, "[T]he agreement plainly says she was to bee an obedient child: She hasent dun five dolars worth of good with peace and pleasure cince we took her."[169] Children, like their parents, were not always successful in achieving their desired outcomes, but some made their preferences known.[170]

Perhaps because of their age, teenagers were the most vocal, expressing their desire to control their own futures, including determining where they would live. When a committee visited Laura Zisser in her indentured home, they reported, "Laura of age now and seems determined to go to her relatives." The managers recommended the family "pay Laura the [indenture] money and take her receipt."[171] Clarence Ransom was not even a year old when his mother died in childbirth and his father, a carpenter from Tarentum, gave him and his two sisters to UPOH to find them homes. The orphanage adopted out the girls and indentured Clarence to a family in Fort Dodge, Iowa. When he was nineteen, and presumably still under indenture obligation, his foster family wrote, "Clarence had taken a notion about a year ago to go farther west and is now in Washington Oregon." The mother added, "He writes her often," implying that it was still a cordial relationship but that Clarence had taken control of his own destiny, moving away from his indentureship.[172] When children left their indentured families before the expiration of their contracts, they generally forfeited the right to claim their indenture payment (typically one hundred dollars for boys at twenty-one and fifty dollars for girls at eighteen). Yet teens frequently left before coming of age, choosing to give up a sizable payment to instead have greater control of their lives.

Indentured teens particularly resisted certain work assignments, such as housework and farming, when they did not like the tasks or viewed them as unhelpful for their futures. In the process, the teens may have contributed to the declining feasibility of the indenture system at the turn of the century. Indentures had been largely premised on housework training and agricultural apprenticeships, which young people appear to have viewed as decreasingly relevant for their lives. For instance, the HCC recorded that Earl Landau, with the help of the family that had indentured him, "will enter Booker Washington school as he does not like housework."[173] Walter Olson, after being indentured for a number of years to a family in rural Butler County, visited a UPOH manager to tell her, "He is dissatisfied with his present arrangements, would like to be released in order to take a position offered him in the city and that he may improve himself by going to school at night." When Olson's uncle in Chicago agreed "to assume the entire charge" of him, the orphanage complied and canceled the indenture.[174] Olson preferred the promise of work in the city and the chance he would have to attend night school while earning his own wages. Similarly, after seven years with his indenture family, Wilber Lowman "had grown tired of farming," and worked "away from home" for the last two years of his contracted time, during which time his foster parents had paid him a monthly wage. In light of what they viewed as a generous arrangement, the managers voted to suspend the final indenture payment, and interviewed Wilber, who "said he had left . . . because he did not wish to do farm work and that he had fully understood he was breaking the contract . . . and it was perfectly satisfactory to him."[175] Teens such as Landau and Olson dreamed of more than housework or farming and viewed education as a key to their aspirations, while others such as Lowman simply wished to get away from the farm and were eager to begin earning their own wages.

Indentured children sometimes used their connection to the orphanage managing boards for their own purposes. For instance, they occasionally requested visits from managers, using these women to intervene in their relationships with their foster families. UPOH reported they had a "[l]etter from Bella Barnstable . . . asking that some of the ladies come to visit her. . . . Bella will be of age in January and would like to learn a trade." Bella's indenture family insisted she remain another two months until her birthday to entirely fulfill her contract, but agreed to pay her the hundred dollars she was due. Barnstable then used the affiliation she had with the managers to get on her feet when she was released from indenture, moving back into the orphanage for a time and earning ten dollars a month in wages from the board for helping around the home.[176] Similarly, Chester Carson returned to the HCC after several years at Thorn Hill, a public industrial school for boys. Carson had spent six years at the orphanage, from ages two to eight, before going to the school, and the managers noted he "came back to the only home he knows. He is permitted to stay until he finds work."[177] These were vulnerable young people that the orphanages charitably continued to support, but the children were not entirely helpless, making requests for assistance beyond the usual age limits.

Occasionally, young people newly released from their contracts engaged the managers as a bargaining tool to collect their indenture payments from reluctant families. Eliza Bailey's case proved somewhat extreme but nevertheless illustrates the way in which some children and young adults used their relationship with the orphanages to their best advantage. After coming of age and failing to get her payment, Bailey sent at least three letters to UPOH "stating she had never received her money" and asking for their help. The managers contacted the indenture mother, who replied she did not have the money just then. After another month of waiting, Bailey paid a visit to the president of the board, apparently without success: three years later she was still frustrated in her attempts to collect and wrote to the managers yet again. This time, the managers took the case to their attorney and the UPWANA board of directors, who, another year later, "recommended our Board pay Eliza Bailey 50.00 of the money coming to her . . . and we wait for the money as Eliza is very much in need of it during her [nurses] training in Columbia [Hospital]." By this time the indenture mother had died and "there [was] no money left in the estate to pay Eliza with," and nothing more their lawyer could do. Finally, another year later—five years after she first sought their assistance—the managers paid Bailey, who was now twenty-six and working as a nurse, the balance of fifty dollars.[178] Bailey may also have used her connections with the managers to gain entry to the nursing training program at Columbia Hospital, UPOH's sister organization, also operated by UPWANA.

In addition to seeking the manager's involvement with their placements and help in collecting payments, indentured and adopted young people further used their association with the orphanages to collect information about their families. For instance, UPOH noted, "Margaret Williams whose brother James has been [indentured] for ten or twelve years called the other day and seemed anxious to locate her brother."[179] Similarly, the managers received a "Letter from Mrs. L who adopted Jenny Blight stating she was very anxious to hear from her brother William."[180] Jenny and her brothers, William and Henry, were orphaned in 1897 when both of their parents died within a few months of each other. Their aunt and uncle gave them "absolutely" to UPOH (meaning they gave up any custodial rights), who indentured out the boys and found an adoptive home for Jenny in Youngstown, Ohio. When he was twenty-five, William himself wrote to the managers, "asking for his history when he was placed in the Home." In this case, William's request directly resulted in new institutional policy, as the managers decided "that hereafter when a child leaves the Home we give the family taking this child a type written history of the case."[181] Children and young adults actively sought out their siblings during and after placement, sometimes hoping to reunite their families, and insisting on their right to learn about their own histories.

While under contract and after their release, indentured teens also protested their treatment. For example, in the only case of abuse recorded at either orphanage during this fifty-year period, fourteen-year-old Ethel Moore took the initial step in contacting the managers, sending a "[l]etter . . . stating she did not like her home." The managers responded swiftly, questioning Ethel's younger sister, Geraldine, who was in the same home, bringing them both back to the orphanage, and initiating a highly unusual lawsuit against the indenture father. The case made its way quickly through the legal system in Ohio, where the indenture family lived, but in the end, "the Grand Jury . . . ignored the case against [the father] for want of corroborating evidence."[182] The managers, however, clearly believed the Moore sisters and acted quickly when Ethel raised the alarm.

Other young people, such as Lydia Wharton—whose indenture parents were the ones who returned her, complaining she "hasent dun five dolars worth of good with peace and pleasure"—contacted the managers only after their contracts expired. When she was approximately thirty years old, Wharton called the orphanage "to learn something of her history." Although she hoped to gain information, she also took the opportunity to object to her indenture conditions, and the managers noted she "[c]laims to have been badly treated."[183] Wharton may have been a child with unusual pluck and a determined spirit that got her in trouble: a few months after their mother died, she and her two brothers set out from England to join their father in Pittsburgh, but "they not having written him when they would leave England they were kept at the Union Depot and an advertisement put in the papers which reached the father and he claimed them at once." The father was boarding with someone himself and could not keep the children, so "he found places at once for the boys but not being situated so he could care for the little girl gave her absolutely to the Home." After the first indenture failed, a second indenturing family complained that "she gave much care and . . . finally gave such evidence of a diseased mind that she was placed in the Insane Asylum." The managers remarked that eventually she "[w]as restored and married" and had moved to Akron Ohio.[184] But twelve years later, Wharton was still angry enough to protest her treatment under indenture during her phone call with the managers.

For some children, their ultimate power lay in simply leaving or running away. Just as younger children regularly ran away from the two orphanages, many teens found their placements quite difficult and chose to leave, even at the expense of forfeiting their indenture payments.[185] For example, when seventeen-year-old Henry Blight grew unhappy with his indenture, the president of the Bessemer Gas Company where he had been working wrote to the managers on his behalf to say he "feels that this [indenture] home needs investigation." Eight months later, Blight's indenture mother wrote, "stating Henry is dissatisfied and wishes to leave," but by the time a committee arrived a few weeks later, they "found Henry had left on account of their treatment and was working for a neighbor." The committee added they were "very much pleased with Henry and all they heard of him," and the managers agreed to cancel the indenture contract, just two months shy of Blight's eighteenth birthday when he would have presumably earned his payment.[186] Similarly, Wilma Edwards, who had been indentured to an HCC board manager, "left her home two months before expiration of agreement" and would have to "forfeit the $50." Despite the managers' "unanimous opinion" that their colleague "had been very kind to Wilma, training her with great care, providing her with very good clothing and greatly interesting herself in her welfare," Edwards preferred to run away rather than remain the final two months of her contract.[187] As this case suggests, teens did not necessarily run away from abusive situations, but contested the terms of bound labor by choosing to strike out on their own.

Both young people and their parents, then, helped to erode the indenture system, just as they had negotiated the boundaries of the orphanages' power in the admissions and dismissal process, and during the children's stay in the institutions.

⌘ ⌘ ⌘

In 1950 UPOH changed its name to the United Presbyterian Home for Children; as the managers explained, the name was "more truly expressing our purpose; in this day of medical advances few young children are so unfortunate as to lose both parents, but there are half-orphans and many unhappy little victims of broken homes who need our care."[188] Yet few children who lived at UPOH during its first fifty years had lost both their parents; indeed, most residents of both UPOH and the HCC were half-orphans, and their parents played an active role in their care at the institutions. By the mid-twentieth century many former orphanages had closed, and others, such as the HCC and UPOH, transformed into specialized care homes for teens, shifting their mission from families-in-trouble to troubled families. Thus, in 1949 the HCC spoke of its "transition from an institution which gave custodial care to one giving treatment care."[189] Now seventy years old, the orphanages were reimagining their own past—aided in part by the way in which they had constructed the "orphan" problem all along—as institutions that had served children left tragically alone in the world.

Yet, while the orphanages had never emphasized their presence, parents were active participants in the institutions, using them for their own child care purposes. Parents initiated the admissions and dismissal processes, negotiating with the managers over such things as clothing and boarding fees. They viewed the institutions as both a charitable system they would have to navigate and a service for which they were paying. Families remained involved in children's institutional lives through letters and visits, supervising, for instance, their medical care. At the same time, parents and children resisted indentures and the terms of bound labor, contributing to the system's demise in this turn-of-the-century period when foster care emerged in its place.

CHAPTER FOUR

FATHERING ORPHANS
Gender and Institutional Child Care

> Grandpap was a machinist by trade. He helped build the
> Duquesne Works of the United States Steel Corp. (USX) He was
> a Jack-of-all-trades. It was said, "If Jimmy Caldwell couldn't fix
> it, it couldn't be fixed." He belonged to the Masons in Carnegie,
> PA. He was an intelligent, self-educated man.
> —Alberta Gordon Kostry, "The James Caldwell Family," 1976

In 1880, at the age of twenty-three, James Caldwell and his new bride, twenty-year-old Jessie, set sail from Scotland. James had a career as a police officer but had already made at least one trip to the United States to scout out a new future for himself. During the voyage across the Atlantic, Jessie gave birth to their first child and, after landing in Philadelphia, the new family soon set out on foot to cross the state of Pennsylvania. They stayed with other Scottish families along the three-hundred-mile journey west to Pittsburgh, where James found work as a cemetery caretaker and then in the electric light department of one of Andrew Carnegie's steel mills. Their family grew quickly, and ten years later they had six children and were expecting a seventh when tragedy struck. First, one-year-old Joseph died, and a few months later, Jessie died shortly after giving birth to Alexander. Suddenly widowed, with a newborn and five other children to care for, James turned for help to the United Presbyterian Orphan's Home run by the women of his church.

The orphanage managers would not take infants, so James likely placed baby Alexander in a private home or with a wet nurse, where he survived only seven months. They would also not accept nine-year-old Katiebell, who had epilepsy, and whom they judged to be "feeble minded." The managers helped James get her admitted to Elywn, a state-run institution near Philadelphia that developed a specialization in epilepsy in this period, and he paid the fees. James later moved Katiebell to the Polk Institute, another state facility closer to Pittsburgh, where she died at the age of eighteen. In the meantime, the remaining four Caldwell children spent between one and nine years in the orphanage, with James paying fifty-cents apiece every week for their board. After a year, Susie aged out of the institution, and she returned home to keep house for her father. Archie got into some mischief when he was eleven, and James had to remove him from the home. Roberta stayed a few more years until she, too, aged out, and James made informal indenture arrangements for her to join Archie, working on a farm in Butler County, forty miles north of the city. Finally, in 1900 James took home his youngest daughter, the managers noting, "Mr. Caldwell having established a home at McKees Rocks in charge of his eldest daughter Susie removed Mamie . . . as she was past twelve years of age."[1]

When his family faced the catastrophic loss of its wife and mother, James used the orphanage as child care, remaining involved in his children's lives. He visited them at the home, as evidenced by this photograph taken on Federal Street in Allegheny City (now Pittsburgh's Northside neighborhood) near the institution (see figure 4.1). He even made a generous financial contribution when he attended an annual Donation Day fundraising event.[2] For James, orphanage care served as a family survival strategy, permitting him to maintain ties to his children and between the siblings.

The James Caldwell story brings the experience of fathers into sharp relief—a significant, and all but forgotten, aspect of orphanage history—as well as the broader history of child care, in the United States. While many orphanage children had living fathers, the institutional managers constructed "orphans" as fatherless, perpetuating a gendered and racialized logic of dependency. Yet for those men using the orphanages as a form of child care, their experiences as widowers differed from those of solo women with children. Furthermore, the experiences of African American and white working-class men were also quite different. Ultimately, the orphanages help reveal the extent to which each group of men was involved with the care of their children as well as the connection between their breadwinning role and family life.

"The parting with his children was the saddest one witnessed in the Home": White Fathers' Use of UPOH as Child Care

One of the most surprising findings of this study is the large percentage of white men who used UPOH to care for their children. During its first fifty years, the institution served a nearly equal number of children of solo fathers and solo mothers (41 vs. 42 percent, respectively, of all children). In addi-

Figure 4.1. James Caldwell with children Mayme, Roberta, Susie, and Archie, circa 1891, after he placed them in the United Presbyterian Orphan's Home. *Source:* Collection of the author.

tion, a handful of fathers were still living with their wives in intact nuclear families when their children entered the orphanage. Altogether, 46 percent of UPOH children in this period claimed a living father.[3] This figure reflects the status of children's parents, alive or dead, regardless of who admitted them to the orphanage. For instance, some children had living fathers but were admitted to UPOH by a grandparent. Looking at who did the actual placing and retrieving of children from the institution further reveals the substantial involvement of fathers.

Over time, the proportion of children admitted by their fathers alone rose steadily, from one-third to nearly one-half of all admissions (see table 4.1). While some of these children also had living mothers, they were generally ill or institutionalized, leaving the fathers saddled with child care duties they struggled to fulfill. The proportion of children retrieved by their fathers is even more striking: while just over a quarter of the children went home to fathers in the 1880s (versus 37 percent to mothers), by the 1920s over

Table 4.1. Number of Children Admitted to and Dismissed from UPOH, by Decade and Parent Involved

	Placed by father		Retrieved by father		Placed by mother		Retrieved by mother	
	N	Percent of total admissions	N	Percent of total dismissals	N	Percent of total admissions	N	Percent of total dismissals
1878–1889	73	33	41	26	111	50	58	37
1890–1899	43	35	17	24	36	30	25	35
1900–1909	37	35	31	53	45	42	11	19
1910–1919	38	38	28	24	40	40	37	32
1920–1929	33	49	28	56	26	39	14	28

Source: UPOH admission and dismissal records.

half went to fathers (versus just over a quarter to mothers). In other words, within a few decades of its inception, UPOH was admitting and dismissing more children of solo fathers than solo mothers. At least one other white Pittsburgh orphanage, the Children's Temporary Home, served "a disproportionate number" of widowers' children.[4] Furthermore, a 1907 report of institutionalized children throughout the city found more children of widowers than widows living in orphanages and other homes.[5] Historians have reported mixed findings in other U.S. cities: one of three orphanages Nurith Zmora examined in Baltimore, the Hebrew Orphan Asylum, served nearly equal numbers of widows and widowers, while the other two served mostly widows. Where Kenneth Cmiel found that mothers brought children to the Chicago Nursery and Half-Orphan Asylum twice as often as fathers, S. J. Kleinberg studied the St. Vincent's Home in Fall River, Massachusetts, among others, and concluded, "Children's homes housed a disproportionate number of widower's children."[6] The Pittsburgh data suggest that, at least in the Steel City, orphanages served a crucial child care role for working-class, solo, white fathers.

Historians have barely begun to tell the story of working-class fatherhood. Reacting to early masculinity studies, which largely ignored men's role as fathers, scholars in the 1980s and '90s began drafting the broad brushstrokes of the history of fatherhood.[7] But their work, drawing on evidence such as letters, diaries, and advice literature, focused on white middle-class men living in the American North. Influenced by the notion of increasingly gendered "separate spheres," a model first put forth by women's historians in the 1960s and '70s, these scholars viewed the nineteenth century as a period of decline for fathers.[8] Starting in the early nineteenth century with the changes wrought by industrialization and urbanization, men's patriarchal power within the family eroded as work took them away from the home.[9] In this view, women's responsibility in the home increased (giving them authority in the domestic sphere) as men's family role narrowed to breadwinning (accomplished in the masculine, public sphere); where they were once involved with children and caretaking more directly, fathers fell to a more peripheral status, reduced to distant disciplinarians and occasional playmates.[10] In a parallel trend, sociologists also began critiquing masculinity studies and started describing the decline of fatherhood.[11]

By the 1990s, however, some historians were challenging this declension model, observing that the nineteenth century was not a simple, downward trend of fathers' role in the family. These scholars also noted that there are multiple "fatherhoods," with variations by race, ethnicity, class, and other categories.[12] At the same time, women's historians themselves questioned the usefulness of a strict separate spheres model. While it had created an interpretive framework in which to view the rise of women's maternal power, its limiting rhetoric (of complete "separation") effectively shaped how historians represented the era (as separate entities with no common history).[13] Not only did some historians of the family find the domestic realm to be more of a common meeting ground than implied by separate spheres, but several historians of fatherhood have also recently challenged the notion that men withdrew altogether from child-caring responsibilities. On the contrary, they argue that fathers maintained a child care role in the nineteenth century; many were present at their children's birth, helped make key decisions about issues such as infant feeding, had important emotional connections through their role as playmate, and continued to guide their older children into adulthood, ensuring a secure future for them.[14] In this revised view, breadwinning did occupy men's time and attention, but it did not necessarily shift all of their thought and emotion away from the home or cause them to grant less importance to it.

While historians to date have looked exclusively at white middle-class men, the experience of UPOH fathers suggests that their central observation may also apply to white working-class men. Specifically, the fathers who turned to the orphanage did so largely as involved parents: for many of them, the institution provided a form of child care, allowing them to maintain connections with their children. Historians have suggested that working-class families maintained an instrumental, economic view of children through the nineteenth century, well past the time when the middle class had shifted to a more sentimental, emotional view of children, free of any income-producing expectations. Because the working class continued to see the family as a collective effort, a working unit in which all members contributed to its viability, these scholars have argued that the middle class used its own, new perception of children as a way to distance itself from those below them in the social hierarchy.[15] While this may have been true of middle-class attitudes, actual working-class behavior was far more complicated. UPOH fathers supervised their children's care at the institution, worked to reestablish their homes, and displayed intense emotional bonds. For these men, the orphanage served as a means of family survival rather than an abdication of their parenting responsibilities.

The vast majority of UPOH fathers were coping with the loss of a spouse: unable to replace their wives' domestic labor, they turned to the orphanage in times of acute family crisis when they were left as a solo parent. For some, this occurred when their wives were incapacitated due to physical or mental ailments (see table 4.2). Sometimes the managers labeled the mothers "incompetent," a judgment rendered by the manager's home investigation committee and not necessarily a legal designation. For instance, when James McGregor, who worked in the jewelry business, placed his daughter in UPOH, the managers noted, "[the] mother living but insane and in the County Home."[16] Similarly, Fred Seldon, a stationary engineer, sent his two-year-old son, Douglas, to stay at UPOH after his wife, Ruth, "being insane, had been two months confined in St Frances Hospital." Seldon found it impossible to juggle the demands of a toddler and wage labor: he could not even leave work to sign the admission papers, instead sending a friend in his place to deliver Douglas to the orphanage. After three months, Ruth "recovered and came for Douglas," and the family was reunited.[17] No solo fathers reported their wives as "deserted" when placing their children at the orphanage, though 18 percent of children of solo mothers had fathers who had deserted their families.[18]

Far and away more often, fathers turned to the institution for assistance when they were widowed. Ninety-five percent of children placed in UPOH

Table 4.2. Spousal Status of UPOH Solo Parents

Spouse is:	Mother living		Father living	
	Number of children	Percent	Number of children	Percent
Dead	162	66.1	218	94.8
Incompetent	2	0.8	4	1.7
Deserted	44	18.0	0	0.0
Separated/divorced	7	2.9	3	1.3
Status unknown to placing parent	4	1.6	3	1.3
Status not recorded	26	10.6	2	0.9
Total	245	100.0	230	100.0

Source: UPOH admission and dismissal records.

by their fathers were motherless. Because many mothers died in childbirth or with babies still at home, widowers were often in an especially difficult situation, since the orphanage would not accept children younger than the age of two, necessitating other arrangements for infants and separating siblings. For example, the managers could only take three of the four children of a Hungarian man "whose wife was burned to death shortly, and the neighbors were trying to care for the family."[19] As the managers noted in their 1896 report, "This year we have received infants, as we had been so often asked to take motherless babes. In one case the little one was only a few days old, and we were obliged to give it to a competent nurse to care for till it is old enough for us to take."[20] Occasionally, the managers helped fathers locate help for their infants: for example, after a man applied to the orphanage, they decided, "We suggest to this father that he place the baby with Mrs. Hickey of Shousetown until it is a year old and then we could take it."[21]

Solo fathers in this period had more trouble maintaining their own households after the loss of a spouse than their female counterparts. For example, instead of remaining as heads of households, widowers were much more likely to become boarders or to move in with other relatives. Furthermore, in the early twentieth century, widowers had an increasingly difficult time keeping their families together. The proportion of widowers heading their own households dropped significantly, particularly among men aged twenty-five to thirty-four, those most likely to have young children at home. Older men, aged thirty-five to fifty-four, were somewhat more likely to remain heads of their own households, but their rate also declined after the turn of the century, as more of this cohort also went to live with relatives and in boarding homes.[22]

To illustrate, in 1900, when James Caldwell retrieved his youngest child, Mayme, after nine years in UPOH, he had two of his daughters living at home and helping to keep house. Yet within a few years, Caldwell was unable to maintain his own home: by 1910 Susie had married and moved to her husband's farm, and James became a boarder with another family. Caldwell had placed out two of his teenaged children on a farm in a neighboring county and brought two others home to live with him, but his mix of strategies ultimately failed to produce a stable household in the long term. Ten years later, he was sixty-two, still working as a factory machinist and boarding with yet a different family. Sometime after 1920 James started to alternate staying with Susie and Mayme, the two daughters who had lived with him and kept house for him during their teen years.[23]

Newly widowed fathers struggled to keep their children at home, and like widows, often did not immediately turn to the orphanages for assistance (see table 2.2 and related discussion). For example, when John Humphrey admitted his two boys to the home, the managers noted that "his wife died . . . and since then he has been keeping house, but finds it impossible to do so any longer."[24] Similarly, Stanley West "struggled to keep his family together for a year and then was compelled to place [his five children] in the Home as no suitable person could be found to take care of them."[25] While some fathers turned to the orphanage for help in the hours and days immediately following the death of a spouse, UPOH men waited an average of sixteen months to institutionalize their children.[26] Although this was ten months sooner than their female counterparts—widowed white mothers waited an average of twenty-six months—the long delay from the time they were widowed to the time they placed their children suggests that most fathers tried other strategies, possibly including providing day-to-day care themselves.

The women who ran UPOH viewed widowed fathers with great sympathy but also questioned their ability to provide adequate parenting. In fact, the managers implied that children of solo fathers might be better off in orphanages, where they could receive surrogate mothering. For example, they lamented, "[T]he most helpless being in the world is a man bereft of the mother of his children." Pointing to the inevitable collapse of a home without a mother, they continued, "Heart sick at the sight of their neglect as he returns night after night from his daily toil to his desolate home, he gives up the effort longer to maintain a home, and turns in his distress to the Home *his church* has provided to shelter such motherless ones."[27] When UPOH donor Ella Hamilton sent a quilt she had made for the orphanage, she enclosed a note saying, "especially should we love and pity those little ones who have been deprived of dear mothers."[28] In the view of these women, the orphanage residents required mothering; they pitied solo fathers but felt that men could not sufficiently parent their children alone.

Yet the actions and words of UPOH fathers suggest that many maintained close emotional bonds with their children and remained involved with their lives while supervising their care in the institution. When Jeremiah Greeley, a potter from East Liverpool, Ohio, lost his wife, he found that his own ill health prevented him from caring for his two boys. The UPOH managers noted that "the father was in such delicate health that he decided to go to Florida hoping the change of climate would benefit him. The parting with his children was the saddest one witnessed in the Home." Greeley was only separated from his boys for the winter season, however, as he found a way to quickly retrieve them: "It was but a few brief months before the father returned, married again and took his boys to his new home."[29] Historian Judith Dulberger has demonstrated the intense emotional ties working-class parents maintained with their children during their stays in an upstate New York orphanage. Using a remarkable cache of highly sentimental letters, Dulberger disputes the prevalent notion that the working class was merely instrumental in their treatment of children, viewing them primarily as potential laborers. Rather, she found that even before the turn of the century, orphanage parents displayed strong attachments to their offspring, suggesting this was not a uniquely middle-class phenomenon.[30]

While the UPOH managers rarely preserved correspondence from parents, a surviving letter illustrates one father's struggle to remain geographically and emotionally close to his children. A farm laborer in nearby Ohio, widower Wallace Taft tried for nearly a year after his wife's death to keep his three boys, aged eleven, nine, and four, near him. But he was not "able to provide a home for the children and they were for a time in the County Home in Dayton [Ohio]." That institution wanted Taft to give up custody of his boys, however, so they could place them out, which he refused to allow. Instead, he admitted them to UPOH, paying ten dollars out of his monthly sixteen-dollar wage.[31] In the fall, seven months after the boys arrived at the orphanage, Taft wrote to the managers asking, "[D]o you think that i can get any thing to do in your City as i will [be] out of work when we get our corn gathered." He informed them that he would be "coming out to see the boys in 2 or 3 weeks" and offered to bring references. He was concerned with more than simply finding work, however, as his letter revealed his longing to be with his children: "[I]f you can find me any thing to do i would be very happy as i want to be neer my boys." He asked the managers to "tell them that i am coming to see them and i hope that they will know me when they see me . . . i dream of them almost every night."[32]

For this father, and doubtless many others, wage labor played an essential role in allowing him to support his children, but fathering went beyond breadwinning. Taft longed to be close to his children, worried about their relationship with him—fretted even that they would forget what he looked like after seven months in the orphanage—and dreamed of them at night. He acknowledged his role as financial provider, saying, "i must have some thing to do or i will no be able to pay for my boys this winter as it takes all of my wages in the summer to pay for them." Yet Taft combined his desire to support his children with his desire to be near them, closing his letter to the managers with "if [I] could just get work there i would be all right."[33] There is no indication that the managers helped Taft find work, but he was eventually able to retrieve all three of his boys from the orphanage.

In addition to maintaining close emotional attachments to their children, UPOH fathers stayed involved in their lives. Men wrote letters to the managers (there are many references to such letters in the meeting minutes, though very few were saved), came to the institution on weekly visitation days, and occasionally made special requests to see their children. For instance, one father wished to sit with his children in church as a means of staying connected with them, and another asked to take his little girl home for the weekend to celebrate her birthday.[34] As discussed in the previous chapter, fathers were vocal in directing the care their children received at the orphanage, resisting plans to cut children's hair and intervening in medical decisions. A few fathers even volunteered in the home: when his wife died, Mr. Pelham, a "physical director in the public schools," placed his three children in UPOH as "there was no one to care for them." But he "volunteered to come Saturday afternoons and instruct the children," an offer the managers gladly accepted, suggesting he could conduct fire drills.[35] However, most UPOH fathers likely did not have much time for volunteer activities, as they were consumed with the wage earning that would eventually allow them to reestablish their households.

Solo white fathers appear to have had a more difficult time reestablishing homes for their children than their female counterparts. Children of widowers stayed in the orphanage, on average, five and a half months longer than children of widows (14.5 months total vs. 9.2 months).[36] Men frequently negotiated with the managers to keep their children at the orphanage when threatened with their dismissal for owing board money, or when children got into trouble or became too old to stay. Oftentimes, fathers were no longer maintaining their own homes and had no place to keep children. For instance, James Schneider, a basket maker living in Allegheny, managed to keep his three children for two years following the death of his wife, apparently in childbirth with the youngest. When he placed the three in UPOH, he told the managers it was "only until he gets work," but ten months later he was behind on his board bill and they were threatening to return the children. Schneider "paid some on his bill" and appeared in person before the board "to see about our keeping the children as he has no place to take them." Evidently persuaded, the managers voted "we reconsider the action in dismissing these children and keep them as long as the man is making an effort to pay for them."[37] Similarly, when "Stephen Moore stole a cake after Donation day," the managers notified his father, who replied that "he cannot take him as he has no place for him," and they chose not to dismiss him "on account of this offense."[38]

While working-class men tended to earn higher wages than women and would seem to be more likely to afford bringing their children home, the very nature of men's employment could prevent this. For men, wage labor generally meant working outside the home for long hours, which necessitated help with domestic tasks such as shopping, cleaning, food preparation, sewing, and child minding. If they did not have friends and family to assist with these tasks, men had to rely on their earnings to pay for help, as they had little time to perform these duties themselves (and often no training or experience in things such as cooking or mending). For those laboring in many factories, the common "swing shift" kept home and work schedules in flux and meant frequent night work. Some fathers faced parenting challenges unique to their sex, such as Mr. Walton, who, with the involvement of the United States in World War I, asked the UPOH managers "to keep his children until he knows whether he can take them or not [as he] may have to go to war."[39] Solo mothers were likely able to bring their children home sooner because they juggled part-time labor with their family responsibilities and often combined wage and domestic work, by, for instance, taking in boarders or doing piecework. This meant, of course, that many women and their children barely scraped by on miserably small incomes.[40] But the structure of men's labor also impeded their ability to reestablish their households.

While it took longer for white fathers to reunite their families, they eventually succeeded in taking home nearly as many of their children as did solo mothers. Both men and women took home the good majority of children they had placed in UPOH, with solo fathers retrieving 68 percent of their offspring and mothers retrieving 71 percent (see table 4.3).[41] Solo fathers were slightly more likely than mothers to see their children dismissed to other relatives or friends but were less likely to send their children to another institution or school. Neither solo mothers nor fathers permitted the adoption of more than a few of their children. For example, when James MacLeod, an electrician living in Homestead, remarried, he found he still could not take his son and asked the managers to "find a home for him." He consented to the placement of eleven-year-old Liam in a foster home but specified his son was "not to be adopted."[42] Though far less common than going home to a parent, the second most likely dismissal outcome for children of solo mothers and fathers was an indenture or foster placement.

Formal indentures gradually gave way in this period to the emerging foster care system, but solo fathers and mothers largely resisted both forms of "placing out" their children in private homes. For example, the widower D. M. Christopher turned to UPOH only when he became "prostrated by disease and entirely without means of support for himself or his children." He told the managers, "If he be restored to such a condition that he can provide for his children he desires to do so. Otherwise, good homes are to

Table 4.3. Dismissal Outcomes of UPOH Children, by Sex of Child and Solo Parent

| | Children of solo mothers | | | | | | Children of solo fathers | | | | | |
| | Boys | | Girls | | Total | | Boys | | Girls | | Total | |
Dismissed to	N	Percent	N	Percent	N	Percent	N	Percent	N	Percent	N	Percent
Solo parent	79	72	67	71	146	71	96	69	65	67	161	68
Relative/friend/guardian	5	5	7	7	12	6	14	10	6	6	20	8
Adoption	2	2	3	3	5	2	2	1	5	5	7	3
Indenture/foster	8	7	14	15	22	11	18	13	18	19	36	15
An institution/college	7	6	4	4	11	5	2	1	1	1	3	1
Juvenile court	0	0	0	0	0	0	0	0	0	0	0	0
Died	4	4	0	0	4	2	6	4	0	0	6	3
Ran away	5	5	0	0	5	2	1	1	2	2	3	1
Total dismissals	110	100	95	100	205	100	139	100	97	100	236	100

Source: UPOH admission and dismissal records.

be found for them."[43] Occasionally, fathers preferred to make these arrangements themselves. For instance, after Ernest Coulter lost his first wife and remarried, he discovered that "[t]he second wife was not a good woman and [she] finally left the family," forcing him to admit his three children to the orphanage. Eleven months later, the managers placed eight-year-old Mary in a private home, "at the written request of the father."[44] Children of solo fathers went to indentures or foster homes in 15 percent of all dismissals, while children of solo mothers were placed out 11 percent of the time.

However, these figures reflect the dismissal status of all children of solo parents, regardless of who admitted them to the orphanage. In other words, it includes some children with a living solo mother or father who were sent to UPOH by relatives, a private institution, or even the courts. If we look at just children actually admitted by a solo parent, there is a more striking difference in the rate of placement: of all children admitted by their fathers, 11 percent went to indenture or foster placements versus 6 percent of solo mothers' children.[45] Viewed this way, solo white fathers were nearly twice as likely to place out their children than were mothers. These numbers suggest that men either viewed this type of training and care more favorably than women, or had more difficulty in bringing children back into their households (for reasons such as the structure of men's employment)—or both.

The sex of a child also influenced parent's decisions when retrieving children, including the choice to indenture them. Solo fathers and mothers both placed out proportionately more of their girls than boys: 19 percent of girls versus 13 percent of boys of fathers, and 15 percent of girls versus 7 percent of boys of mothers went to indentures or foster homes. Fathers allowed more of their daughters to be adopted than their sons, though the overall numbers remained quite small. Fathers were also somewhat more likely to send their sons to stay with a relative or friend after leaving the orphanages, while mothers sent more of their daughters. Overall, the children of solo mothers stood a slightly greater chance of reunification with their parent, while fathers' children, and in particular their girls, were the least likely to go home again. Yet, again, the larger point is that the great majority of men's children eventually went home to their fathers.

A child's sex also factored into his or her length of stay at the orphanage. Boys of solo mothers not only went home in the greatest proportion, but also the quickest, staying a median of 6.3 months (see table 4.4). Fathers were slower to bring home both their boys and girls but took the longest to reunite with their sons, at a median 15.5 months—more than twice that of widow's sons. If teenaged boys were providing remunerative work for their mothers, an incentive for them to be brought home quickly and in larger numbers, then

Table 4.4. Median Length of Stay for UPOH Children of Solo Parents, by Sex of Child and Parent

	Boys		Girls		All	
	N	Months	N	Months	N	Months
Solo mothers	86	6.3	85	9.5	169	9.2
Solo fathers	110	15.5	75	13.0	185	14.5

Source: UPOH admission and dismissal records.

we would expect them to be equally valuable laborers for their fathers. Yet fathers took the longest to reunite with their sons, suggesting that potential wage earning was perhaps not the decisive factor in their choice of when to retrieve boys. Furthermore, in Pittsburgh during this period, white widows with children actually decreased their families' dependence on child labor, gradually replacing the income contributed to the family economy through child labor with their own waged labor.[46] Working-class fathers, too, then, may have been depending less on their sons for financial contributions to the family.

We might also expect fathers to take home their older daughters to keep house for them and to take care of younger siblings, yet that also does not seem to be the general trend. By the early twentieth century, one reason may have been Progressive era compulsory education laws, which required daughters to be in school rather than keeping house for their fathers. Overall, girls of widowed fathers returned home less often than any other group, and stayed nearly as long as widower's boys, with a median stay of thirteen months. While this data does not reveal fathers' internal decision-making processes regarding the role of children in the family, it does illuminate working-class men's behavior, which suggests that they were not strictly interested in using their children as potential laborers to contribute to the family economy.

One final factor affecting children's chances of reunification with their fathers was remarriage. In the general population, widowers were more likely than widows to remarry, and they tended to do so to obtain child care assistance from their new brides.[47] For instance, UPOH managers noted they "returned [Colin] to his father . . . because Mr McDougal had been married and has a home of his own in which to care for him."[48] A railroad brakeman, James McDougal had managed to keep Colin for seventeen months before placing him in the orphanage, but required the domestic labor of a new wife before he could bring Colin home again. Widows bereft of their husbands' income discovered it was difficult to find a new partner, a particularly daunting predicament for women with young children. In turn-of-the-century Pittsburgh, 10 percent of widowers but only 2 percent of widows remarried.[49] These findings have led some scholars to assume that widowers with young children frequently remarried and did so quickly after the death of their spouses.[50]

However, the large number of solo fathers who resorted to orphanage care for their children tells a different story. Indeed, in countering this faulty assumption, historian S. J. Kleinberg concludes, "Widowers and younger widows were most likely to marry again, but it was never a common occurrence."[51] Statistical data from UPOH support this assertion. While the proportion of children returned to a parent upon a remarriage was greater for fathers than mothers, in neither case was it the primary reason children returned home (17 percent of widowers' children returned home after a remarriage vs. 4 percent of widows' children).[52] In addition, of those children who did eventually return to their fathers, only a quarter did so because of their fathers' remarriage.[53] For widowed men, remarriage was not the most likely path to family reunification, nor was it necessarily quick. The data suggest that men did not rush out to find new wives: the median length of time elapsed from the death of a spouse to remarriage was two years.[54] Thus, remarriage was neither common nor speedy among UPOH widowers, though it contributed to fathers' ability to retrieve their children from the orphanage.

The story of white working-class fatherhood, as reflected in the experiences of UPOH men, is one of involvement and reunification. These fathers were nearly all widowers, struggling to care for their children, and they made the choice to institutionalize them only after a considerable length of time. What's more, UPOH fathers remained connected with their children while in the orphanage and worked to bring them home again. Though family reunification was clearly more difficult for men than women, white fathers succeeded the majority of the time in using the orphanage as temporary child care for their children.

"He having neither place nor means to care for him": African American Fathers' Use of HCC as Child Care

Where the vast majority of white men using UPOH to care for their children were widowed, most of the African American men using the HCC were not. More black fathers actually had surviving spouses than were solo parenting when their children were admitted to the orphanage. Twenty-three percent of children had two living parents, while 18 percent had solo fathers: overall then, 41 percent of HCC children could claim a living father (see figure 2.4). While this figure was fairly close to that of white UPOH children with a living father (at 46 percent), there were significant differences in the experience of African American fathers and their children. First, far fewer men actually interacted with the HCC. Although the orphanage served children from families with two living parents, it appears that many of the fathers in those families were not in residence, and it was the mothers who interacted with the institution. Second, the structure of men's employment affected their involvement with children while at the orphanage. And third, black fathers had a much more difficult time reestablishing their households and retrieving children.

At first glance, it appears that fathers are strikingly "absent" from HCC families. Because the HCC managers recorded information about the party retrieving a child at the time of dismissal far more consistently than the placing party at time of admission, the orphanage's dismissal records provide the principal data source for gauging actual parental interaction with the institution. Overall, fathers retrieved 14 percent of the institution's children compared to 55 percent by mothers (see table 4.5). Over time, fathers retrieved roughly the same small proportion of children while solo mothers retrieved an increasingly large proportion of the orphanage residents. In other words, black fathers held steady but made no gains in their ability, relative to mothers, to reunite with their children. In sharp contrast, African American mothers retrieved a substantially larger proportion of the orphanage children than either their male counterparts at the HCC or white women at UPOH. These numbers suggest that, at least in Pittsburgh, orphanages served an important role as temporary child care for black mothers, but the story is less clear for black fathers, who appear from the retrieving party data to be largely missing.

Table 4.5. HCC Dismissals by Decade and Retrieving Parent

| | Retrieved by mother | | Retrieved by father | |
	N	Percent of total dismissals	N	Percent of total dismissals
1878–1889	5	36	2	14
1890–1899	10	28	6	17
1900–1909	77	51	28	19
1910–1919	92	57	14	9
1920–1929	116	64	28	15
Total	300	55	78	14

Source: HCC dismissal records.

Indeed, the alleged absence of fathers has been the subject of much of the historiography of the African American family over the past thirty years. Reacting to work in the 1950s and '60s that had characterized black families as dysfunctional and matriarchal, scholars began challenging the idea that slavery had permanently damaged black family stability.[55] Historians argued that bondage had not necessarily emasculated men and found evidence that nuclear families were common on plantations across the South.[56] But women's historians countered that these efforts to reclaim the role of men went too far in emphasizing the patriarchal ambitions of black fathers and challenged the notion that black families were either patriarchal or (dysfunctionally) matriarchal. Rather, they suggested that slavery separated so many fathers from their families that women created matrifocal family forms.[57] Enslaved men might live apart from their wives in "abroad marriages" on separate plantations, could be hired out to perform labor elsewhere, and could be forcibly separated through sale. Mothers, then, primarily raised children but also relied on supportive relationships with other enslaved women. After emancipation, these extended networks of kin and fictive kin played a crucial role in child care.[58] During its first fifty years, HCC served many children who appear to have been raised in this matrifocal family form.

Furthermore, labor shaped gender role expectations and family relationships, including the position of fathers. Under slavery, men did not control their own labor and could neither protect nor provide for their wives and children, a situation that may have blunted patriarchal tendencies for fathers.[59] During Reconstruction, white agents of the Freedmen's Bureau and other reformers wanted to impose white standards of family and gender roles, insisting that women and children become dependents of black men. These fathers were to be patriarchs of their own homes, yet they had almost no power outside of them given the economic, political, legal, and social constraints working against them. In reality, African Americans maintained distinct ideas about gender roles: realizing that fathers were not going to be able to support their families on meager incomes, they were more accepting of women combining wage work and motherhood, and at the same time, they understood that fathers' masculinity was not necessarily dependent on bread winning.[60]

In tandem with these historiographic lines of inquiry, sociologists, alarmed by the growth of single motherhood in the latter part of the twentieth century, have focused on the role of African American men in families. Their work, too, has challenged the idea of disorganized, broken matriarchies and introduced terms such as "live-away" fathers.[61] These scholars view modern black family forms, such as extended kin networks, subfamilies, and serial families, as coping mechanisms employed in place of inadequate social welfare policies.[62] Similarly, some had assumed that the instability of families in the urban North—measured by the dissolution of marriages and the rise in desertion rates and out-of-wedlock births—had arrived with Southern migrants. But recent scholarship demonstrates that these ills lay instead with structural racism, under- and unemployment, and the poverty people encountered after they reached the city.[63] Finally, sociologists argue that even nonresident fathers played, and continue to play, an important role in children's lives. They counter that the focus on "absent" fathers and narrow emphasis on breadwinning has obscured the family role of men's other contributions and erased the fathering tasks performed by other men in the community through "social fatherhood."[64]

The experience of HCC fathers would appear to support these recent historical and sociological arguments. African American men were not the chief users of the institution; mothers, who had the primary responsibility for children, had far more contact with the orphanage. Yet men were not entirely absent either, as revealed by a closer examination of solo fathers and the married, though probably largely nonresident, partners of mothers who admitted their children to the HCC. In fact, the very first residents of the HCC were the four sons of Robert Highland, ages ten, nine, three, and two. A laborer living in a boarding home with three other men, also laborers, Highland had migrated to Pittsburgh from his birthplace in Virginia and was thirty-five at the time of his children's institutionalization. He was illiterate and had been unemployed for five months during the previous year, hinting at the perilous financial situation that may have prompted him to admit his children to the brand new HCC. It was also not a quick path to reunification with his children: though there is no record of when the older two left the orphanage, the younger two were dismissed after two and a half years, likely back to their father as the managers did not record a different retrieving party in the ledger.[65] Bringing men such as Robert Highland into view complicates the nascent history of working-class fatherhood, introducing the lived experiences of black men as fathers dealing with child care responsibilities, rather than merely absent, ghostlike figures.

Like white UPOH fathers, most of the solo men with children at the HCC were widowers. However, a slightly larger proportion reported living wives who were unable to perform domestic labor due to mental illness or desertion (see table 4.6). For example, Jonah Harley's wife, Annette, was "insane and . . . sent to City Farm." The managers accepted five of his seven children, but eighteen-month-old Fannie was too young. Two years later, Harley sent her to join her siblings in the orphanage, where she died

Table 4.6. Spousal Status of HCC Solo Parents

Spouse is:	Mother living		Father living	
	Number of children	Percent	Number of children	Percent
Dead	142	39.6	87	64.4
Incompetent	1	0.3	6	4.4
Deserted	14	3.9	1	0.7
Separated/divorced	0	0.0	0	0.0
Status unknown to placing parent	10	2.8	1	0.7
Status not recorded	192	53.5	40	29.6
Total	359	100.0	135	100.0

Source: HCC admission records.
Note: Percentages do not total to 100 due to rounding.

at the age of four. A year later, he retrieved his oldest son when he turned twelve and returned for each of the others as they aged out of the institution.[66] Harley paid eighteen dollars a month for the care of his children and continued making payments for more than six years while they lived at the HCC. In another case, the managers were forced to refuse the "admission of 3 children whose mother deserted them four months ago" on account of space. They noted the "father has been caring for them since that time" and agreed to "place the Johnson children . . . in the Home as soon as there is a vacancy" at a dollar per week for each child.[67] Yet these cases of desertion and incompetence were few and far between, and no African American parents at all reported being separated or divorced.

Instead, like white men, the majority of solo African American fathers using the orphanage—at least 64 percent—had lost a wife to death and were struggling to replace her domestic contributions. Because many African American women continued to work after having children, widowed fathers may also have experienced the sudden loss of their wives' income, a double blow to the family's stability. These newly widowed fathers struggled to keep their children with them, exceeding white men's efforts by several months: they averaged 21.1 months elapsed time from the death of a spouse to the admission of their children versus 16.5 months for white men (see table 2.2). For example, James Matthews, a porter on the railroad, waited twenty-one months after losing his wife before sending his two sons, by then aged nine and seven, to the orphanage. When Matthews was "accidentally killed at work" two months later, the managers took full responsibility for the orphaned siblings and eventually sent them to college.[68] African American women, however, succeeded by far the longest in keeping their children after losing a spouse, averaging 36.5 months, fifteen months longer than widowed men. This suggests that orphanage care was truly a decision of last resort for these mothers and for black fathers, who took nearly two years to admit their children, likely not their first child care strategy, either.

At the HCC, more children actually had two living parents than a solo father. Although the managers noted that 23 percent of the children had both a mother and father (versus 18 percent with a solo father), these were not necessarily intact, nuclear families (see figure 2.4). They were obviously struggling through some form of crisis necessitating the use of orphanage care, and few of these children actually returned to homes with both parents. Only 5 percent of children with two living parents at the time of their admission were retrieved by both parents. While 13 percent were retrieved by fathers alone, mothers returned by themselves for the majority of these children (see table 4.7). A handful of children left the orphanage to live with relatives, stay in a foster home, or attend another institution. And a small number after 1903 were dismissed to the juvenile court, which operated a "Home Finding" department with social workers who helped locate foster families or made other arrangements. For instance, Albert and Harold Johnson's parents were both alive when the boys were admitted to the orphanage at the ages of two and four, but apparently the parents were unwilling or unable to take them as they aged out of the home years later. Albert went to an adoptive home but was returned after just a few months and then sent to the juvenile court's Home Finding department a year later. The managers noted that his brother, Harold, "had low mentality only of a 9 yr old" and sent him to the court as well, when he reached the age of fifteen. In turn, the court sent him to a trade school.[69] Most children with two living parents did not appear to hail from or return to nuclear families with a father present in the home.

Table 4.7. Retrieving Party of HCC Children
with Two Living Parents at Time of Admission

	Number of children	Percent
Both parents	6	5
Mother	71	55
Father	16	13
Relative	7	5
Adoption/placement	7	5
Another institution	6	5
Juvenile court	11	9
Died	4	3
Total	128	100

Source: HCC admission and dismissal ledger.

But rather than merely "absent," evidence suggests many HCC fathers were nonresident, a not uncommon pattern for African American families in which fathers (and sometimes mothers) lived apart from partners and their children, often because of work. Although some men may not have married the mothers of their children, this was not typical of black families in this period.[70] The managers marked only five children as "illegitimate" in their ledger book in this entire fifty-year period. Rather, most African American families from the 1880s through the 1920s, in both the rural and urban North and South, contained two parents with the husband or father in residence.[71] This pattern persisted tenaciously through waves of northern migration, though by the turn of the century the number of women over forty heading households increased due to both widowhood and men living elsewhere for work.[72] This was evident among HCC families. For example, James and Emma Hastings admitted three of their four children, ages nine, eight, and six, in March one year. In June, both parents retrieved the children; but two months later, they were back in the orphanage, and their youngest sister, aged three, joined them within a few weeks. The older children stayed at the HCC three times each, and it was Emma who retrieved them, without James, all but that first time (she also retrieved the youngest after her one stay).[73] For the Hastings family, it appears that James was involved in the admission and retrieval of his children one spring, but for the next three years, the records show no sign of him, and the orphanage interacted solely with Emma, suggesting that he was no longer making decisions about the children, possibly because he had moved away.

Similarly, even when the managers noted that both parents were living at the time of a child's admission, in many cases, they communicated solely with the mother during the child's institutionalization, suggesting the father was not living with the family. For instance, while both Earl and Sarah Dennis were living at the time their three children entered the HCC, it was Sarah who paid for their board each month and she who corresponded with the managers about the care her children received. When an employee in the orphanage wrote anonymously, "telling her that her children were being abused," she "caus[ed] a great deal of trouble in the Home . . . accusing [the matron] with beating them" and "threaten[ing] to take her children out."[74] For families such as these, fathers were alive, but appear to have been only peripherally involved in their children's institutionalization, if at all.

One might presume that these fathers had deserted their families, but evidence supplied by solo mothers suggests otherwise. When the HCC managers noted that mothers were alive at the time children were admitted to the orphanage, they indicated that those women had been deserted only 4 percent of the time (versus the 18 percent of white women who told UPOH managers they were deserted). Another 40 percent of African American women claimed to be widows (versus 66 percent of white mothers) (see tables 4.6 and 4.2). Far more often—55 percent of the time—the HCC managers did not record the status of children's fathers at all. This can be partially explained by the managers' lax record-keeping style: indeed, they failed to record any parent information at all for nearly a third of the children in the home, the kind of less-than-thorough documentation that was a source of consternation for Progressive reformers.[75] Yet the managers were not consistently lax: they far more often accepted children from mothers without recording the status of fathers (54 percent of women's children), while failing to note the status of mothers only 30 percent of the time when recording the father's information (see table 4.6). This record-keeping gap reveals a sex bias on the part of the managers: it appears they were more likely to simply accept solo mothers' children without asking for information about fathers than they were to accept father's children without knowing something about the mother.

It seems quite likely that a large proportion of these women's mates were nonresident, living elsewhere perhaps temporarily, or even permanently. Given the focus of many white reformers in this period on making African American men financially responsible for their families—and thereby decreasing the dependency of black women and children—the HCC managers' apparent laissez-faire attitude toward solo mothers is curious. While they vetted all applications for admission, accepting only "worthy objects" and rejecting those children who had parents or relatives able to care for them, they were less particular about verifying the status of live-away fathers. It may be that the managers, with their maternalist ideology, sympathized with the plight of solo mothers; at any rate, they did not penalize them for having living spouses by refusing to admit their children (as occurred regularly at UPOH). They may have asked about the men during the admission interview, but their failure to record any information about them so much of the time suggests they deemed the men unimportant and ancillary to the process of institutionalizing children. This "invisibility" was both a negative assessment of black men's ability to father, especially as defined by breadwinning, as well as a more positive, and pragmatic, assessment of women's urgent need for childcare assistance. For instance, the Pennsylvania Department of Welfare complained to the HCC managers that the institution had been "caring for three boys whose father has been living in Chicago for more than a year." While the state was concerned about making him "provide for his family," the orphanage clearly knew where he was and had not gone after him.[76]

Migration and the structure of men's employment would have acutely shaped the experience of live-away fathers. The majority of HCC parents (69 percent) hailed from the South and migrated to Pittsburgh during turbulent times: at first during the Civil War and Reconstruction, and later in the post-Reconstruction and Jim Crow era (see appendix C). In search of a meaningful freedom, migrants moved for many reasons, seeking better jobs, more control over the labor of each family member, educational opportunities for their children, and an escape from violence.[77] When they encountered northern racism and persistent under- and unemployment, some men (and women) were forced to repeatedly move, leaving behind children with a solo parent or other kin.[78] This may have been the case with John Banner, whose wife was also living when his two daughters, Rachel, aged four, and Harriet, aged two, entered the orphanage. After four and a half years, the girls went home to their father, who was now living back in North Carolina, where both he and his wife, Grace, had been born. In the North, the Banners had been unable to keep their family together, and John returned south, possibly seeking work, a supportive kin network, or both.[79] African American men were forced into occupations at the bottom rungs of the economic ladder, with low pay, high rates of injury, and persistent unemployment. The cyclical nature of the industrial economy meant that men were frequently out of work and searching for the next job, pulling them away from families who may have only recently arrived in the city.

For men who did stay involved with their children's care at the HCC, family reunification proved difficult. Children of solo fathers stayed by far the longest in the orphanage—ten months longer than children of African American mothers and twice as long as their male peers at UPOH (see table 4.8). Both black and white men kept their sons institutionalized longer than their daughters. It is possible African American fathers were keeping their sons at the orphanage until they aged out. For example, the HCC managers "decided that Mr. Corning and Mr. Hampton take their boys as they are too large and too old for us to care for longer."[80] However, this was not the typical experience, and of those children who went home to fathers, most were below the home's upper age limit of twelve. At nearly two and a half years, boys of solo fathers averaged the greatest time in the orphanage, but black men also took a long time to bring home their daughters, suggesting they, like white men, had more trouble than solo mothers in reconstituting their homes.

An analysis of the dismissal outcomes for fathers supports this observation: the majority of children of solo fathers returned home (57 percent), but in a much smaller proportion than those who returned home to solo

Table 4.8. Median Length of Stay for HCC Children of Solo Parents, by Sex of Child and Parent

	Boys		Girls		All	
	N	Months	N	Months	N	Months
Solo mothers	73	22.0	75	15.1	147	18.3
Solo fathers	48	29.5	35	20.4	83	28.1

Source: HCC admission and dismissal ledger.

mothers (82 percent) (see table 4.9). In addition, the proportion of children returning to African American fathers was significantly smaller than that of those returning to either white mothers or fathers (see table 4.3). In other words, children of solo black men were the least likely to be reunited with their fathers. While it is possible, of course, that these fathers resisted re-unification with their children, there is no evidence to suggest they dragged their feet for any reason. Rather, when the HCC managers notified men that they must retrieve their children—when they aged out or had broken house rules, or when board fees went unpaid—these fathers routinely asked for more time or even financial assistance, citing their housing and wage earning situations.

Like many white men, black fathers often did not have homes to take children into. For example, when the managers wrote "to Mr. McCrary telling him of his son's having set fire at 3 different times to building . . . he wrote back asking to please give him another chance, he having neither place nor means to care for him." A widower, James McCrary had placed his three boys in the orphanage five years earlier but still did not have a home or income enough to support them. The managers agreed to "keep the McCrary children and give them the food they need to keep them until Oct.," though James managed to keep them in the home until the following March.[81] Similarly, many solo men lived in boarding homes that were often overcrowded and provided no room for parents with children. Nevertheless, the HCC managers noted, "The two little Horst girls Sadie and Cassie were taken home by their Father to the house where he was boarding to assist the family."[82] In this case, the father may have expected the children's labor in the boarding home to pay for their keep. Other men were willing to take their children home but lacked ready funds to pay for immediate needs. For instance, when the managers learned "John Pelquist's father will take him if Board will pay transportation," they agreed, "that [the] board defray expenses."[83] These fathers showed no unwillingness to retrieve their children, but rather expressed their difficulty in finding suitable housing, adequate income, and even cash on hand to pay for the carfare home.

Table 4.9. Dismissal Outcomes of HCC Children, by Sex of Child and Solo Parent

	Children of solo mothers						Children of solo fathers					
	Boys		Girls		Total		Boys		Girls		Total	
Dismissed to	N	Percent	N	Percent	N	Percent	N	Percent	N	Percent	N	Percent
Solo parent	63	82	56	81	119	82	31	67	16	43	47	57
Relative/friend/guardian	3	4	3	4	6	4	3	7	8	22	11	13
Adoption	0	0	0	0	0	0	0	0	0	0	0	0
Indenture/foster	3	4	8	12	11	8	4	9	7	19	11	13
Another institution/college	2	3	1	1	3	2	5	11	5	14	10	12
Juvenile court	5	6	0	0	5	3	1	2	0	0	1	1
Died	1	1	1	1	2	1	2	4	1	3	3	4
Ran away	0	0	0	0	0	0	0	0	0	0	0	0
Total dismissals	77	100	69	100	146	100	46	100	37	100	83	100

Source: HCC admission and dismissal ledger.
Note: Percentages do not total to 100 due to rounding.

The HCC solo fathers also leaned more heavily on family for help in retrieving their children. These men were more than three times as likely as mothers to send their children from the orphanage to live with relatives (13 percent vs. 4 percent of children). Scholars have repeatedly noted the reliance in the black community on networks of extended kin and fictive kin, non–blood relations who are emotionally close and act in the place of family. The HCC noted the same thing, reporting one year that "many children . . . accepted into the Home only remain for a few months when some relative or friend takes them for adoption."[84] Relatives who expected to be able to take children from the orphanage were sometimes frustrated by managers who did not necessarily recognize their kinship claims. For example, when Laura Washington's aunt "asked permission to take . . . her neice into ther family," the managers "decided that as Laura had been placed in the Home by her father and she was now placed in a good [foster] home, we would not make any arrangements with the Aunt."[85] Furthermore, not a single solo mother or father permitted the adoption of their children by non-kin.

Fathers were far more likely than mothers to allow their children to be sent to another institution or placed out in private homes. Thirteen percent of men's children went to indentured or foster homes versus 8 percent of women's children. Sometimes fathers made placement arrangements themselves. For example, Mr. Long admitted his three sons to the HCC, and eight years later, the managers contacted him to "find out if he could take his son Harold who has been placed in a home." The man "who had taken him was not willing to sign indenturing papers," so they instructed him to "return Harold to the Home" and then asked "to have Mr Long take Harold out of the Home and arrange for his future with this person."[86] But the proportion of black men's children in placements was somewhat less than that for white men (13 percent versus 15 percent of dismissals). While both black and white parents generally resisted foster placements, African Americans had particular reason to distrust such a system given the legacy of forced apprenticeships foisted upon families after emancipation.[87] Nonetheless, black men's greater use of indentures and foster placements, relative to their female counterparts, speaks to their difficulty in reconstituting homes with their children.

The sex of children also affected their likelihood of being reunited with their fathers. While HCC men were less likely overall to retrieve their children than women, they were significantly less likely to reunite with daughters. Proportionally, solo fathers took home only 43 percent of their girls compared to 67 percent of their boys. Instead, they sent girls in far greater number to stay with relatives (22 percent versus 7 percent). Fathers also placed a greater proportion of their daughters in foster homes and sent them to other institutions. By contrast, solo HCC mothers retrieved nearly equal proportions of their boys and girls, and brought home considerably more of their children than any other subgroup, male or female, white or black.

Remarriage may have also played a role in allowing HCC fathers to reunite with their children. Although the data do not permit this level of analysis (as the managers did not record case histories to the extent that UPOH did), it is quite possible African American widowers were able to remarry and bring home children just as some white fathers did. For instance, widower Ezekiel Tine placed his three sons in the orphanage nine months after his wife's death, but was able to retrieve them two years later when he remarried.[88] Nationally, throughout this period, African Americans actually had the highest rate of remarriage.[89] However, as the bulk of fathers with children in the HCC were not in fact widowers, this was not likely to have been a common path to family reunification.

Rather, the story of African American fatherhood as seen in the history of the HCC is one of struggle, separation, and loss, and eventual reunion for the majority of families. The fathers who turned to the orphanage for child care help had few resources and were unable, or unwilling, to call on extended kin networks. Men like Charles Wagoner, whose wife Esther was living when their three children were admitted to the institution, faced great financial hurdles. The siblings, aged three, four, and seven, came to the orphanage from the Allegheny City Home (a public almshouse), where they may have been living with one or both of their parents, a sure sign of the family's impoverishment. Five years later, Wagoner's oldest son, John, was dismissed to the juvenile court, which may have helped locate a foster home for him. But two years later, when Chester and Ruth aged out of the orphanage, Wagoner was able to retrieve his children and take them home with him to Rochester, Pennsylvania, about thirty-five miles northwest of Pittsburgh along the Ohio River.[90] Far from "absent," fathers like Wagoner represent the experiences of many HCC men. Thus, while women were the predominant users of the orphanage, fathers were not entirely missing either, as many were likely nonresident and others struggled as solo fathers.

᙮   ᙮   ᙮

Around 1921, James Caldwell visited the grave of his wife, Jessie, who had died in childbirth thirty years earlier, leaving him a widower with six children to care for. On that sunny day his daughters Bertha and Mayme and

Figure 4.2. James Caldwell, circa 1930 *(top)*, and visiting the grave of his wife and three deceased children with some of his surviving children and grandchildren, circa 1921 *(bottom)*. *Source:* Collection of the author.

their families accompanied him to the cemetery, where someone captured the scene in a snapshot, showing James surrounded by babies and young children, living testaments to his struggle to keep his family together despite tragedy. By this point in his life, he lived part of each year with Mayme and part with another daughter, Susie. Many years later, his grandchildren remembered him teaching them the Highland Fling and other dances, the way he would sing in his Scottish brogue, and the money for candy that always accompanied his visits.[91] For James, placing his children in an orphanage had served as a family survival strategy and allowed him to keep most of his children together. What's more, he was able to sustain those relationships throughout a lifetime and provided a generational connection between adult siblings and their families. He died in 1935 at the age of seventy-eight, and his children buried him next to their mother.

The experiences of men like James Caldwell remind us that fathers have often played significant roles in child care, especially in times of family crisis. Like many other widowers, Caldwell found breadwinning and parenting difficult to combine, and institutional managers were ready to take pity on his motherless children. But his ongoing involvement with them through their time in the orphanage, indentureships, and beyond, reveals the ways in which fathers did successfully deal with their child-rearing responsibilities. Indeed, the lived reality of both white and black men—solo, married, or nonresident—challenges us to reconsider how child care has been constructed and reconstructed solely as "women's work."

CHAPTER FIVE

REFORMING ORPHANS

Progressive Reformers and Staff in the Development of Child Care Organizations

> In 1878 the Legislature passed a law prohibiting the keeping
> of children under fifteen years of age in the Almshouses of the
> State. At that time there was in the Almshouse of Allegheny
> a little colored girl, two years old named Nellie Grant. The
> Women's Christian Association of Pittsburgh and Allegheny was
> notified of this act of the Legislature. They took charge of this
> child.
> —"Fiftieth Anniversary of the Home for Colored Children N.S.
> Pittsburgh, PA," 1931.

On the occasion of its fiftieth anniversary, the Home for Colored Children (HCC) recorded this version of its founding story, tracing the genesis of the institution to a state law. Several succeeding versions of this tale cite the role of legislation in prompting the formation of a new institution for African Americans, suggesting that the state acted as a progressive agent, forcing changes in the handling of all dependent children.[1] The Women's Christian Association (WCA) is even presented here as a passive entity: it "took charge" of Nellie Grant, but only after it "was notified" of the new act, suggesting it was unaware of the law, or at least had not planned to start a new orphanage based on it. However, the law in question—Pennsylvania's "Children's Law"—did not pass until 1883, three years *after* the founding of the HCC. Also known as the "Sixty-Day Law," this legislation excluded "normal" children between the ages of two and sixteen from almshouses for more than sixty days.[2]

Hailed by later reformers as "one of the most significant pieces of legislation" of its era, the Sixty-Day Law was nonetheless difficult to enforce.[3] As late as 1915, social investigators found that "the law is frequently violated," and the state itself subsequently acknowledged, "Many children . . . remain in almshouses despite the law."[4] Yet the act signaled a tide change in progressive thinking about child welfare at the end of the nineteenth century. Alice R. Liveright, Secretary of Welfare in Pennsylvania in 1934, remembered the law as a great advance, as children were no longer permitted "to associate permanently with adult paupers."[5] Considered progressive for its time, the Sixty-Day Law moved dependent children and adults into separate institutions. But by the early twentieth century, progressives put increasing pressure on orphanages to de-institutionalize their populations altogether, favoring foster homes for dependent children over large congregate care. They also called for numerous changes to orphanage policy and practice, for the benefit of those children who did remain in institutions.

Thus, while this version of the HCC's founding story may not be entirely accurate, it contains an essential truth: progressive reform ideas were starting to circulate in this period and had real impact on the development of child care institutions. The story locates the impetus for change outside of the orphanage founders themselves, placing it instead on progressives working through the government to enact new state laws regulating child welfare. Orphanage founders laid the groundwork for the development of child care institutions, based on their gender, racial, and class ideologies, but they did not rule in a vacuum, and their authority was often contested. Progressive reformers urged changes to the institutions from the outside, working from their positions in private agencies and state government. Meanwhile, staff members, working from within the two orphanages, sometimes agreed with the progressive agenda and at other times resisted it. Although the reformers and staff did not gain power equal to that of the managers in this period, both of these groups helped to shape institutional child care policy and practice.

"Spoke kindly . . . but made some criticisms": Reformers Negotiate Policy and Practice

The Home for Colored Children and the United Presbyterian Orphan's Home (UPOH) faced growing pressure from progressive reformers over the course of their first fifty years. Progressivism itself was a large tent, loosely covering and connecting many separate movements, from child labor, food safety, health, sanitation, playgrounds, and education, to the reform of institutions serving criminals, the insane, women, delinquent teens, and dependent children. Progressives had multiple agendas but were generally united in their belief in the use of new scientific methods to address social problems, and they often called for increasing government intervention through protective legislation and stricter regulations. In the late 1800s, concerns about the efficacy of large congregate care institutions—such as prisons, asylums, and orphanages—created a strong wave of anti-institutionalism. After the turn of the century, a younger generation of women often championed the anti-institutionalization movement.[6] But this was not a neat and tidy takeover of progressive ideals, and in some places there was a great deal of resistance as the old tussled with the new.[7] The HCC and UPOH demonstrate just how successful some institution managers were in holding onto older traditions of benevolent volunteerism and fending off recommendations from progressives. These reformers called especially for de-institutionalizing children through foster placements and coordinating admissions with the new expertise of social workers. At the same time, the managers were willing to accept some reforms when they did not threaten their institutions or authority, such as modernization of facilities, new ideas about healthcare and nutrition, and cooperation with the burgeoning playground movement.

In Pittsburgh, reform pressures came from individuals working in local private organizations as well as the state government, which slowly gained a supervisory role over social welfare, including that of dependent children. For example, Helen Glenn Tyson authored several key reports on child welfare in the city and state, served as Deputy Secretary of Welfare for the commonwealth in 1930, and worked for many years for Family Charities in Pittsburgh. She was very active in the Urban League of Pittsburgh, along with her husband, Francis D. Tyson, a professor of economics at the University of Pittsburgh, where Helen earned her PhD.[8] As a highly educated woman—she also graduated Phi Beta Kappa from Vassar College—Tyson personified the new generation of reformers who, after the turn of the century, gradually wrested authority from the older, maternalist volunteers. In the field of child welfare in particular, which previous generations of women had already staked as the unique purview of their sex, reformers fashioned a "female dominion" that extended from hotbeds of progressive ideas such as the University of Chicago and Hull House all the way to Washington, D.C., with the 1912 founding of the U.S. Children's Bureau.[9] Pittsburgh was well connected to this national network: in 1917, for instance, it hosted the annual meeting of the National Children's Home Society, later renamed the National Home and Welfare Association, a federation of thirty-four statewide organizations that did child placing (what evolved into the modern foster care system).[10]

National figures also came to the Steel City to investigate the impact of the industrial economy on families and then published studies on institutional child care efforts. These included Elizabeth Beardsley Butler, Florence Lattimore, Crystal Eastman, and Margaret Byington, who each conducted extensive field research for the groundbreaking *Pittsburgh Survey*, a six volume series published by the Russell Sage Foundation in New York. Butler examined women engaged in wage labor, particularly factory work, and Lattimore tackled child care head-on in her study "Pittsburgh as Foster Mother."[11] Around the same time, William H. Slingerland and Hastings H. Hart, both of the Department of Child-Helping at the Russell Sage Foundation, published an in-depth study of child welfare institutions in the state of Pennsylvania, cataloging and critiquing 343 organizations.[12] Similarly, local academics used Pittsburgh as their laboratory for a slew of studies on child welfare: starting in the 1920s the department of social work at the University of Pittsburgh regularly produced master's theses on children living in institutions, education, child labor, and more.[13] These reformers were a varied lot, with a range of progressive ideas and agendas, but they shared a common desire to de-institutionalize children and introduce new methods of scientific social work.

What's more, progressives obtained key staff positions in the public sector, so that the government itself became an agent of reform. For instance, working for the Public Charities Association of Pennsylvania, a state regulatory body, Abraham Oseroff authored a scathing report of child care institutions receiving public funding, including the HCC. Oseroff used a photograph of the orphanage's basement playroom on the inside cover, representing the institution by this prominent placement as the "poster child" for needed reform (see figure 5.1). In the body of the report, Oseroff described the room as "totally devoid of play things of any sort . . . almost completely underground, with four very small windows at the top of two of the walls."[14] Both the HCC and UPOH came into increasing contact with such agencies intent on supervising orphanage policy and practice. For example, the local Department of Public Health regularly interacted with the orphanages, imposing quarantines for up to months at a time, and through its Bureau of Sanitation, which was responsible for fire inspections, it began pushing for increased safety equipment. Repeated visits and recommendations for installing fire escapes, improving hoses, and implementing fire drills eventually resulted in partial accommodations from the boards.[15]

For many years, the HCC also had to submit reports to the state's Department of Public Instruction since it provided schooling within the institution. In addition, both orphanages increasingly came under the gaze of local private agencies such as the Children's Service Bureau, the Federation of Social Agencies, and the Welfare Fund, who each sent inspectors to

Figure 5.1. Original caption: "Basement Play Room in an Allegheny County Institution." *Source:* Oseroff, *Report of the Allegheny County Committee Public Charities Association of Pennsylvania,* 1915.

review the homes. While the Children's Service Bureau acted mainly as a child-placing organization and lacked any authority over the orphanages, the HCC did eventually cooperate with the progressively minded Federation of Social Agencies, as well as the Welfare Fund, which held the purse strings to a large percentage of its budget by the 1930s.[16] Thus, a range of both government and private organizations slowly gained responsibility for oversight of dependent child welfare.

Yet the orphanages maintained the upper hand in negotiating how much control they would cede to these organizations. This was particularly true in the homes' relationship with Pennsylvania's Department of Welfare, which evolved in the late nineteenth and early twentieth century to have a much greater supervisory role, yet lacked enforcement teeth. The state's department of welfare grew out of the Board of Public Charities, created in 1869, which had five unpaid commissioners who were supposed to inspect all institutions in the commonwealth annually; they could make recommendations but had little real power to enforce changes.[17] For instance, in an early visit to the HCC, the commissioners "spoke kindly" of their work, "but made

some criticisms" including "defective ventilation in the hospital room . . .
the way the nursery is lighted at night and . . . a place in the basement where
the wood work needs protection from a gas jet."[18] State agents relied on
polite negotiations with the managers to entice change, peppering them with
praise, encouragement, and gentle suggestions. For instance, UPOH noted
that a state representative "was greatly pleased . . . and reported that our
Home ranked among the first in the State in methods, management, and
so forth." The visitor "expressed praise for our work and also gave a few
suggestions for changes and an offer of help in any way we may wish."[19]

In conjunction with 1903 legislation creating some of the earliest juvenile
courts in the country, the state established a county Board of Visitors charged
with inspecting each institution in the district annually; orphanages and
other child welfare organizations were also required to submit yearly reports.
The state eliminated the old Board of Charities in 1921 and replaced it with
the Department of Welfare, keeping the county-level Board of Visitors in
place. Subsequent laws split the responsibility for children between two state
agencies: the Department of Public Assistance dealt with children receiving
aid in their own homes, while the Department of Welfare continued to deal
with dependent (and delinquent and neglected) children in institutions and
foster homes. But the state did not gain real teeth until new legislation in
1929 that, among other things, allowed the department to withhold state
funding.[20] For the first fifty years of the orphanages' history, then, the state
lacked coercive muscle and the balance of power in negotiating change to
institutional practice and policy rested firmly with the orphanage managers.

This started to shift somewhat in 1923 when the incoming governor,
Gifford Pinchot, promoted a forceful new personality, Dr. Ellen C. Potter,
to head the recently reconstituted Department of Welfare. A former New
York City settlement house worker and physician trained at the Woman's
Medical College of Pennsylvania (now part of Drexel University), Potter
served as chief of the state's Child Health Division under the previous administration and then led the Bureau of Children in the newly formulated
welfare department. Her promotion to secretary of that department made
her the first female member of a governor's cabinet in the United States. As
a progressive, Potter advocated documentation of research and good practices—what she called "writing it into the record"—and therefore published
many articles herself on social welfare administration.[21]

Potter staffed her administration with numerous women who served as
field agents and increased the frequency of their visits to UPOH and the
HCC. Every Welfare Department agent noted by the two orphanages was
a woman. The county level Board of Visitors and private agencies such as

the Children's Service Bureau and the Federation of Social Agencies also employed many women who visited the homes. Under the new regime, the managers at both orphanages noted yearly inspections, generally followed by a letter from Potter summarizing the agent's findings and recommendations. Potter served only one four-year term as secretary before moving to New Jersey as that state's Director of Medicine in the Department of Institutions and Agencies. But her work in Pennsylvania arguably set the stage for increased government scrutiny and control over child welfare institutions.

Through gentle prodding, Potter succeeded in getting some changes implemented at the orphanages—but only when the managers agreed with the state's recommendations and had sufficient funds to pay for them. For instance, reformers in this period increasingly emphasized the individuality of children and abhorred practices at many congregate care institutions that treated all inmates the same, such as uniform clothing and haircuts. Potter and her staff repeatedly called for individualization and privacy, while also employing the progressive rhetoric of hygiene and sanitation. After

Figure 5.2. Dr. Ellen C. Potter in uniform during World War I, 1916. *Source:* Drexel University, College of Medicine, Archives & Special Collections.

field agent Sarah Spencer visited the HCC, Potter wrote, "[W]e urge that the basement toilets (whose dark location we deplore) be given attention as soon as possible. We would repeat our hope also that arrangements be made for greater privacy." She added, "We are glad to learn of the effort that is being made to provide individual towels."[22] The following year, field agent Elizabeth Wyatt inspected the orphanage, and Potter commended the use of individual combs and toothbrushes, noting also, "We all believe that individual towels are not a luxury but a necessity for health's sake."[23] The managers noted, "After reading the letter from Dr. Potter motion was made and seconded that we had carried out the suggestions given as far as we were financially able to do so."[24]

Though they ignored several recommendations, the managers did cooperate with reformers, willingly taking up some issues, perhaps because they were in line with changes they had been making on their own for many years. As early as 1902, the HCC managers noted, "Each child has its own brush and comb."[25] And while the state may have found the basement toilets dark and deplorable in the 1920s, they were an improvement over the "outside closet" that had "been the cause of much annoyance to [the] neighbors" just twenty years earlier.[26] After reading Potter's letter, "the plumbing and toilet equipment were discussed and extensive changes decided upon."[27] Within a few months "[b]lueprints . . . were shown and discussed," but they decided "that all plumbing work to be postponed."[28] It took several more years to complete the work, but by 1930 the managers boasted of new bathrooms, "complete and modern in every respect," including linoleum floors. They also noted, "Each child has his or her own wardrobe and is provided with play, school, and Sunday clothes. These garments are all marked with owner's name and kept in individual lockers." What's more, they assured investigators, "All toilet articles such as tooth brushes, wash clothes and towels are individually owned and are not used in common."[29]

Similarly, the UPOH managers cooperated by accepting some recommendations while rejecting others. When the state suggested a few improvements such as "fire drill, rearrangement of showers, more bathing facilities, physical examinations once a year, and examination of teeth," the managers assigned a committee "to consider and report at next meeting."[30] The committee made no report and no mention was ever made again of these issues. Yet the managers responded favorably to a state recommendation two years later: field agents "found things in good shape but suggested a few additions—among them drinking fountains." The plural "additions" indicates the welfare department made several recommendations (as was their practice), but the managers responded to only one, promptly voting to "install three drinking fountains."[31] Likewise, when the state Board of Health sent a doctor "to present [the] case for new vaccinations for diphtheria"—a dreadful and deadly childhood disease that generated epidemics in both orphanages—the managers chose to bring in their own experts. After listening to "testimonials" from several local doctors, "including authorities from Allegheny General Hospital," and reading a "New York paper favoring its use," they decided to "consult our staff regarding its use and if they approve the treatment be begun at once."[32] Without compulsory powers, the state could only make suggestions, and the managers were free to pick and choose which ones they would consider.

Even when the state used its legislative authority to regulate institutions, the orphanages occasionally persisted in their practices despite the law. For example, in 1904 the state's Dairy and Food Commission sent a notice to the HCC "citing a law passed by legislature in 1893 making an officer or manager of any charitable or penal institution who shall purchase oleomargarine or butterine for use in these institutions" guilty of a misdemeanor punishable "by fine or imprisonment or both." The managers noted, "This being a rather alarming condition of affairs the purchasing committee were instructed to buy only pure butter."[33] Yet, the orphanage went back to using the cheaper product, and the Commissioner for Public Welfare wrote some years later, chastising the managers that "oleomargarine is not a satisfactory substitute for butter in food for children since it does not contain the growth promoting substances that are found in butter in abundance."[34] The managers may not have agreed with the state on the issue of butter, but their standards for milk quality appeared to exceed state recommendations. When they worried that the milk they were buying was not up to par, they sent some to the state Board of Health for testing. The board concluded it was "very good quality," but the managers were not satisfied and voted "to give the milk subject further investigation," instructing the matron to "take another quart of milk to the Board of Health for further test."[35] In these instances, the managers valued their own judgment as institutional leaders, based on their expertise as homemakers and mothers, above the opinions of state "authorities."

Through the 1920s the managers maintained the upper hand in negotiations with reformers, following their suggestions when it best suited them. Their stance was often not so much anti-progressive, as it was pragmatic: for instance, they agreed with the need to continually upgrade their facilities and generally did so to the best of their financial ability. They also agreed with certain progressive ideas when they aligned with their beliefs about how to best treat the poor children in their care. For example, the middle-class women of the playground movement, which took hold nationally and locally at the turn of the century, advocated supervised play in controlled spaces that freed children from urban ills while teaching moral and social behavior.[36] Both the HCC and UPOH cooperated with the local North Side Play Ground Association, which supplied professional game teachers and storytellers during the summer months and helped them develop formal recreation plans.[37] But on other progressive matters, the managers doggedly refused to budge. For instance, through the 1920s the HCC defied all suggestions to more fully racially integrate its board and staff (see next chapter for further discussion).

The managers particularly resisted the suggestion to coordinate their admissions and foster placements using experts in the newly professionalized field of social work. In 1915 the Public Charities Association conducted a study of child care institutions in Allegheny County and pointedly concluded, "One of the most marked weaknesses" of the orphanages in the county, was "an almost total lack of proper investigation before the admission of a child." The report accused institution managers of needlessly breaking up families and burdening themselves "with the care of children who need never have become institutional charges."[38] That same year, the Russell Sage Foundation, in cooperation with the Pennsylvania State Conference of Charities, published a detailed review of child welfare institutions in the state, scoffing at institutional managers who "still adhere to the supposed advantages of unsupervised volunteer service."[39] This report complained that it was "impossible" for untrained "volunteers to carry on this responsible and exacting work [of admissions and placement] with due efficiency." It argued that home investigation "is a technical work" and that the use of volunteers, however well intentioned they might be, "harks back to the days of spinning wheels and hand looms." The report criticized women such as the HCC and UPOH managers: "The day is past when the interests of a neglected child can be committed to an agent whose chief qualifications are physical courage and general goodwill towards suffering children."[40]

But the orphanage managers fundamentally disagreed, tenaciously holding onto their role in the admissions and placement process that had always been a central part of their work. The State Conference of Charities study probably identified their sentiments exactly when it huffed, "It is held by these organizations that volunteer work is more sympathetic and genuine, and not cold, methodical, and machine-like, as is the work of many paid employes." The report lamented that the volunteers dismissed "any benefits of training in social service" in favor of "the closer relations of those who do the work because of love for humanity."[41] Even after UPOH moved quite a distance to their country location in 1929, they continued to conduct their own admissions and placement investigations.

The HCC, however, slowly moved toward cooperation with other specialists in the field, while keeping control over the process. In 1922 the state Department of Welfare cautioned the managers that they were not performing "sufficiently thorough investigation" of children's homes before admitting them, and that they ought to "meet this need of adequate social investigation by cooperating either with the Children's Service Bureau of Pittsburgh or the Children's Aid Society of Allegheny County."[42] Still lacking teeth, the state could not force this change, but made the suggestion again the following year, adding, "This insures careful handling of this rather specialized type of work and liberates your volunteer workers for other important duties such as raising funds, making community contacts, etc."[43] In a personal meeting with a board representative in the state capital, though, Potter was more forceful, making it "very plain . . . that we should use the Children's Aid to help us in our admissions of children."[44]

In 1924 the HCC chose instead to work with the Children's Service Bureau, another private agency that placed children in foster homes. However, the managers continued to be intimately involved in the admissions process, sometimes collecting applications and then sending them to the bureau for investigation, and other times admitting children directly. For instance, in one "very distressing case" involving two young children, one under the age limit, the managers decided, "This being an emergency case the children were admitted until baby could be placed in a proper home."[45] Bypassing the bureau altogether, the managers took in two-year-old Anna Carlton, who stayed for just nine days before her mother came for her, and her three-year-old brother, James, who remained a year and a half until their "mother remarried" and came for him, too.[46] The managers also continued to negotiate the terms of board payment with families, retaining the right to admit children free of board at their own discretion.

Cooperating with the bureau may have introduced more professional social work methods, but its benefit to poor families was questionable, particularly as it slowed down an already agonizing process for families desperately in need of child care. Parents now submitted an application to a committee of HCC managers, who presented the cases at the next board meeting and then forwarded the paperwork onto the bureau for investigation. For example, Laura Galloway applied for admission of her two-year-old daughter, Dorothy, in October one year; after board approval, the HCC sent her application along to the bureau, which was apparently satisfied with its review, but the little girl did not enter the orphanage until December, two months later.[47]

The HCC and UPOH managers were most resistant to the idea of de-institutionalizing their children. Progressives increasingly called for foster homes to replace institutional care for dependent children. One critic complained of "the tendency in the Pittsburgh district to emphasize institutional care rather than the more modern and more effective system of placing out normal children in family homes."[48] Speaking on behalf of reformers, another wrote, "The advantage to a child of being reared in the normal conditions of a good family circle rather than in the abnormal conditions of an institution, is now too well known to need explanation, and so universally accepted as not to require argument."[49] Yet, the orphanage managers did not universally accept the notion of placing out most of the children under their care. In fact, as discussed in chapter three, many families were adamantly opposed to the placement of their children and effectively prevented the practice, even when the orphanages favored finding foster homes for them. The orphanage managers were not alone: statewide in 1923, 68 percent of all dependent children being cared for outside their homes were in institutions. Sixteen percent were in free foster homes, and another 14 percent were in paid foster homes.[50] Using the language of steelmaking, a 1930 study of child welfare in Pittsburgh concluded, "Allegheny County is over-weighted with provision for institutional care for children," and called for the smaller denominational organizations to be "melted down" and their funds "run into new channels of relief."[51]

The managers responded defensively, emphasizing the homelike qualities of the orphanages. For instance, the HCC told the child welfare study, "It is both the purpose and the desire of the Board so far as it is within their power to make this Home for colored children a real Home, with as much home care and with as many home surroundings as is possible in an Institution."[52] As early as 1898 the UPOH managers were referring to the orphanage as "our foster home," where "cheerful surroundings and comforts" made the children "soon forget the sorrows and misfortunes which darkened their young lives and seem as happy and free from care as most children do in their own homes."[53] In describing their institution as a foster home, the managers often detailed the many outings, entertainments, and holiday celebrations that made orphanage life more normal and homelike: one year the children attended the Pittsburgh Exposition, went on a steamboat ride, and saw "the Haunted Swing," after which the managers reported, "Although living in an Orphans' Home, you will see that they enjoy about as many pleasures as other children."[54] The next year, the managers described another visit to the exposition, complete with ice cream sandwiches and popcorn balls, toy cane whips, a ride on the merry-go-round, "movable pictures in the Theatorium," and a picture card for each child presented by H. J. Heinz himself: "Indeed, they have a happy life; it is our aim to make it 'home-like,' and as far as possible removed from institution life."[55] In a 1938 history of the home, the UPOH managers described the close relationship of the children to volunteer "big sisters," saying, "These little touches show ours is not an Institution but a real home."[56]

When avoiding institutional care was not possible, progressives advocated the use of the "cottage plan" to break up large congregate, dormitory style buildings into smaller "homes." Each cottage would have a small group of residents living in a more family-like environment, under the care of a housemother or other caretaker. Later in the twentieth century, both the HCC and UPOH moved to the cottage plan, but for their first fifty years, they staunchly defended their facilities as homelike. UPOH published photographs and illustrations of the orphanage looking like a large, comfortable house; even its hospital building, constructed behind the orphanage on a steep hillside, was nestled among other homes, keeping in scale with the neighborhood. After 1929 when it moved to Butler County, photographs of UPOH emphasized its pastoral setting and the grandeur of a country estate (see figure 5.3). The HCC made similar claims about its large building, which it constructed on riverfront property somewhat removed from the city in 1893. They published fewer photographs until the 1930s but consistently described the orphanage's parklike setting and spacious grounds (see figure 5.4). Through these images, the orphanages defended their institutions as ideal places for children and appropriate, substitute homes.

Thus, the orphanage managers fended off the most significant changes demanded by progressive reformers: coordinated admissions and de-institutionalization. The reformers, largely women working in private organizations as well as state agencies, negotiated with the managers but lacked real supervisory authority and enforcement muscle until the late 1920s. While the managers maintained the balance of power in the relationship, the reformers did influence orphanage practice and policy in areas such as public health measures, sanitation upgrades, and children's recreation programs. And by keeping the issues of foster care and professional casework methods constantly on the table, they also kept the managers on the defensive, forcing them to justify the institutional care they provided. Eventually, the reformers succeeded in transforming child care in the mid-twentieth century—by implementing the foster care system for "normal" dependent children, introducing

Figure 5.3. Top left: Postcard of original UPOH home on Sherman Avenue, opened 1878; *Top right:* location of UPOH on West Jefferson and Monteray Streets, 1880–1929; *Bottom left:* Hospital building, 1890; *Bottom right:* Mars, Butler County estate, purchased 1929. *Source:* Staff and Board of Directors of the Mars Home for Youth.

Figure 5.4. Termon Avenue location of the HCC, built 1893. *Source:* Library and Archives Division, Sen. John Heinz History Center.

social welfare programs for single mothers, and converting institutions into homes for delinquent youth—but the seeds of these changes were sown in this earlier period, as they negotiated with the orphanage managers.

"Hard work, heavy responsibilities, and low wages": Staff Negotiate Policy and Practice

Like reformers, staff members played an important role in the development of the institutions, influencing both the policy and practice of dependent child care. Where reformers negotiated with the managers from outside the institutions, the staff negotiated from within, from positions as "insiders." They, too, lacked the upper hand in their relationship with the managers, but staff asserted their own ideas and actively participated in the administration of the orphanages, long before the professionalization of institutional staff later in the twentieth century. Despite their close association with the daily management of orphanage life, staff members have received very little attention in the historiography of welfare institutions.[57] This may be due at least in part to the fact that most staff members were working-class women who left few records of their own. But the managers commented frequently on their employees, and their notes reveal the significant ways in which staff shaped the orphanages.

The women on staff at the HCC and UPOH had an enormous impact on the lives of the orphanage children. Nearly all staff members lived at the institutions, in tight quarters with the children, interacting with them both day and night, and sometimes all night long when children were sick. UPOH children left the orphanage to attend the local public school, but until after the turn of the century, HCC children received lessons in the home and rarely left for other reasons, meaning their interactions with adults were almost exclusively with orphanage staff. Both institutions hired a core staff ranging from four to twelve people who lived in the orphanage with the children. On average, six staff members resided in the homes at any given point, usually consisting of a matron, assistant matron, cook, housekeeper, seamstress, and laundress. These positions fluctuated constantly, with, for instance, chambermaids substituting for a housekeeper or a nurse (a caretaker for pre–school aged children) instead of an assistant matron.

The matron's position evolved later in the twentieth century to what is today an executive director, but through the first fifty years, the role was much less independent. The matron ran the home, supervised and sometimes hired staff, and made daily decisions. But she was subject to the constant scrutiny of the managers. The managing women could be quite supportive and respectful of a skilled matron, but they also did not hesitate to intervene in routine matters and expected their chief employee to act as their proxy, placing the matron in a distinct position: above and sometimes in tension with the rest of the staff, yet below and sometimes in tension with the managers.

Both the HCC and UPOH boasted better staff-to-child ratios than the national average yet suffered from the common problem of frequent staff turnover. By the early twentieth century, most orphan asylums around the country had relatively low staff-to-child ratios, with cottage-based institutions having the best ratios of one to ten. Larger congregate institutions were higher (at one to sixteen), while asylums for minorities often had substantially higher ratios.[58] Day nursery staff ratios could be even worse than orphanages, as high as one to twenty-five.[59] By these standards, both the HCC and UPOH's ratios compared quite favorably, averaging around one to six or one to seven.[60] Significantly, all of these ratios measure total staff, not just staff involved in direct child care, though managers frequently tried to press chambermaids, laundresses, and others into child care duties, with varying success. The low ratios at UPOH and the HCC meant that children could potentially receive more individualized care.

Yet staff came and went frequently, undoubtedly adding to the turmoil of the young lives in their care. One reformer examined orphanage staff in Pennsylvania and concluded, "The matrons and most of the subordinates are quite universally loving and sympathetic." And yet, "they are mentally and physically overtaxed, burdened with excessive strain and long hours, and sadly underpaid." He argued that mothers might care for their own children under such conditions, but "the hired toiler" would have to be "far above average in maternal qualities and the higher characteristics of womanhood" to withstand the strain. He summed up the situation: "[W]ith hard work, heavy responsibilities, and low wages conspiring against the institutions working forces, it is no wonder that it is difficult . . . to attract and retain efficient workers."[61]

Both the HCC and UPOH staffs largely comprised working-class women, often from the local community, who shared with the poor client families they served a similar experience in the city's industrial economy. Even the matrons, who were more often middle class, tended to be widows or self-supporting single women, giving them common ground with many of their clients. Although this did not guarantee their sympathies, staff also interacted with parents on a regular basis—on visiting days, while collecting boarding fees, during the admission process—and came to know their personal stories. Staff were "on the front lines," working daily with the children and their families, sometimes serving as a buffer between them and the managers. For instance, staff could selectively enforce the managers' rules, such as allowing parents to visit on nonvisiting days or to bring outside food and treats to their children. Managers' repeated attempts to enforce their own rules on these points, regularly reminding both staff and parents of the visitor and food regulations, suggests some degree of staff collusion in these "petty" offenses.

Through the 1920s, staff received no formal training in child care, and there is no doubt that some arrived unprepared for their positions. Turbulent periods could follow the arrival of a new matron. For example, shortly after Miss Kiefer began at the HCC, the board visitor reported she was "much distressed about the condition of the Home—boys having gotten beyond control of the matron and helpers, the laundresses gone." Kiefer "said she was not strong enough and asked that we relieve her as soon as possible."[62] By 1929 neither orphanage had yet hired staff with specialized training or education, despite the increasing enrollment at social work schools, such as the one at the University of Pittsburgh. UPWANA did hire a professional social worker for their hospital during this time, though it took some time for them to fully commit to the position; this social worker also assisted a small handful of families at the orphanage. Nationwide, many orphanages did not hire their own social workers until the depression.[63] Yet staff could develop a personal interest in the children, as evidenced by Alice Hurst, the UPOH matron who took orphanage children with her for summer vacations, or Jennie Corbett, a former matron who wrote to the home twenty-seven years after she left to find out how many children there were so she could send candy. At both institutions, it was relatively common for former residents to write letters and return to visit as adults, expressing feelings of warmth and gratitude toward the staff and orphanages.

Many staff members also knew firsthand the severe financial repercussions of widowhood, abandonment, divorce, and single motherhood, as witnessed by the large number who brought children with them to the orphanages. Even middle-class women in Pittsburgh during this period could be thrown into dire financial straits with the loss of a husband; widows were particularly vulnerable in the city's heavily industrial economy that favored men's employment and left little room for women's wage work.[64] With steel mills and other factories not hiring women, widows had few employment options, and nearly all meant separation from their children. Widows with young children persistently applied to these Pittsburgh orphanages for work in an effort to keep their own families together. This further suggests the way in which parents preferred orphanage care to day nurseries: historian

Elizabeth Rose found only one matron who became a client at the twelve day nurseries she studied in Philadelphia.[65]

In fact, the very first matron and assistant matron hired by UPOH in 1878 both brought their children with them. Lyde Rose, a white thirty-six-year-old widow, arrived with her three children, ages three, five, and ten. Rose stayed twelve years, resigning in 1890 shortly before her death, and Mary Reid then assumed the matron's responsibilities. Also hired in 1878, Reid was a thirty-two-year-old widow when she started as assistant matron, bringing her three children, ages five, seven, and ten, with her. Reid resigned in 1892, "to provide a little home for her children," though ironically, by this time they were all nineteen or older.[66] Both Lyde Rose and Mary Reid had, in fact, provided "a little home" for their young children precisely by seeking employment in an institution where they could live together.

Both the HCC and UPOH were willing to consider applicants with their children, though it was not a given that they would admit them. For instance, the HCC managers recorded that their employee "Mary had asked permission to have her child at the Home but this was not thought advisable."[67] In 1898 UPOH hired Mrs. Copeland as the new matron, but refused to admit her child. Copeland lasted only three short months after irritating the managers by communicating with parents and acknowledging receipt of donations (tasks the board saw as under their sole purview), but her frustration over their refusal to accept her child and the subsequent forced separation may well have played a role in her departure.[68]

Sometimes staff members leveraged their positions after they were hired to negotiate for the admission of their children. A laundress at the HCC told the managers she would be "willing to stay for $50.00 a month, if she could have her little girl with her." The managers agreed, charging her five dollars per month for the child's board, substantially less than average for that time period.[69] Managers at both institutions found it difficult to keep women to do laundry, labor intensive and low paying work often performed by African American women left with few options outside of domestic service. Black women often preferred laundry work to live-in domestic service, because they could maintain independence from their employers, manage their own work environment, and keep their children with them. They could also resist employers' attempts to control their personal and professional lives by quitting, a strategy threatened here by the HCC laundress.[70] While this woman lived and worked at the orphanage where her labor and personal life were largely under the control of her employer, she successfully negotiated for the admission of her child (and at a reduced rate), keeping her family together.

Anna Elliott, a longtime UPOH employee, was not as successful in negotiating with the managers to keep her older children with her. A recently
widowed mother of two in 1886 and a member of UPOH's "founding congregation" (Rev. Fulton's 4th United Presbyterian Church), Elliot found work
in the orphanage laundry, bringing her children with her. A few years later she
moved up to the housekeeper position, but by 1897 the managers concluded
that "if she decides to stay . . . we will have to dismiss her boys" who were
now well past the age limit of twelve.[71] Elliott resigned instead, and though
the managers clearly expressed their regret at losing her, they portrayed the
decision as entirely hers, stating in their annual report that year, "Her boys
had grown up in the Home, and she felt the time had come for her to leave
and provide for them a home."[72] Like Mary Reid, the former matron, Elliott
used employment at the orphanage as a way to keep her family intact after
losing a husband but found that her mothering responsibilities did not end
when her children reached their teen years. Rather than be separated from
her boys after keeping them with her through eleven years of work at the
orphanage, Anna Elliott chose to resign. A substantial number of women, like
Reid and Elliott, were both clients *and* staff members at these institutions.

Quitting was an effective action that forced management to pay attention to salaries and working conditions, particularly when women left in
clusters, as they frequently did. For instance, an HCC board visitor reported,
"Everything went along smoothly in the home till . . . the cook left without
giving any warning. Left with dinner uncooked, Mrs Black [the nurse] had
to take her place in the kitchen and has been there ever since," leaving
two of the older children in charge of the nursery. The chambermaid was
threatening to leave at the same time.[73] UPOH experienced similar problems,
noting one year, "The lack of competent help has been a great drawback
all through the year, and the prospect for the months to come is far from
encouraging. At present we need two strong, healthy girls for the laundry
and one for chamber work."[74] With few exceptions, matrons also did not
stay very long: the median length of stay was two years, and roughly half
of all matrons at both institutions stayed for one year or less.[75] Quitting
represented, in part, a protest of very low pay for what amounted to nearly
round-the-clock work.

Threatening to quit could be an effective bargaining tool in wage negotiation. For instance, after "the chambermaid informed visitors that unless
her wages be raised she also would leave the Home," she was granted a
raise.[76] Similarly, "The cook asks she be allowed a weeks vacation or be
relieved entirely."[77] She won two weeks vacation and a pledge to try to get
more help. Mrs. Baybutt, the HCC seamstress, asked for a salary increase

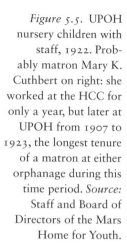

Figure 5.5. UPOH nursery children with staff, 1922. Probably matron Mary K. Cuthbert on right: she worked at the HCC for only a year, but later at UPOH from 1907 to 1923, the longest tenure of a matron at either orphanage during this time period. *Source:* Staff and Board of Directors of the Mars Home for Youth.

after the managers assigned her the extra, labor-intensive work of making children's jackets, but "[t]he Board could not see it in this way and it was [decided] that no advance be given to the seamstress."[78] Baybutt resigned instead. Quitting, or threatening to quit, were important tools of resistance for laboring women and reflect the ways in which working-class people employed multiple strategies to control their work lives.

Staff particularly resisted managers' efforts to control their nonwork hours, forcing the boards to accommodate new boundaries on their authority. Because the staff lived and worked at the institutions, they were subject to intimate observation, both by managers and by more senior staff. At the HCC, for example, "[t]he laundress' bed was reported in bad condition," and a manager was assigned "to tell her she must clean it."[79] UPOH managers discovered a staff member getting the secular Sunday paper in the home and immediately passed a rule against such reading material.[80] By 1929 UPOH employees still only had one day off per week plus one Sunday a month and could not stay out "all night without permission from the President or some member of the Executive Committee, and on such occasions, must report as early as possible the next day." Rules also dictated that "[e]very member of the household must be in and house closed at eleven o'clock every night, except by special permission."[81] Similarly, the HCC ruled that "no friends or relatives of employees be allowed to remain over night in the Home except by permission from the Executive Committee."[82] One critic of Pennsylvania's orphanages during this era surmised, "Another reason for the unrest and frequent changes among institutional workers is the nagging supervision many of them receive from officials and managers."[83]

With little privacy, staff attempted to protect their leisure hours and resisted changes to work assignments. For instance, when the HCC laundresses requested a wage increase and a washing machine to help with their work, the managers granted both, "providing they take their turn on Sabbath in caring for the children." But the board immediately learned the "[l]aundresses are not willing to assist in caring for children."[84] Similarly, their seamstress "refused to accompany the children to church."[85] The UPOH managers also experienced resistance when they ruled that children were no longer allowed to wash dishes (only to dry them). The visitors reported it made for a "very strenuous month. . . . Matron complains of House-keeper not doing anything but baking. Does not try to obey orders in regard to childrens washing dishes, because she could not get employees to do so." That very same week, the infirmary nurse left "rather than wash dishes," and the children's nurse left "rather than do her ironing." As a final straw, the managers lamented, "Matron very unwilling to try using parlor for worship under her supervision."[86]

Here the staff resisted intrusions into their personal time, especially requests to care for children on Sundays, traditionally a day off. In addition, the very presence of rules regulating staff curfew and overnight visitors suggests these were areas in which staff had been exerting control over their after-work hours. They also resisted efforts to assign additional work duties such as child care, dishwashing, or leading worship when they viewed these tasks as outside their job responsibilities. In turn, the managers were often forced to accept these narrower job definitions. With tight budgets limiting their ability to hire additional staff, this could result in fewer staff members providing direct child care or restrictions on the children's activities (such as attending church).

Staff members also pushed to control their own labor through the common practice of wage negotiation. Staff insisted on adequate compensation for their work and frequently requested salary increases, to which the managers acquiesced more often than not. For instance, the HCC managers were "very much pleased with the nurse in the nursery," but she sent a letter saying she was "not . . . satisfied with the money paid to her," and they agreed to give her an additional day's wages.[87] A UPOH laundress won a raise after several rounds of negotiation. She began by requesting a monthly increase and offered to provide her own assistants. When the managers refused, she again asked for additional wages, and they agreed to pay her a dollar per day if she would give them additional hours of work. A few months later, "the laundress had asked for $1.25 per day," which they granted.[88] Sometimes staff negotiated for compensation in the form of paid vacations or reduced boarding rates for their children. When Mrs. Westlake started as the new nurse and kindergarten teacher at UPOH, the managers decided to pay her fifteen dollars per month and ask her for ten dollars in boarding—a full two-thirds of her salary—for her three children. After a few months, however, Westlake succeeded in having the boarding fees reduced to five dollars, though she still fell into arrears trying to keep up with payments.[89]

Occasionally, staff resorted to other strategies to control their labor and compensation. For example, UPOH visitors once reported, "Matron suspects laundress of keeping her family in bread and soap."[90] While the managers viewed this as stealing, the laundress may literally have been "keeping her family" with critical supplies in the tradition of pan-toting, sometimes practiced by domestics who would take home leftover food and house goods with the tacit consent of their employers.[91] At the HCC, the mother of an employee threatened to "make trouble for the Board" if they did not pay the wages owed her daughter. The managers had hired Mary Payne to work "where her services would be most necessary," but agreed to pay her only $25.00 per month, arguing that she was "mentally deficient and had never before worked for wages having come from Polk [a state-run institution]." When they asked Mary to "[take] the place of the regular laundress she and her mother thought she should have extra wages." The managers agreed to pay her $7.50 for five days of work, then hired another laundress at twice the rate they had paid Mary. But they still had not paid her six months later when Mary's mother resorted to threatening the board with "trouble."[92] Staff rarely received salary increases without asking, and though raises were not always granted, these requests, combined with other compensation strategies—such as the occasional theft or pan-toting—forced managers to regularly attend to the wage needs of the employees as they developed increasingly more sophisticated operating budgets for their institutions.

It is tempting to speculate that Mary and her mother contacted the Bureau of Labor in their frustration, as the bureau sent an agent to investigate "supposed difficulties" that had been reported in the home. The board reported the investigation and eventual settlement with Mary in back-to-back statements in their minutes, suggesting a connection. It is impossible to know who called them, of course, but the bureau's response nevertheless illuminates working conditions for the staff: the agent "advised to try not to have our help work over 54 hours a week and to try and have our help satisfied." The managers were relieved to learn that they "would not be expected to handle our help as in factories"—where presumably stricter labor laws applied—and assured the investigator that "our help was not overworked and were satisfied." They also agreed to frame the bureau's laws and hang them in the building.[93] If a dissatisfied employee had been the one to call the bureau, she may have been disappointed to learn how weak the government's ability was to protect her as a worker. Staff could use complaints to the labor department as a strategy for controlling their own work lives, but the managers maintained the balance of power in this triangular relationship.

The case of Mrs. A. M. Gebhart, a UPOH housekeeper, provides a highly unusual window into the tensions that could exist between staff and managers and the ways in which at least one employee attempted to negotiate over working conditions in the orphanages. Hired in June of 1897, within a few months Gebhart was deeply unhappy. Through a series of letters that fall, she directly confronted the UPOH managers, making her complaints clear: "When I applied it was [as] a housekeeper, but I have found it as a drudge. I have not had proper help. . . . I have no Sabbath, not time to read a chapter in my bibel . . . and have not had time to read a word in a paper since I have been here." In another letter, she wrote, "I never saw such oppression as is here in every department of work. . . . [Y]ou cannot put enough work on them." She accused them of "pretending to be such a Charitabel board of women" while "oppressing those in charge of work," and concluded, "I do not see the charity here and shall say so." She told the managers, "I cannot live that way" and "I do not feel it is right to live as a heathen."[94]

In turn, the managers accused Gebhart of not giving the children enough to eat and gave her thirty days notice. She resigned instead, accusing them of being "inconstnt" in their actions, and responded, "I think it very strange when you say I have been starving the dear children, you permit me to remain and keep on starving them another month." Gebhart reminded the managers that she was not completely dependent on them and could control her own labor: "I have a home and enough to keep me without drudging as I have here . . . I have eaten my last bite in this house will go out and get what I want." Furthermore, she suggested that working women were familiar with the reputation of employers and would avoid the institution if it treated them poorly: "[Y]ou will find every person is not so anxious to come here to work as you would like to make out."

Gebhart reserved the right to have Sundays off, time to read, and sufficient help to perform her job, then quit when conditions became unbearable, admonishing the managers to think about the reputation of the institution among potential employees. Through her letters, Gebhart demanded respect and promoted a sense of equality between herself and the managers, diminishing class differences through shared religion. She explained, "One great inducement in my applying for the place here that I would be in a Christin home among Christin peopel of my own Church." She wrote, "I do not feel kindly" toward the managers, as "they have not treated me as a Christian or a lady." Gebhart maintained her worth as a member of the same church as the managers and expected them to treat her as a "lady," a status-laden term placing her on equal footing with the managers. She closed this letter saying the work "has been nothing but slavery," a common rhetorical device of labor writers in this period.[95] Gebhart may have sensed that she had pushed things too far with the managers, and followed this letter shortly with another, apologizing and asking for forgiveness. However, she maintained her innocence—"I do not want you to think I was angry without a caus, for I still think I have been wronged"—and feared the managers would think she had "not acted the part of a Christin." She humbly added, "I know better than anyone that I come very far short of a Christin duty." The managers accepted her apology and asked Gebhart to stay. But within a month they had changed their minds and hired a new housekeeper, and at a higher salary. Gebhart's negotiation ultimately failed to win her a permanent position, yet it underscored employees' view of working conditions in the orphanage and their expectations of contract labor.

Staff asserted their own ideas about how to run the orphanages, and while they obviously never had power equal to that of the managers, they influenced both institutional policy and practice. For example, the HCC decided that they would not permit children to work outside the home, but "the matron was not satisfied with the action of the Board at a previous meeting not permitting Mrs. Holmes [a part-time employee] to have one of the boys to deliver milk to her customers and she thought Mrs. Holmes was so helpful in the Home that we could not dispense with her services." The managers rescinded their ruling and allowed Mrs. Holmes to have a boy "for the present" as long as he returned in time for school.[96] Similarly, when the UPOH managers instructed the matron to fire Miss McDade, the nursemaid, the matron resisted, saying she felt the employee was "satisfactory." The managers replied that "the Board desire[s] a change be made," but the matron delayed in carrying out their wishes. After another month elapsed, the managers relented, reporting McDade "[i]s proving most satisfactory."[97] Another UPOH matron exasperated the managers by refusing to allow children to run errands in the rain: the local store, "who have been sending bread, rolls and cakes [as donations to the orphanage] complain that one day when they called up for boys to come for same, were told the children could not be sent in the rain, have since been giving to Sisters of the Poor."[98] These matrons asserted their beliefs about child labor, children's working conditions, and employee retention, and, at least in these instances, they got their way.

Sometimes matrons resisted managers' efforts to modernize child care practices. For example, Elizabeth Dalzell, the sixty-one-year-old Irish-born matron of the HCC in 1910, resigned over disagreements about proper punishments for the children. At a board meeting, Dalzell reported on "punishments administered—and in view of her inability to comply with the rules of the Board about punishment—resigned."[99] Though she later agreed to stay, she clearly had administered punishments out of line with the managers' new guidelines. In fact, one reformer investigated the home and criticized Dalzell's discipline quite pointedly, saying that "the children were at times subjected to severe punishments, totally unjustified under any circumstances in the care of children."[100] Reformers had been targeting disciplinary techniques at institutions for several decades, and at least in this case, the orphanage managers appeared to be softening their approach. Where in 1884 the board visitors reported being pleased when they dropped in at teatime and found the "children enjoying there bread and milk [the matron] presiding with rod in hand," by the 1910s they were moving away from corporal punishment. In 1916 a new matron, Isabella Rowell, reported to the State Board of Public Charities that while whipping was still allowed, it was "not often" that she used it, "this is the worst punishment and only for the older ones." Instead, she found that when the children were "not allowed to go walking with me . . . [this] punishment . . . is the one that really punishes."[101] The managers relied on their employees, especially the matron, to implement their disciplinary policies, and some stubbornly resisted change.

Similarly, at least some of the HCC managers wished to change the long-standing, and often criticized, practice of maintaining absolute silence during mealtime. But they faced resistance from Mrs. Edwards, the matron. A board visitor at mealtime reported, "The children were all obedient and Mrs. Edwards upon being asked about allowing the children to talk while in the dining room at meals, said that it would not be possible for her to obtain any degree of order if such freedom was given."[102] While progressive reformers faced resistance from managers on many issues, in these cases it was staff who resisted managers' more progressive ideas of child care, reflecting not only the difficulty in effecting institutional change, but the crucial role staff would have to play in modernizing child care practice.

Some staff members did bring new, progressive ideas of child care with them to their work. After 1900 the staff became increasingly professional, though the transition was neither straightforward nor complete until after the 1920s.[103] For instance, matrons increasingly had prior, professional experience working in child care institutions. In 1904 UPOH hired Mary Shaw as the new matron, and the managers reported, "She has inaugurated a new plan for caring for the boys and girls, having each under an excellent woman, called a 'care taker,' who gives them their constant attention when they are not in school, teaching them to be useful in various ways and thus far the plan works well."[104] Shaw's specialized "care takers," however, soon found themselves assigned additional house-cleaning duties, taking them away from their child care responsibilities, illustrating the tension between progressive child care techniques and the reality of institutional finances and staffing. Shaw herself did not last long, resigning in 1906 at the request of the board, which had split thirteen to nine over the decision to keep her. The uncharacteristic choice to record this tally in their minutes reflected an unusual level of disagreement among the managers over retaining Shaw and, perhaps, over her progressive agenda.

The HCC also experimented with some progressive changes, particularly after 1929 at the urging of the new matron, Jean McClaren Jones. A forty-eight-year-old Scottish-born widow, Jones brought many progressive ideas with her, emphasizing record keeping and professional development. The very first month on the job, Jones requested a scale to regularly weigh the children, as well as a filing cabinet and desk for her room.[105] Within the first two years she had also convinced the managers to let her attend several professional conferences and lectures on child behavior. Jones also began submitting detailed, typed reports to the board, clearly illustrating her expanded, professional role, assuming responsibilities once belonging solely to the managers, such as making information-gathering trips to other orphanages in distant counties, personally admitting children in emergency cases, visiting parents in the hospital, and checking on children in their foster homes.[106] Even the changing title of the matron's position after the turn of the century reflected the orphanage's experimentation with progressive ideas: In 1908 they voted "the name of 'Matron' of the Home be changed to 'Superintendent.'"[107] By midcentury they changed the title again to "Director" and later "Executive Director."[108] For both the HCC and UPOH, the transition to a fully professional staff and acceptance of more progressive child care methods was set in motion during the period of this study, but not fully realized until several decades later.

Staff played a crucial role in this transition, embracing and promoting some changes, while resisting others; at times pushing progressive ideas on reluctant managers, and at others rigidly holding onto traditional child care methods while managers urged more modern techniques. While the matron position slowly, and unevenly, began shifting in this period to a more professional occupation that would be filled by specially trained, typically middle-class women later in the century, through 1929 the vast majority of staff members remained working-class women. Indeed, a substantial number of staff members were also clients, bringing their children with them to live at the orphanages. These working-class women shared similar backgrounds with the families they served, and while this did not guarantee their sympathies, many understood firsthand the ravages of the city's industrial economy on solo parents with young children. Staff members thus brought a distinct working-class experience to the orphanages, shaping both the policy and practice of institutional child care as they negotiated the boundaries of their professional and personal lives, sometimes resisting managers, and at others nudging them in new directions.

⌘ ⌘ ⌘

In 1906, on the occasion of the HCC's twenty-fifth anniversary, the managers recalled their founding, noting that "an article in one of the daily papers called attention to the fact that while homes were being provided for orphaned and destitute white children there was no such a refuge for the colored. From this a meeting was called . . . which was well attended and resulted in a Board of Managers being appointed."[109] Like later origins stories that emphasized the role of new state laws instigating the founding of the HCC, this version pointed to forces outside the managers themselves, crediting a newspaper article for calling attention to a racial disparity in child care. Whether they recalled actual events or not, these tales of the orphanage's genesis highlight progressive sentiments that were beginning to circulate in Pittsburgh around the turn of the century. In some ways, these versions of the HCC's founding story reflect the thinking about child welfare of their own moment, more than accurate historical memory. They emphasize legal changes—such as the Sixty-Day Law, which did not actually pass until after the orphanage's founding—as well as newspaper reports, suggesting that the founding managers tuned into new ideas. These post-1900 versions of the founding story have the women responding to external stimuli, rather than conceiving of the home themselves, yet they also underscore their receptiveness to those new, progressive ideas.

Indeed, from their very inception, the HCC and UPOH faced mounting pressure from progressive reformers working at the local, state, and national level to transform child welfare. Orphanage managers cooperated with the reformers on many issues, especially pertaining to facilities upgrades, sanitation, health, and recreation, but clearly maintained the upper hand in the relationship through the 1920s. Yet they were constantly pushed and pulled from without and within: progressives urged the de-institutionalization of orphanage populations through the emerging foster care system as well as coordinated admissions and dismissals overseen by professional social workers. Meanwhile, working as "insiders," staff members urged change at times and challenged it at others. They negotiated with the managers for control of their professional and personal lives, and some even used the institutions for their own child care needs. Ultimately, the staff was on the front lines of child care and shaped orphanage practice and policy in its day-to-day implementation.

CHAPTER SIX

SEGREGATING ORPHANS
The Home for Colored Children

About 30 years ago Rev. Mr. Fulton of the Fourth United Presbyterian Church, Northside, one dreary, rainy morning found a little Afro American girl of 4 or 5 years of age wandering in the streets of Lower Allegheny. After seeking admission, in vain, for this little outcast in the various institutions, he finally appealed to the late Mrs. John K. Blair to assist him. "What can be done for this little girl," said Mr. Fulton, in presenting the case to her. "The only thing to do is to make a home for her," said Mrs. Blair.
—*Pittsburg Dispatch*, January 30, 1916

In 1916 the *Pittsburg Dispatch* published this account of the founding of the Home for Colored Children, capturing nearly all the details of what would become the institution's modern origins story: a rainy day, a lost little girl, Reverend Fulton, and Mrs. Julia Blair. While the little girl, Nellie Grant, was not named in official histories until the orphanage's fiftieth anniversary, she has come in recent years to symbolize the founding and very mission of the home. The HCC's successor organization, Three Rivers Youth, today presents "Nellie Leadership Awards" each year, recognizing local champions of children's services. However, accounts of the Nellie Grant story vary widely, and for its first several decades, the orphanage does not appear to have promoted the tale at all. For instance, in their twenty-fifth annual report, the HCC managers recalled their beginnings, explaining "an article in one of the daily papers called attention to the fact that while homes were being provided for orphaned and destitute white children there was no such a refuge for the colored." This report also noted, "The Home was started with five children," which probably counted Robert Highland's four sons in addition to Nellie Grant.[1] In fact, according to intake records, the

Highland brothers were the first actual residents of the orphanage, arriving almost two full weeks before the little girl.

Yet Nellie was almost certainly integral to the founding of the home. She was around seven years old when she arrived at the HCC, though her age was sometimes reported as young as two, no doubt increasing the dramatic effect of the rescue narrative.[2] She was likely fully orphaned or abandoned, as no parents ever appear in connection with her, though whether she was wandering alone in the streets or was living in an almshouse remains un-clear. Several sources credit the Reverend James Fulton with rescuing Nellie, though one history published by the orphanage credits a founding manager with her actual discovery.[3] Other sources trace the origins of the HCC to Pennsylvania's Sixty-Day Law, claiming that the Women's Christian Associa-tion (WCA) removed Nellie from the Allegheny City Home after the law was enacted (though this historical memory inaccurately transposes events).[4] It is possible, of course, that Nellie had been discovered on the streets and then placed in the almshouse for a time before the WCA women, moved by her plight, founded the orphanage. Some records indicate that she was placed for a time at the Young Women's Boarding Home, undoubtedly referring to the institution the WCA had founded in 1870 to house single women work-ing in the city.[5] More recently, it has been suggested that Reverend Fulton's black maid cared for Nellie until the orphanage was ready, though there is nothing in the historical record to support this assertion.[6] Despite their discrepancies, all of these variations of the founding tale point to Nellie's rescue as the pivotal moment that launched the HCC.

Rather than discrediting the validity of the story, the competing versions go beyond a single, literal "truth" and speak to a larger truth about the grim reality facing many African American families and their children in the post-Reconstruction, industrializing North. Most telling, all versions of the origins story share a single common detail: the crucial context of racial segregation and its insidious effect on child welfare. The *Dispatch* article calls Nellie a "little outcast" and explains that Fulton tried "in vain" to have her admitted to the child care institutions of the city. This would have included the United Presbyterian Orphan's Home, founded by the women of his own church at his instigation just two years earlier. Another version of the story records that the WCA did the searching, but did "[n]ot [succeed] in placing her in any of the Homes for Children on account of her color."[7] Today, the Three Rivers Youth Web site summarizes, "She was an orphan seeking shelter, but found no help because of the color of her skin."[8] Just three years after its founding, Julia Blair addressed supporters of the or-phanage, explaining its mission as "the care of destitute and orphan colored children who have been so long neglected and oppressed."[9] Blair's comment acknowledged not only the neglect that African American families faced in the lack of social services, but the oppression of racial discrimination. The managers viewed themselves as countering the dearth of institutional child care options as well as racial oppression, and later generations constructed their founding stories around this central theme.

The story of Nellie Grant and the founding of the HCC, then, highlights many of the salient threads of the institution's history. Over its first fifty years, the HCC both reinforced and resisted racial segregation and discrimination. This tension was particularly apparent in the educational opportunities provided by the orphanage. It also saw moments of interracial cooperation through its partially integrated board of managers, raising questions about racial attitudes and the motivations of both the white and black women who served in its early years. The orphanage had complicated relationships with both whites, who proved deeply ambivalent about the institution, and with African Americans—including members of the middle class, who urged strengthening ties to the black community, as well as the poor African American families it served. Yet the orphanage manager's initial resistance toward, and eventual shift to, further racial integration, was set in motion during this period through the persistent efforts of progressive reformers and African American leaders.

"The only thing to do is to make a home for her": Reinforcing and Resisting Segregation

To understand the position of the HCC in Pittsburgh's child welfare scene, it is crucial to recall that the orphanage served African American children yet was not so much a "black orphanage" as an institution for black children, run by whites. With increasing migration from the South after the turn of the century, the African American population of the city leapt to 54,983 residents by 1930, or 8.2 percent of the total population. But when the HCC opened in 1880, the city's African American population was very small—only 6,136 people, or 3.9 percent of the total population—and the black community had not yet launched the bevy of social institutions it would later support.[10] Founded in the transitional period following Reconstruction and before migration yielded a more sizable black community, the HCC reflected the practice of white charitable activity in the tradition of the Freedmen's Aid movement. This movement included many northern white middle-class women who sent resources and personnel, such as teachers, to the South during the 1860s and '70s to assist newly freed people. The effort involved some middle-class black women as well, who found some common ground along gender lines, yet occupied a difficult place somewhere between the white women and the freed people they were helping.[11]

The HCC board of managers included three African American women from its very inception, yet the orphanage remained a culturally white institution through its first half century, maintaining an arms-length relationship with the growing black community. To be sure, the race of the children complicated the managers' relationship with other whites, particularly potential donors, as discussed further in this chapter. Lying at the heart of the orphanage's mission to care solely for African American children, racial categories were the very foundation upon which the institution was built—a notion constantly referenced with each repetition of its name. Segregation was built solidly into that foundation as well, as the managers alternately reinforced and challenged racial hierarchies and the logic of racial separation in working with dependent children.

Indeed, by launching a separate institution for African American children, the managers seemed to reinforce racial segregation. When James Fulton appealed to the white philanthropist Julia Blair to help find a home for little Nellie, she responded, "The only thing to do is to make a home for her," implying, at least on the surface, that separating dependent black and white children was necessary, perhaps even natural. Yet, Fulton, Blair and the other founding managers did challenge the racism of segregation, even while working within its constraints. In several versions of the founding story, different white community leaders tried to gain admission for Nellie into the various orphanages in the two cities. (In one version it is Rev. Fulton who requests admission for Nellie, in another it is the all-white Women's Christian Association, and in still another, it is a manager herself who finds Nellie and tries unsuccessfully to get her into an orphanage.) They knew these were "white" institutions, yet challenged that designation by the very act of requesting admission. As the "founding father" of UPOH just two years earlier, Fulton was certainly connected to the field of child welfare, but the issue went beyond the simple matter of "pulling strings" to get one little girl admitted to an orphanage; the founders saw a greater need in Pittsburgh for a new institution to provide refuge for many poor black children.

While the managers never offered a radical critique of segregation, they elevated the needs of African American children to the level of those of poor white children. For instance, when the managers boasted shortly after the founding of the HCC of the "comfortable home and pleasant surroundings" they provided the children, they implicitly suggested that African American children were worthy of such treatment.[12] Similarly, historian Leslie

Harris found that the white managers of the New York Colored Orphan Asylum never intended to challenge racial inequalities, but did try "to give black orphans some of the same privileges of childhood accorded to white orphans."[13] Significantly, the HCC managers also challenged segregation by establishing a highly unusual, albeit limited, interracial board. Thus, while reinforcing the racial segregation practices of their day, the founding managers also challenged some of the racist assumptions at its core.

Yet their preoccupation with racial categories and the boundaries of those categories reflect the managers' reluctance to challenge racial hierarchies altogether. When the managers did speak directly of race, it was a bifurcated notion—split into black and white—common to most of the United States at that time. While some historians have argued that certain European ethnic groups such as the Irish and Italians were only "marginally" or "conditionally" white in this time period, for the purposes of child care, Pittsburgh institutions considered these groups entirely white.[14] The city was home to many of these immigrant groups that faced their own demeaning stereotypes and discrimination, but orphanages did not segregate their clientele along these ethnic lines: the only racial line that mattered when it came to classifying dependent children was the one separating "colored" from "white." This construction of race rested on the notion of fixed, biological categories, an identity of "blackness" (though not necessarily "whiteness") that children inherited from their parents. Yet these categories were fraught with ambiguity, as they depended on appearance and could be open to interpretation.

In an extremely rare articulation of their own ideas of racial categorization, the managers struggled in 1902 to define the identity of a young girl: "The case of Esther Lion was brought up and most of the managers expressed their opinion that she was not a colored child. Miss Clark [a board member] was appointed to investigate the case—consult physician and get information about the mother."[15] Clearly, those who had placed her in the home (quite probably her mother, who was living and retrieved her later) felt Esther was "colored," or they would have sent her to another orphanage, but to the managers, the little girl was not colored enough. Esther seems to have failed the manager's simple visual test of skin color—she just did not look dark enough to them. Yet, curiously, it took them several years to arrive at this decision, further reflecting ambivalence on the managers' part: Esther was placed in the home in March of 1899, and the census lists her as in residence the following year (and categorizes her as "colored" along with the rest of the children). Though she may have been dismissed and readmitted, or possibly living in a foster home during the next two years, the managers waited three years before taking issue with her racial designation.

The managers then chose to consult a doctor, whom they presumed could locate the child's race in her physiology, and to inquire further about her mother, who would hold clues to Esther's heredity. This case demonstrates the managers' use of skin color, physical examination, and family history to determine racial categories, and illustrates their discomfort with individuals who threatened to blur racial boundaries with an ambiguous identity. Apparently satisfied with their investigation, Esther remained in the HCC until the following summer, when her mother fetched her, four years after her initial placement.[16]

Just a few years later, however, the managers seemed to accept some racial ambiguity when it did not involve whiteness, as two of their boys crossed a different color line, transforming from African American to Native American. Horace and Jonah Matthews, aged nine and seven in 1913 when their father placed them in the HCC, spent ten years there together before the managers sent them to college in Kansas. The boys' mother had died in 1911, and their father, a porter on the railroad, held the family together for nearly two years before placing them in the HCC; he died just two months later in a work accident, and the boys were fully orphaned (a fact that may have contributed to the managers' willingness to keep them well past the usual age limit). In 1923 the matron personally escorted Horace and Jonah to Lawrence, Kansas, where they attended the "Haskell Institute for Indians."[17] Founded in 1884 as the United States Indian Industrial Training School, the institute had expanded to postsecondary education in a variety of fields by the 1920s, and today continues to serve Native American students exclusively as the Haskell Indian National University.[18] It is entirely possible, of course, that the Matthews boys had some Native American heritage and were accepted at the institute for that reason. Nonetheless, the racial transformation of two young men, who had lived for ten years as "colored" boys at the HCC and then became "Indians" for the purposes of higher education, provides a fascinating insight into the sometimes-fuzzy boundaries of U.S. racial definitions that could exist around orphaned children. Similarly, historian Linda Gordon analyzed the racial transformation of New York City Irish foundlings who became "white" to the Arizona Anglos who wanted to "save" them from their intended Mexican Catholic foster families, illustrating a different set of racial boundaries in the turn-of-the-century American Southwest.[19] The HCC managers were uncomfortable with a child who appeared too white, but they would allow two of their own boys to slip across a different racial line, albeit one that did not challenge the seemingly fixed boundary between black and white.

Education provides a particularly salient example of the managers' simultaneous accommodation of and challenge to segregation. African American education was a prominent cause among both black and white reformers throughout this period. Following emancipation, former slaves across the South quickly built school buildings in their communities, which were often targeted by white violence as obvious symbols of freedom.[20] Despite some managers' assumptions to the contrary, most African American families in Pittsburgh also believed strongly in the promise of education: for instance, in 1882 the board visitors recorded, "Visited . . . children in the school room, reading a Bible story, we are often taken by surprise at the knowledge shown by these, hitherto uncared for children."[21] Of course, the very fact that these children had such knowledge contradicted the visitors' characterization of them as "uncared for," and most did have families. Similarly, in their 1911 annual report, the managers noted, "The scholars show themselves unusually well informed in the myths, stories and legends of good literature and display an interest and enthusiasm in this line that many white children might envy."[22] These poor African American children were clearly coming to the HCC with education already under their belts and a cultivated "interest and enthusiasm" for school.

Since Pittsburgh's public schools accepted African American children, the institution's decision to provide instruction within the home for several decades suggests an accommodation to racial segregation. In 1880, the year of HCC's founding, Pittsburgh had desegregated its schools and dismantled its single African American school; an act of the legislature the following year officially desegregated schools throughout the state, though trenchant de facto segregation led to court mandates later in the twentieth century.[23] While UPOH sent their children to public school, in-home schooling was actually quite common in congregate care institutions of the era—white and black—as many orphanages tried to isolate the children under their care from the urban ills outside their walls, literally providing "asylum" to their inmates.[24] Keeping children out of public schools could also protect them from epidemics, which regularly swept through urban areas.

In the HCC's second year of operation, there is some evidence that at least a few children actually did attend public school. A board visitor reported that she "[g]ot school permits for two boys," and the following week, "One of the boys, for whom I got a permit, had taken whooping cough and another boy was sent to school in his place."[25] But by the following year, all the children attended school in the orphanage under the instruction of the matron, Mrs. W. A. Ware. The managers highly praised Ware's teaching skills, but she had to split her attention between household and educational duties: "We only wished Miss Ware might have more time to devote to this [teaching] branch of her work. . . . She is a faithful worker, but she has her hands more than full."[26] In 1884 they hired a separate teacher, a considerable financial commitment for the young institution, which reflected their preference for in-home schooling and willingness to support education despite limited resources.

A few years later, Margret Kemp, a single white woman in her late thirties, joined the staff as a full-time teacher and stayed for twenty-two years until her death. The managers enthusiastically supported Kemp's work with the children, offered her generous wages, treated her more as a professional employee and peer (compared to other staff members), and even fitted up a small house on the property for her residence in her declining years. In 1907 the board defended their decision to keep the children out of public school, arguing, "they are taught the same studies and graded as if they were attending the Public School but are better prepared in their work as each child is a special study to Miss Kemp and in this way she makes their minds more active and retentive."[27] Shortly after Kemp died in the early 1910s, the managers began sending the children to John Morrow, the local public school. Thus, their decision to school the children within the orphanage for so many years may have had as much to do with the managers' admiration of Margret Kemp's abilities as a teacher as with any segregationist tendencies on their part.

Nonetheless, in keeping the children within the walls of the institution, the managers bucked the tide of progressive educational thought. The Pennsylvania State Department of Welfare, for instance, expressed relief when the HCC finally reversed course, saying, "We are glad to learn that the children are now going out to public school; the contact with the children in the community is necessary if we want this group of dependents to return to a normal home with an understanding of normal community relationships." By the 1920s the Welfare Department consistently pushed a reform agenda, arguing that children should be in institutions only as a last resort. Here the state suggested that orphanage children could return to "a normal home," implying institutions were anything but, and that public schools would allow children to develop "normal community relationships." Reformers working for the state believed that public education would "give these children good standards of living to take back into their own homes." And since "most of them have come from poor homes where the little refinements of life are unknown," public schooling would show "every child . . . what he can attain if he will but work for it, later."[28] The HCC took issue with the state's characterization of institutional child care and consistently resisted the department's efforts to modernize their child welfare techniques, yet it did eventually send the children to public school. Their delayed decision, waiting until the 1910s to do so, reflected their strong belief in the orphanage's ability to best serve the needs of its children, yet also effectively kept the children racially segregated.

The fact that the HCC emphasized education, requiring all school-age children to attend classes twice each day, indicates the managers believed strongly in the importance of schooling. In fact, education was written into the organization's constitution: "The object is to provide a home for orphan . . . colored children, and to . . . educate the same."[29] Fifty years later, the HCC continued to emphasize its educational mission, declaring, "The aim of the organization is to . . . send the children out with sound bodies and trained minds."[30] But training minds had multiple purposes. For instance, during this period that overlapped with the southern educational movement, many of the sympathetic white northerners supporting universal schooling for both African Americans and whites hoped to create better citizens and future laborers. This educational ideology had more to do with maintaining social and economic stability than with upsetting racial and class hierarchies.[31] Indeed, many of the philanthropists who bankrolled the southern movement maintained highly racist ideas about the mental abilities of black students.[32]

The HCC managers were certainly interested in fostering good citizens and workers, yet they also recognized the intellectual potential of African American children. For many years, Margret Kemp submitted a school report every month to the board of managers, who would proudly record the full roster of students on the Honor Roll and Honorable Mention list in their minutes; most months, this list occupied a great portion of the recorded activity. Occasionally, the managers would allow older children to stay in the home past the age limit, particularly if they were enrolled in school. In one notable case, the managers allowed Gwyneth Johnson to remain in the home as she attended high school, and then paid her tuition to Geneva College. Located in the neighboring county of Beaver, the college opened in 1848 under the sponsorship of the Reformed Presbyterian Church of North America and operated as a stop on the Underground Railroad. Following emancipation, nearly half the students were freed people, and the college was also one of the first institutions to admit women to a full degree program.[33] Gwyneth graduated from Geneva College in 1926 and headed south for a teaching position. She was clearly an unusual young person in whom the board placed an enormous amount of trust: at one point they even left her in charge of the home for two weeks while the matron took her annual vacation. Gwyneth remained in touch throughout her college years with numerous letters thanking the board for their support and received a watch from them upon graduation.

The managers took obvious pride in children's academic achievements after they left the home. In a similar case, Adam Washington arrived at the HCC in 1884 at the age of three and spent some time in a foster home before going to Lincoln University, "preparing himself for a physician." Located outside of Philadelphia and now part of the Pennsylvania state system of schools, the university was the first in the nation to provide arts and science education to African American boys. Over the course of its first century, Lincoln graduated nearly 20 percent of the black physicians and over 10 percent of the black attorneys in the United States (as well as Langston Hughes, Thurgood Marshall, and the first presidents of Nigeria and Ghana).[34] In 1904 Adam wrote to say that "he had taken second honors in Latin and Greek. This report naturally pleased the managers very much."[35] Through education, the managers challenged the racist assumptions underlying segregation and asserted their belief in the intellectual capacity of African American children.

The HCC viewed education as an integral part of its mission, occasionally admitting a child just so he or she would have access to schooling. For example, Jeannette Jenkins arrived in 1895 at the age of two, the youngest of six fully orphaned siblings, and was adopted a few months later. But when she was seven, the board voted that she "be taken [back] into the Home that she may receive some education."[36] Several other adoptive, foster, and indenturing parents returned children to the home, claiming they could not educate them according to the standards set by the board in the agreement papers that all parties were required to sign. For instance, "Mrs. Wright who has Walter Jennings does not wish to keep him longer than fall as they can not . . . send him to school."[37] Even Elizabeth Beighel, who taught the manual training program at the HCC, returned Wyatt Farmer, a child she was fostering, because she "could not send him to school."[38] Wyatt was seven when he arrived at the home after his mother died; his father was still living in Pittsburgh, but was either unable or unwilling to take him several years later when he reached the age limit, and Beighel had agreed to care for him. It is unclear why Beighel could not send him to school—it was certainly not for lack of interest in education, since she herself was a teacher—but the decision to return Wyatt to the home proved deadly, as he contracted scarlet fever upon reentering the orphanage and died the following month.

Unlike Beighel, many foster and indenturing families never intended to educate the children they took, as indicated by the managers' reservations in placing out young children. They explained that they had to turn down many indenturing requests for children, "as the majority are too young. Under ordinary circumstances we prefer keeping them in the Home until they are twelve years of age, that they may get as much schooling as possible."[39] The managers clearly took education seriously and were even willing to bend their own rules to facilitate that process, taking children back from (what they presumed were permanent) adoptive homes and re-admitting children over the age limit.

The type of education provided by the HCC further underscores the managers' implicit, though limited, challenge to racism. The managers emphasized a wide variety of topics, reflecting their belief in general education for African American children. For instance, until the 1910s, when the children began attending public school they studied a range of disciplines, including "Reading, Arithmetic, Writing, Geography, History and Native [Nature] Study" in the orphanage classroom.[40] The managers also embraced domestic and industrial training. They instructed "that the children be taught in the kitchen how to prepare vegetables for cooking, as it will be useful to them in the future."[41] By 1908 they had formalized this domestic training, appointing a Domestic Science Committee to visit local public schools to learn about setting up a program, then hiring a teacher to hold classes each Saturday, "to prepare our children to go out and help themselves to earn their livings."[42] Similarly, as early as 1900, the board experimented with an "Industrial Manual Training" program, and for many years the children were "instructed in basket weaving, wood carving, joinery, pasteboard work, mat weaving, paper folding, mechanical drawing and the care and use of tools."[43] The children also made yards of carpeting out of rags and sewed small articles each year that the managers sold to raise money.

Supported by some African American leaders such as Booker T. Washington, industrial training offered a pragmatic education, but was potentially limiting, as other black leaders argued, since it did little to prepare children for lives beyond manual labor.[44] When the managers chose to formalize their industrial training in 1901, rather than turning to Washington's model, they selected the "Sloyd System of Manual Labor."[45] Popularized in Europe by Otto Saloman, the "Educational Sloyd" system taught woodworking as a way of building children's intelligence, moral character, and hand–eye skills. Teacher's schools in the United States promoted Educational Sloyd around the turn of the century as an alternative to the more traditional "Russian system," which emphasized more purely vocational training. The Sloyd system was closely associated with Froebelian education, inspired by the work of Friedrich Froebel, founder of the Kindergarten movement. Sloyd advocates insisted that children should gain a general education through the system, rather than intensive training in a single field, and thus introduced it in the primary grades. One disciple of Otto Salomon explained Sloyd in a talk to a group of parents as "a system of educational school hand-work. . . . EDUCATIONAL, because it is not in any sense intended to give mere technical instruction, to teach a trade, but—in the highest sense—to educate."[46] In choosing the Sloyd system, the HCC managers may have believed they were providing children with a more progressive training that emphasized general education.

Nonetheless, Educational Sloyd was still, at its core, industrial training designed to move the children of the working class into positions of manual labor. Saloman himself listed as the first two "formative aims" of his system: "1) To instill a taste for, and a love of, labour in general. 2) To inspire respect for rough, honest, bodily labour."[47] While the HCC managers were delighted when the occasional child went on to higher education and pursued a professional career (such as the doctor Adam Washington, or the teacher Gwyneth Johnson), they knew the vast majority of the orphanage residents would go into industrial and domestic work. Furthermore, racism meant that even those opportunities would be limited, as many factories refused to hire or promote black men, and African American women faced few opportunities beyond domestic service and laundry work. Implementing Sloyd, then, was both practical and at the same time, hopeful, as the managers put considerable faith in its potential to create educated (not just trained) future workers. The progressively minded State Commissioner of Public Welfare praised the home's industrial and domestic training efforts that continued long after the children started attending public schools, saying, "We ought also to commend the training that is given to the older children, putting them through high school and giving them domestic science training. It is very unusual to find these opportunities given especially to colored children."[48] Thus, the mere act of providing such training challenged segregated education, while simultaneously accommodating the race- and class-based assumption that African American children would necessarily lead lives of manual and domestic labor.

While the managers were never radical in challenging the segregation of child care or the racism at its core, they did offer a degree of resistance. By working within the constraints of segregation and establishing a separate institution, they nevertheless challenged its most racist assumptions by insisting that African American children were worthy of a pleasant, homelike refuge. Through the Sloyd system, they further implied that black children deserved an education as well as industrial training. And in their support for higher education, the managers asserted that African American children possessed great intellectual capacity.

"Three of these women were Negroes": Interracial Cooperation and Ambivalence

The composition of the HCC board reflects a degree of interracial coopera-tion, however tentative, unseen elsewhere in Pittsburgh child welfare until well into the twentieth century. As the HCC noted in an institutional history, of the thirty-five original managers, "[t]hree of these women were Negroes, and among the Board members were represented some of the most prominent names in Pittsburgh."[49] Though their numbers remained quite small until the later twentieth century, and could arguably be viewed as mere tokenism, the African American women of the HCC board challenged this role. They played a crucial part in the institution's founding and development, often serving as a bridge between the white women of the board and the black community. Yet the HCC remained in many ways a culturally white institution. For example, the board minutes presented whiteness as the presumed norm: the race of various employees was only mentioned when they happened to be black. Thus, the managers called attention to a "colored plasterer" or painting work donated by "colored men," but never identified white workers by race, since whiteness was normative in this discursive construction of race.[50] Even more tellingly, the managers hired only white employees in key positions such as matron and teacher, ignoring recommendations from progressive reformers until at least the 1930s. Yet as an institution serving African American children, the HCC was not entirely white either: the orphanage's ambiguous identity complicated relationships between the predominantly white managers and other whites. Consequently, the orphanage reflects both early, hesitant steps toward interracial cooperation and deep ambivalence among whites.

The initial HCC board boasted three African American women: Henretta Golden, Maria Gross, and Amanda Ware. The biographies of these early African American board members illustrate several common themes among Pittsburgh's black families in this turn-of-the-century period, including mi-gration experiences, labor patterns, and the struggle for financial success.[51] All three of these founding women hailed from the South—North Carolina, Virginia, and Kentucky—reflecting early black migration to the city. As in other northern cities, the later dramatic surge of newcomers from the South amplified intraracial tensions with established black families.[52] Yet the HCC represents a very early example of Pittsburgh's "old elite"—migrants themselves—reaching out to the new arrivals.

Henretta Golden, for instance, was born around 1840 in Kentucky to parents who had also been born in that state. She was a second wife to

Samuel, a Maryland native who had migrated to Pittsburgh by 1860 and had seven children with his first wife, Margaret, before she died. Samuel Golden was unusually successful, though he was always listed in records as a "porter, driver, or laborer, and he signed his will with an 'X,'" suggesting he was not literate.[53] Yet he accumulated considerable wealth, which allowed him to purchase or build at least five homes. A study of African Americans in Pittsburgh investigated Samuel Golden's story and found that while he "cannot be considered typical of Pittsburgh blacks . . . his experience, pieced together from census rolls, wills, deeds, mortgages, and city directory, are revealing of what was possible."[54] His oldest son, who lived with Samuel and Henretta through their deaths, worked as a barber, a relatively high-status occupation in the black community. Even more tellingly, Henretta did not work at all—the census listed her as a housewife—and became an active community volunteer, serving on the HCC board with high-profile white women. As the wife of one the most prominent African American men in the lower Hill District (home of Pittsburgh's growing black community), it is perhaps not surprising that she was recruited to serve on the orphanage board. Her position also reinforced her husband's status. Henretta Golden resigned from the board in 1891 and died shortly afterwards.

Maria Gross also migrated north with her husband. Her journey included a series of moves that suggest a connection to the Underground Railroad, though the link is uncertain. Born in North Carolina around 1845, Gross moved with her Maryland-born husband, Benjamin, to Canada, where their oldest son was born just as the Civil War came to a close. They immigrated back to the United States around 1869, and their second son was born in Pennsylvania, but Gross apparently maintained ties to Canada, where she was living when her third and fourth children were born, before returning once again to Pennsylvania for the birth of her last child. In all, Gross had six children, five of whom survived to adulthood. In 1880, when she helped to establish the HCC, all of her children were still living at home, supported by her husband's job as a janitor. Her eldest son, at the age of fifteen, was also a janitor. Within twenty years, Benjamin was working as an elevator operator and the Grosses managed a mortgage on their own home; by 1920, shortly before her death, Maria was widowed, had paid off the mortgage, and was taking care of her sixteen-year-old grandson. Gross's larger migration story, from the South to the North, is representative of black migration patterns in this period: their stopover in Canada during the Civil War hints at an escape from slavery, and their multiple moves (in this case back and forth to Canada) reflect African Americans' attempts to find a meaningful freedom.[55]

Amanda M. Ware migrated north from Virginia, where her parents had been born, and lived with her Pennsylvania-born husband, George, a head-waiter. They had no children, but their thirty-four year-old niece lived with them and worked as an assistant housekeeper. George's occupation, though fairly high-status, did not pay enough to support both a wife and niece at home, nor did it leave much of a nest egg for Amanda when he died. By 1900 Ware owned her own home free of a mortgage, but as a widow, was forced to support herself working as a ladies' maid, one of the few occupations open to black women, regardless of their stature in the community.

After the turn of the century, with Henretta Golden deceased, Hallie James joined Maria Gross and Amanda Ware on the board. A member of the younger generation, James had also moved north, though from a free state: she was born in West Virginia just after emancipation to West Virginia–born parents. Described by the *Pittsburgh Dispatch* as an "excellent uplift worker," Hallie James married the Virginia-born David, who also worked as a waiter in a hotel, and they had no children. In 1900 the Jameses rented a home and had two boarders, but by 1910 David had moved into a very good job as a steward in a steel mill, and they purchased a home in the prestigious Schenley Heights neighborhood. Interestingly, while the census had listed Hallie as "black" in 1900, the next two censuses listed her as "mulatto." Though her skin color likely did not literally change, lighter skin was associated with higher status, and it is quite possible the later census takers interpreted the now Schenley Heights resident differently and assigned her to a new racial category based on perceived wealth and class.

While their numbers remained small, these African American managers served as more than silent tokens of integration. Gross, Ware, and James each served on the board nearly forty years, though no additional African American members joined until 1926 with the arrival of Mary (Mattie) C. Glasco. Wife of Bidwell Presbyterian pastor Rev. Benjamin F. Glasco, Mattie brought with her connections to the Urban League of Pittsburgh—a group that grew out of the interracial Association for the Improvement of Social Conditions in the Hill District, formed to address problems faced by black migrants. One of the earliest affiliates of the National Urban League, Pittsburgh's chapter attracted social reformer Helen Glenn Tyson, active in child welfare reform in the city, and her husband, Francis, a professor of economics at the University of Pittsburgh.[56] The Tysons lived around the corner from Hallie James in the Schenley Heights neighborhood in Oakland. HCC board minutes show that Gross, Ware, James, and Glasco all participated fully in monthly meetings, raising issues and voting on motions, and served on many committees, including the powerful visitors committee. While African Americans did not constitute a significant portion of the board until the 1950s, the HCC managers were an interracial group from their very inception and, if not fully integrated, represent a rare instance of interracial cooperation in the field of child welfare.[57]

More commonly, institutions established for the care of African American children were founded and managed entirely by whites or blacks. In Pittsburgh the Colored Women's Relief Association Home, also known as the Davis Home for Colored Children (1908), the Coleman Industrial Home for Colored Boys (1908), and the Fairfax Baby Home (1910) were founded and managed entirely by African Americans.[58] Other homes were founded by whites, such as abolitionist Charles Avery, who left a sizable estate for "the education and elevation of the colored people of the United States and Canada."[59] The resulting Allegheny Institute, also known as Avery College, served as a stop on the Underground Railroad and probably housed needy children on an informal basis as early as 1849.[60] A wholesale druggist, Charles Avery had developed an interest in the plight of slaves during buy-

Figure 6.1. HCC Board member Mary (Mattie) C. Glasco. *Source:* Collection of Bidwell Presbyterian Church, Pittsburgh.

ing trips to the South, and upon his death, he also left $20,000 to Oberlin College, the first college in the United States to admit African Americans. The trustees of Avery College made substantial contributions to the HCC, beginning with $500 in 1882 (worth $11,152 in 2010); their 1884 donation of $1,500 far exceeded the total received from other donors and families' board payments combined.[61] By the turn of the century these payments had ceased, and the Avery trustees had apparently decided to open their own institution, a residential trade school that could house fifty adolescent boys and girls aged ten to twenty. The HCC maintained its ties to this white-run institution, developing a formal agreement in 1905 to exchange some of their children, "the Avery School taking some of our older children and giving us the younger."[62] Though Avery always seemed to have more room for girls than boys (a situation similar to the HCC), the two institutions continued the arrangement at least until 1910.

In the field of African American child welfare work, then, the Home for Colored Children stood alone for decades as an experiment, however tentative, in interracial cooperation. Though it far preceded other better-known interracial efforts in Pittsburgh, such as the Urban League, by the 1920s the HCC was under increasing pressure from the black community to more fully integrate its staff and board, as we shall see in a moment. Eventually, both Avery College and the Coleman Home partially integrated their directors and staff, though neither institution outlived the HCC. Before it closed in 1917, Avery hired a black principal, along with black teachers and directors, but enrollment dropped, and the black community began complaining. African American progressive reformer Helen A. Tucker was particularly critical of the school: in a 1909 article published in *Charities and the Commons*, the premiere social work journal of the period, Tucker accused the school of mismanagement.[63] The Coleman Home also partially integrated its board, adding several white directors by 1923, but closed in 1945–46.[64] In general, the increasing professionalization of institutional staff also meant a loss of control for African Americans over the care of black dependent children.[65]

In the context of the 1880s, however, we might consider what motivated the black and white women of the HCC board to work together. For the white managers, their work with African American children may have sprung from a combination of religious and charitable convictions, as well as class and social control motives. Some may have had personal experiences, such as one white manager, Amanda Neale, who was married to an African American man: census takers listed him and their eight children as "mulatto," a designation that rendered Neale's entire family essentially black in the eyes of white society. For the African American women of the board, willingness to work with whites—despite what must have been painful treatment at times—likely stemmed from a combination of pragmatism, shared religious purpose, and belief in their own power to shape the institutions from within. In 1880, the relatively small black population had not yet launched the string of relief organizations that would be established after the turn of the century, and for those women interested in child welfare work for African American children, it was likely a pragmatic choice to join forces with the white women of the HCC. Though it was surely tiring to be in the small minority, and the board as a whole steadfastly refused to recruit additional African American members until much later, the African American managers nonetheless tenaciously stayed with the organization for decades.

Furthermore, African American women had multiple avenues for social activism, and many engaged in numerous activities, including all-black organizations. In her analysis of African American women in the larger YWCA movement, historian Judith Weisenfeld notes that their continued commitment to associational work "reflects a confidence in their own ability to engage and transform the movement and its institutional structures in significant ways."[66] Black women were drawn to the YWCA's—and arguably the WCA's—focus on working women in cities, traditionally a critical population and space for their relief work.[67] Lastly, African American Christianity contained a longstanding corollary tradition that "had long emphasized the responsibility of all Christians to deal with social ills as a necessary component of Christian commitment, with racism representing the most significant American malady."[68] The African American women of the HCC board, then, were likely willing to work with whites both as a practical matter and through a sense of shared religious commitment to social activism, even if their understanding of that religious mandate differed from their white "sisters."

Yet even in death, these women endured slights: the full measure of respect granted to other founding members of the board appeared conspicuously absent in 1921 when the managers learned of Maria Gross's death. Where deceased white board members had full page tributes entered into the official minutes as a memorial, the managers merely noted, "Word was received of the death of Mrs. Gross once a Board member. [The secretary] was asked to send her daughter a letter of sympathy. Which was done."[69] For Gross, Ware, Golden, and James it may have been a practical decision to work with the HCC, but surely not an easy one. However, their persistence on the board, some for forty years or more, suggests they viewed their work with the HCC as valuable and a positive contribution to the black community.

While the HCC represents an early experiment in racial cooperation, it was limited by white ambivalence toward closer affiliations with African Americans. This was reflected in the orphanage's parent organization, the WCA. The partially integrated HCC board served, by default, to partially integrate the WCA leadership, as the orphanage managers were also members of the parent association. In fact, the Pittsburgh WCA may mark the first involvement of African American women in the country with what became the YWCA movement (historian Judith Weisenfeld has previously traced African American women's participation to 1893 in Dayton, Ohio).[70] The Pittsburgh work, however, was highly atypical of the broader YWCA, which gave rise in most cities by the turn of the century to separate, racially segregated chapters. The all-black chapters suffered from overt racism, particularly evident after 1905, following a national merger that formed the modern YWCA. The new national office issued a policy mandating that new local chapters be sponsored by existing ones, effectively allowing white groups to exclude newly forming black groups. African American chapters were literally and symbolically subordinated to local white chapters under this sponsorship arrangement.[71] The Pittsburgh WCA refused to join the new national YWCA, for reasons that remain unclear, and it continued its commitment to the HCC, providing financial support as late as 1921.[72] Ironically, by midcentury, after years of work by African American women in the movement, the national YWCA signed an "Interracial Charter," committing itself to becoming a fully interracial organization and today is known for its racial equity work.[73]

In 1925 three other Pittsburgh "Y" chapters combined, again without the WCA, which continued to use its original name. The newly united YWCA included the WCA's own daughter branch in the East Liberty section of the city, yet histories written since then have tended to overlook the founding role of the WCA in the local movement, missing, too, the early role of African American women. For instance, a 1950 official history of the Pittsburgh Y states, "There are scattered references to Negro girls and women . . . from the start although they had little part in the YWCA life before the organization of Centre Avenue Branch in 1917."[74] If on the one hand, the WCA was more willing to be racially inclusive, on the other hand, it does not appear to have invited any additional black women to join the board of its many affiliated organizations. The WCA, like its subsidiary organization the HCC, remained hesitant about forming closer ties to African American women, despite its early track record of limited inclusion.

White ambivalence toward African Americans was further evident in the orphanage's relationship to prospective white donors. The managers had difficulty finding crucial broad-based financial support from a large group of smaller donors (as UPOH did). This kind of dispersed support provides much needed cash flow and donated goods that keep institutions afloat through difficult times. Particularly in its early years, the orphanage occasionally struggled to meet even the most basic of needs. For example, in a highly critical report, manager Emily Hunnings informed the board, "Small chairs for the little children are needed very badly . . . there being only 12 chairs with seats in the house" to accommodate "28 children now in the Home and three grown Persons." Furthermore, "[t]he children are crowded entirely too much in their cots—two and three and sometimes four sleeping together," because so many of the beds were broken and there was "an insufficient supply of bed clothes." It was winter, and Hunnings worried, "I don't see how they are kept warm. . . . The house is very dirty. . . . It lays us open to severe and deserved censure."[75] Hunnings's report, though highly unusual—most were not nearly so grim—suggests the difficulty the managers sometimes had in finding financial resources to pay for an adequate supply of beds, chairs, blankets, and heating fuel.

Over time, the HCC did acquire endowment income from bequests left by a handful of wealthy white donors and occasionally received donated items from white women's groups like the Needlework Guild, but the managers did not attempt to solicit contributions directly from the public until the 1920s. Where UPOH held annual "donation days," a sort of open house for the community that yielded considerable in-kind contributions, HCC waited until 1931 to try a similar event. UPOH's annual reports routinely acknowledged scores of individual donors, where the HCC rarely saw more than a dozen or so donors in a year. Although this could indicate a general reluctance on the part of the managers to perform the labor intensive and socially uncomfortable work of soliciting individual donors—who would generally have been the managers' friends, acquaintances, and church colleagues—it seems more likely, given the institution's persistent financial difficulties (and the women's general tenaciousness), that this was a fundraising strategy they believed would not work. White donors may have been unwilling to support what they saw as a "black" institution, despite its largely white management.

Instead, the managers turned to the state for support. Pennsylvania provided critical cash support to the HCC, whereas public officials in other states were at times unwilling to fund black orphanages. For instance, the white managers at New York's Colored Orphan Asylum had trouble raising money outside a small circle of donors, were criticized for detracting from efforts for needy *white* children, and found their institution treated as nonwhite (and unfundable) by public funding authorities. State support for the HCC, when combined with boarding fees paid by families, was often the only source of external funding.[76] As early as 1885, the HCC succeeded in petitioning Pennsylvania for an appropriation of $5,000 (worth $119,756 in 2010); through the 1920s the managers requested annual appropriations of up to $10,000, though they rarely received more than $1,500–$3,000. In contrast, UPOH did not apply for public funds at any time during its first fifty years, relying instead entirely on private contributions. Many years the HCC also had to dip into its endowment to make ends meet. After the turn of the century, progressives increasingly criticized state support for private institutions. Even some state officials objected, as the managers discovered in 1924 when their representative went to Harrisburg to meet with Dr. Ellen C. Potter, State Secretary of Welfare, and reported back: "Dr. Potter does not favor drawing on the Public treasury for any of the institutions and is trying to discourage the practice as much as possible."[77] Some progressives believed that public support would make it more difficult to convince private donors of the need for their dollars. But these objections did not take the complications of race into consideration, and the HCC managers may have felt they had little choice but to continue their reliance on public dollars. Nevertheless, in petitioning the state for funding, the HCC managers always sought support as a charity: they did not posit parents' "right" to public money for their child care needs.

When the HCC did finally reach out to a larger group of prospective white donors, it chose to do so through a third party—the new Welfare Fund—which meant that contributors had a much more distant relationship with the organization. Like most institutions of this era, it took many years for the managers to develop the direct solicitation techniques so commonly used today. The HCC actually waited until 1921 to organize its first direct appeal, which never made it off the ground, and like many other orphanages around the country, eventually opted instead to join a collaborative fundraising effort.[78] The managers sought and received endorsement from the Chamber of Commerce and then drafted a fundraising letter with the goal of raising $12,000 ($144,952 in 2010 dollars). But each time the board considered sending out the letter, they decided not to, because other groups in the city were conducting their own, competing campaigns. In 1922 they discussed starting an annual Christmas letter, but in 1925 they were still talking about it and had apparently not yet sent any direct solicitations. It could take years to develop the fundraising expertise, including the timing of appeal letters, along with a funding base of individual donors necessary to support an institution.

Perhaps due to its own frustrating experience with direct solicitation, the HCC chose to join the Welfare Fund in 1929. The managers did so with great trepidation, realizing that participation in this joint fundraising effort could create problems for them. The Welfare Fund, a precursor to the modern United Way, raised money on behalf of member organizations: in 1930, for instance, it hoped to raise an astonishing $1.2 million for social service agencies in Pittsburgh.[79] But because the fund imposed its own set of rules, and becoming a member meant increased oversight and reporting burdens for the HCC, the board voted to "enter an application for the Welfare Fund of Pittsburgh and if found irksome after one year we withdraw."[80] By the following spring, Welfare Fund representatives were asking to visit during board meetings (an unwelcome and unprecedented intrusion) and were late making promised payments, causing trouble for the HCC in paying its own bills. The process of submitting budgets each year to the Welfare Fund's all-male board also meant a loss of autonomy for the HCC women, who were forced to negotiate over individual line items. For instance, the fund agreed to a budget increase for the orphanage "in the amount of $724 which, in the opinion of the committee, should be sufficient to enable you to complete these bathrooms as planned," but the HCC had to agree "to postpone the purchase of linoleum."[81] Despite the intrusions and budgetary oversight, the HCC chose to remain with the fund, receiving a full 30 percent of its budget from this source by 1931–32.

Collaborative fundraising meant the HCC had a less intimate relationship with the Welfare Fund's largely white donors, mediated through a third party, but it also meant a substantial and more stable funding base for the orphanage. The difficulty the managers experienced in raising funds through direct solicitation, and their unwillingness to approach prospective white donors, illustrates the deep ambivalence of whites toward the orphanage: the HCC proved to be a highly unusual, if tentative, experiment in interracial cooperation, yet race and racism complicated the task of finding broad-based support for dependent African American children. At no time did the HCC managers make a case for child care as a right for working parents, but rather, they petitioned the state's Department of Welfare for charitable support for dependent children.

"A campaign among the colored people": Relationship to the Black Community

Despite its handful of African American members, the HCC board also largely functioned as a white institution in relationship to the black community. Increasingly acting as a voice of progressive reform, the state urged the HCC to strengthen its ties to African Americans, but lacking coercive powers, it could not force change on unwilling institutions, and the managers consistently rejected their advice in this area. In particular, the board resisted recruiting additional African American women as managers, hiring black staff, or reaching out to black donors for financial support. Not until the 1920s, under increased pressure from the state, new staff members, and, crucially, the black community itself, did the HCC board slowly relent and begin to deepen its ties. What's more, the black community was not monolithic: to speak of it as a single entity implies a false notion of uniformity. The "black community," while perhaps lumped together in the eyes of whites, was actually divided along many axes, including class, gender, and even "race" itself, with lighter skin tones often equating with higher status. The HCC eventually strengthened its relationship with middle-class African American supporters and child welfare workers, while its relationship with those poor black families it served remained more distant and, sometimes, distrustful.

For instance, after the turn of the century, the origin of client families became an increasing concern. Prior to 1900, the managers did not routinely ask parents where they had been born. But beginning in 1901, this information was carefully recorded in the admissions log for nearly three-quarters of the children.[82] Of those parents for whom they recorded place of birth, only 13 percent were Pittsburgh natives. Nearly two-thirds of the newcomers hailed from the South, predominantly the Upper South (in this case, Virginia, Maryland, and Washington, D.C.). These numbers mirror the larger trend in Pittsburgh, with southerners arriving in pulses of northward migration and accounting for most of the black population growth in the city between 1910 and 1930.[83] The HCC managers may have been sympathetic to the plight of these families, but may have also seen the dramatic influx of migrants as threatening. By 1924 they had instituted a residency requirement for parents that excluded at least one little girl from admission: "Geraldine Dickson not admitted on account of mother not living here one year."[84] The new policy prevented recent arrivals from seeking aid for their children, yet these were the very families who often most needed help, frequently eking out a living at the margins; with unpredictable and unstable employment, housing, and health, the loss of a spouse or job could easily push a family into crisis. The residency requirement, then, suggests a new degree of suspicion held by the managers toward poor African American families and a desire to discourage their migration to the city.

By contrast, the institution's relationship with middle-class African Americans warmed over time, prodded along by progressive state reformers and black leaders themselves. But that change came slowly, as their unwillingness to recruit new African American members to serve on the board illustrates. In 1924 State Secretary of Welfare Dr. Ellen Potter urged the managers to consider such recruits, saying, "Would it not be possible to interest more of the persons who should be active in this work by including on your board influential members of the Negro community who will be able to get from colored people themselves a more adequate support of the work?"[85] This recommendation rested on the notion that black managers would provide an entrée into the community for fundraising, but also subtly suggested that African Americans needed to finance child welfare "themselves." In 1929 white Pittsburgh reformer and social worker Helen Glenn Tyson reissued the call for more black board members in her prescient report, "Institutional Care for Dependent Colored Children," adding a subtle critique of decades of essentially white control over black children: "During recent years the feeling has been growing among the colored group that they should have more responsibility and control over the care of the children of their own race." Tyson listed as her very first recommendation, "[t]hat the Board of the Home be enlarged to include more representatives of the colored group."[86] The board's glacial pace of diversification was not simply a matter of overt resistance to the idea. With managers and officers elected yearly, but frequently serving decades in the same position (and often bringing in their daughters to join in the work), the board's stability and continuity provided structural inertia that made it difficult to diversify.[87] Yet the managers could take years to fill even those "slots" left open by the few African American women upon their deaths.

The HCC managers also resisted hiring African Americans into senior staff positions. During the period of this study, the matrons and other key members of the staff (such as the assistant matron, cook, housekeeper, or resident teacher) were exclusively white, while black women sometimes filled laundress, chambermaid, and nursemaid positions. A field representative of the state Welfare Department visited the home in 1929 and recommended that "the children should come in contact with their own people, girls and boys should have an educated worker of their own race to look after them."[88] Shortly thereafter, the newly hired white matron, Jean Jones, "asked permission to employ a refined colored woman to act as care taker of older girls." The board agreed to her request, perhaps in part because Jones pragmatically suggested this "refined colored woman" could also "act as a relief to all other employees."[89] But the board could be testy on this point. Responding to criticism from the Pittsburgh Child Welfare Study, they wrote a letter defending the composition of their staff: "The entire force of workers has been re-organized and at present there are four colored members."[90] Like the managers, however, the HCC staff did not include a significant number of African Americans, especially in senior management, until much later in the century.

While Jean Jones quickly introduced a wave of progressive reforms to the HCC, the continued presence of a predominantly white staff created friction with some in the black community. For instance, the city's premier African American paper, the *Pittsburgh Courier*, reported an abuse scandal that had as much to do with displeasure over the race of the staff as with any real abuse occurring at the orphanage. A banner headline, printed on page 1 above the masthead, screamed, "Children's Home 'Cruelties' Exposed" and went on to outline charges of children's mistreatment lodged by a white former cook in the home. Jones admitted she punished a boy by locking him in a dark basement storage room for "several hours," upsetting several managers when they heard this news, but she denied the rest of the accusations. The article overlooked any possible motives the fired employee may have had in making her charges, and repeatedly mentioned the racial composition of the staff. For example, it reported "no demonstration of affection toward the children was shown by the white members of the home staff" and that a "white janitor" administered floggings. The *Courier*'s reporters visited the home and found its physical plant "ideal . . . beautiful . . . strikingly neat and immaculately well kept," and approvingly noted that Jones had hired a new "colored janitor" and had plans for "gradually taking on personnel for the home which will include mostly colored employees." The *Courier* ran the identical article a week later on page 6, but the "scandal" did not get further traction.[91] Eight years later, the *Courier* carried another story on the HCC, this time nearly hagiographic in its praise, noting, "The children are under the direct supervision of caretakers of their own race" before listing each of the African American employees by name.[92]

The experience of an African American dentist hired by the orphanage also serves to illustrate black middle-class response to the institution's history of predominantly white staffing. Some time in the 1910s, the HCC hired Dr. Henry M. Garrett to care for the children's teeth, but the managers also apparently contracted with a white dentist at the same time, angering Garrett. In a 1919 letter, Garrett complained that Dr. Bishop, the white president of the Allied Medical Association, had been boasting of his affiliation with the orphanage: "This seemed to me a case of my doing the work and someone else getting the credit." Garrett tactfully explained that since "the ethics of the profession forbids intruding or encroaching on the practice of a fellow practitioner, I do not feel free in continuing the work until this point is cleared up." Lest he appear ungrateful for the work the HCC was doing for "his" people, he closed his letter saying, "Perhaps in such a worthy cause, after you and yours are doing so much for mine, such hair splitting technicalities should not arise. But at the same time it is best to know our status."[93] Garrett held his ground and was still affiliated with the orphanage several years later, though the board voted to offer him only "a nominal sum to take care of the dental work."[94] While the managers were willing in this instance to hire an African American, their poor treatment of him provides insight into the institution's relationship with black professionals. Yet Garrett's insistence on "knowing his status" forced the board to acknowledge that treatment; and by using the rhetoric of the "ethics of the profession," he further asserted his status as a professional, equal to his white colleague and deserving of the same professional courtesy. Garrett's actions strengthened the HCC's connection to the black middle class, but also revealed the ways in which that group pushed back, helping to slowly change the institution.

The managers also resisted reaching out to potential black donors until the 1920s, though African Americans did support the HCC from its inception. For instance, Wylie Avenue AME Church sent $11.67 (worth $269 in 2010 dollars) from their collection in March 1883, and their Infant Class (Children's Sunday School) sent another $2.50 the next month. The following year, board manager Maria Gross secured $20.68 from the Grand United Order of Odd Fellows, a black fraternal organization. Of course, the African American population was quite small until after the turn of the century and not likely to have enormous cash resources like those of some of the HCC's wealthiest white donors. Yet even after the surge of African American migration in the early twentieth century, the managers did not actively reach out to the black middle class and elites, who were actively supporting a host of other institutions in the city.[95] For example, a review of Pittsburgh Courier articles reveals that the black-managed Coleman and Davis homes held frequent fundraising events and received considerable financial support from readers of the paper.[96]

The HCC managers instead seemed content to passively accept those contributions that did arrive without obligating themselves to interracial socializing. For instance, in her 1903 annual address to association members,

Secretary Julia F. Blair announced that four African American congregations had sent "their Thanksgiving offering which amounted to $20." The donations were "sent through Rev. I. S. Lee . . . with the promise that in the future they would make Thanksgiving Day a day for annual contributions to the Home." She concluded, "We hope that the pastors of these churches will remind and encourage their people to generous giving."[97] Blair's comments illustrate the managers' gratitude for contributions yet at the same time demonstrate their reluctance to approach black congregations directly, preferring to instead have Rev. Lee coordinate efforts on their behalf with other churches. The managers' historical disinclination to view African Americans as potential donors may have stemmed partly from racial assumptions—about who had wealth and who could fund their work—but black donors had supported the institution from its inception, and often with collaborative donations. Collecting from a large group of people, such as by passing the plate at church, allowed people of limited means to participate as donors.

More likely, because the white managers were accustomed to a personal, face-to-face fundraising process that often involved social functions (teas, benefit concerts, dinners), they may have been reluctant to engage with prospective black donors in this way. It may have been one thing to manage an institution serving poor African American children, but quite another to commit to deeper interracial social engagement, which required meeting as social equals in order to solicit funds. Dr. Potter at the State Department of Welfare prodded the managers in 1923, writing, "We realize the financial limitations under which you are working but trust that the institution may more and more gain the confidence and support of the community."[98] In response to Dr. Potter's urging, the managers did discuss launching "a campaign among the colored people to try and get $1.00 from each person."[99] This campaign strategy necessitated less social interaction, as it would not depend on special events, such as benefit dinners, and would not rely on personal connections to reach donors, as the managers hoped to again have an African American minister solicit on their behalf.

In fact, it was only through the persistent efforts of African Americans themselves, that the HCC slowly began strengthening ties with the black middle class. In November 1924 the HCC sent a white manager to speak with Rev. Benjamin Glasco, the African American pastor of Bidwell Presbyterian Church, about the prospective campaign. Glasco had been volunteering with the children for several years, but his relationship with the orphanage was complicated, and he responded that "before doing anything he would like to come and speak to the Board."[100] There is no record that the managers ever invited him to speak with them nor that "a campaign among the colored people" ever occurred. This would not have been for lack of interest on Glasco's part, since he had clearly been working patiently to build a relationship with the orphanage. On New Year's Day the previous year, "a reception was held at the Home by the colored people, friends of Mrs. James [the only African American manager at the time] and the Rev. and Mrs. Glasco. They left a purse of $20.60 [worth $261 in 2010 dollars]."[101] When the matron, Isabella Rowell, retired in 1924, the Glascos presented her "with a handsome reference Bible . . . and the Young People's society [of Bidwell church] gave her a ten dollar gold piece in recognition of her work for their people."[102] The managers may not have achieved their hoped-for campaign, but Glasco and others were already actively raising money.

Glasco clearly took a strong interest in the HCC and no doubt hoped that some of the children would connect with his church. After Glasco took some orphanage residents to the Shriner's picnic in the fall of 1921, the matron "asked permission to take older children to Rev. Glasco's church Bidwell St.," but "[n]o decision was reached."[103] The children continued to attend nearby

Figure 6.2.
Rev. Benjamin F. Glasco.
Source: Collection of
Bidwell Presbyterian
Church, Pittsburgh.

Brighton Road Presbyterian, a white congregation, yet Glasco persisted in his efforts to work with the HCC. He treated the children at Halloween the following year, and a full year after that, "[s]everal of the older boys . . . expressed a desire to join Rev. Glasco's church."[104] The managers appointed a committee to look into it, but ultimately decided—another year later—to keep the children at Brighton. Brighton was certainly closer, but in 1930 when the children eventually did start attending Bidwell, Glasco solved the problem by hiring cars to provide transportation each week. Though cost could have been a consideration—the fee in 1930 came to $1.25 per car—the managers chose a few years earlier to not only keep the children at Brighton, but to send $2.00 per month to that church, so at least some extra funds had been available. The glacial pace of the managers' response to both the matron's and the children's own requests indicates their reluctance to have the children switch churches, even though the change would have kept the children in the same denomination. Clearly, religion was not the issue for the managers: in this case it appears race was at the heart of their concerns.

It was just after they had refused to send the children to Bidwell Presbyterian in 1924 that the managers approached Rev. Glasco about the proposed campaign. Perhaps it is not surprising, then, that he asked to meet with the board before agreeing to help. A founding member of the National Urban League and board member of the Coleman Industrial Home for Colored Boys, Glasco was no stranger to child welfare or civic institutions.[105] He could have disconnected from the HCC, maintaining his focus on the needy children at Coleman, but clearly he felt he should persist in his work with the HCC. Most telling, his wife, Mattie Glasco, became an HCC manager in 1926, joining Hallie James as the only other African American member at that time. This was a politically savvy recruit on the part of the board, but it also indicates the Glascos' continued interest in the institution and determination to be a part of its work.

The home's relationship with the Glascos and Bidwell Presbyterian illustrate the complicated nature of its relationship to the expanding black middle class. On the one hand, African American women had been a part of the board since its inception, and black donors were among the institution's earliest supporters; on the other hand, the managers waited until the 1920s under pressure from state authorities to consider a coordinated capital campaign. Their refusal to allow the children to attend a black church risked alienating key African American leaders, yet those leaders persisted in their efforts to work with the orphanage's children, even strengthening ties through Mattie Glasco's board membership. Change came slowly; in this case, it took nine years to get the children to Bidwell Presbyterian from the time the matron first made the request, and then it was only "through the successful efforts of Rev. Glascoe securing conveyances to and from the church."[106] It may well have been the "successful efforts" of Glasco and other African Americans that ultimately tipped the balance in favor of strengthened ties with at least some segments of the black community.

Staff members may also have played a crucial role in that process. For instance, the matron, Isabella Rowell, made the initial request to have the children join a black church in 1921, but she retired in 1924 just as the board decided against the church transfer. Her replacement, Margaret Johnston, worked for six years at the home with no record of similar outreach to the black community—and no record of gifts from Bidwell congregants upon her retirement in 1929, suggesting a possibly cooler relationship than had existed with Rowell. Johnston's successor, Jean Jones, however, initiated a series of rapid changes in the institution, bringing with her new methods of professional management. Her very first month on the job, the board learned, "Matron would like the children old enough to go to their own church." They decided, "Mrs. Jones, Miss Stewart [another board member], and Mrs. Glascoe to try to work out a plan for sending children to church."[107] The timing here suggests that staff played a pivotal role in the HCC's relationship with the black community—and reminds us that, just as that phrase incorrectly implies a monolithic group, there was no corresponding "white community" of uniform opinion. Managers and staff could have distinctly different ideas about appropriate ties to African Americans, whether established elites or impoverished clients.

Two of the matrons, Rowell and Jones, provide an unusual glimpse into the relationship between at least some of the white staff of the home and the black community. In a rare articulation of race relations, Rowell took a trip through the South in 1921 and returned to report "the conviction that all colored people fortunate enough to be in the North should by all means stay here."[108] Working and living with African American children for many years, Rowell was surely aware of northern racism and segregation, too, but what she saw in the South clearly shocked her. Rowell had been badly burned in 1917 while trying to put out flames from a gas heat-stove that had engulfed a child. While financial need for employment may have combined with Rowell's professional and ideological commitment to the HCC, she remained at the institution long after that tragic accident, in which a little girl died and Rowell permanently lost the use of her hand.[109] Rowell retired in 1923 with the obvious respect of the Bidwell congregation.

By 1931, when Jean Jones held the matron's position, state officials expected staff to play a pivotal role in bettering race relations. Jones advocated hiring African American child care staff and sending the children to Bidwell Presbyterian, among a host of other progressive ideas. Elizabeth T. Shipley, field representative for the state's Bureau of Children, wrote to Jones, saying, "[Y]ou are giving service in a field which is one of the most difficult and complicated that we have in America, this field of creating better interracial understanding." Shipley added, "It is encouraging to find that you do realize the significance which the work of the . . . Home may have in the whole field of interracial understanding."[110] Here, the state acknowledged the work of the staff, specifically Jones, rather than the managers, in strengthening interracial relationships.

Just as the HCC was slow to build relationships with African American leaders and donors, succumbing only after steady pressure from state authorities and the persistent efforts of individuals such as the Glascos and staff members, the orphanage also hesitated to connect with other institutions serving black children. At the turn of the century, with the black migrant population starting to climb, the HCC was still the only orphanage in the Pittsburgh region accepting African American children, and there was mounting need for additional services, particularly for adolescents and older teens. In 1903 the HCC managers asked rhetorically, "[W]hat shall we do with the children after they have reached the age limit which is twelve years and for whom we can find no desirable home? Can this problem be solved by the Colored people of Allegheny and Pittsburg?" Answering their own question, they proposed, "There are enough colored people in these cities—intelligent, responsible colored people to form an association whose object will be to look after these children when they cease to be our charges."[111] Indeed, black social activists did not need to have whites raise their awareness of this issue: by 1908 they had opened two institutions, the Davis Home for Colored Children (run by the Colored Women's Relief Association) and Coleman Industrial Home for Colored Boys, both quite independent of the HCC. The short-lived Fairfax Baby Home opened shortly after that.[112]

The Davis and Coleman homes illustrate the ways in which black community organizers viewed the needs of African American children differently from the largely white-run HCC. For example, both of these institutions served a broader age range than the HCC: Davis accepted children from two to fifteen, and Coleman, boys aged eight to fourteen. And both discharged children by age sixteen, thus providing four additional years of coverage for children who would ordinarily have aged out at the HCC. For years, the HCC had an upper age limit of twelve, though it reported in 1929 that it kept children until fourteen. Occasionally, the HCC allowed teenagers to remain even longer, particularly when they were full orphans and had been raised at the home or were promising scholars performing well in high school. However, clearly neither Davis nor Coleman saw itself as a mere companion institution, picking up services where the HCC left off. Rather, each accepted younger children in age ranges overlapping with the HCC. Furthermore, each established itself in a separate neighborhood of the city where African American migrants were quickly swelling the population, and there is no record that the HCC discharged any children to either institution until well into the 1920s. Progressive reformers balked at the inefficiency of these "duplicated" services, but at the time of their founding, their managers clearly saw overwhelming community need (the HCC had a waiting list nearly every month) and responded with their own distinct vision of black child care.

For instance, Davis added a day nursery by 1912 to provide families with nonresidential daytime child care.[113] It also streamlined applications, as one reformer scornfully noted: "The management prides itself on the lack of red tape and the absolute ease with which admission of new children is allowed."[114] Though to the reformer this was evidence of neglect in the admissions process, to anxious African American families seeking child care it was no doubt an enormous benefit. The African American managers clearly "prided themselves" on speeding up a process that could take several weeks at other institutions. Similarly, at the Coleman Home, this same reformer found that the managers were willing to admit children based simply on "the statement of the individual boy or the recommendation of the person by whom he is sent."[115] In fact, Coleman's decision to house only boys may have also reflected the black managers' response to the greater need for such services: girls were in higher demand as domestic servants, and families could more easily find live-in positions for daughters than sons.

A survey of *Pittsburgh Courier* articles reflects the relative high esteem in which many African Americans held these two institutions compared to the HCC. In its first twenty years, the newspaper printed only two articles mentioning the HCC, while it featured numerous stories about the Davis and Coleman homes.[116] When Mrs. Delia F. Arnold, the matron at the Davis Home, died, the *Courier* announced "Community Mourns Loss of Prominent Citizen," calling her a "prominent club and social worker" with "great foresight and a strong belief in the possibilities of her own people."[117] The number of articles, combined with items submitted by readers about the Coleman and Davis homes—announcements of meetings, fundraisers, notes in the social register—suggest the way in which many African Americans embraced these two orphanages as their own, while holding the HCC at arm's length.

The attitude of the HCC toward Coleman and Davis was equally distant. Despite their similar missions, and a precedent of exchanging children with

Avery College, the HCC appears to have had little contact with the two largely black-run institutions until 1927 when, once again, the state Welfare Department intervened. (By 1923 the Coleman home included several whites on its board of directors, but it remained primarily a black-run home.)[118] After finally succeeding in getting the HCC to use the Children's Service Bureau to screen its applications, the state then called a roundtable meeting of representatives from the three orphanages (Avery and Fairfax were closed by then). Managers from each institution met with a bureau agent to hammer out an agreement whereby the HCC would accept children under the age of ten, while older girls would go to Davis and older boys to Coleman.[119] The bureau coordinated admissions for all three. The HCC managers appeared content with the arrangement, commenting in June of 1928, "Plans for 3 homes to take care of the children according to age and sex working out very well."[120] Perhaps they were satisfied that at last the solution they had proposed in 1903 was in place; namely, black community organizers were running their own institutions dedicated exclusively to the older age group, leaving the care of younger children under what they saw as their rightful purview.

But connections between HCC and the other organizations remained tenuous. In 1929, a full two years after the roundtable agreement, "Rev. Askin and several women connected with the Davis Home visited the Home and were surprised at the size and furnishings."[121] Their surprise at the impressive size of the institution and its interior appointments indicates these black leaders had never been to the HCC before. The next month the HCC had "two ladies from the Coleman House to visit the Home and they were very much pleased with the home and children."[122] Since these two instances were the first mention of guests from either of the other institutions, and the managers carefully recorded visits from "outsiders" in their minutes, it seems quite likely that these were the first formal visits from Davis and Coleman representatives. The HCC did not bend over backward to maintain ties with the two: a full year later, the Urban League sent a request asking the managers to meet with representatives of Davis and Coleman. The managers put them off for several months, saying they would meet when it was more convenient, reflecting their uneasiness with further deepening ties to their institutional colleagues.

Perhaps it is not surprising, then, that the three institutions strongly resisted combining services when urged to do so in a 1929 report, "Study of Institutional Care for Dependent Colored Children." Stemming from the earlier roundtable discussion (that resulted in altered admission patterns) and authored by Helen Glen Tyson, the report surveyed the three orphanages, concluding, "the colored and white groups should throw their efforts back of one institution best equipped in ground, building, etc. to give all necessary care." Since the HCC had such accommodations and "an endowment fund," Tyson recommended that it "be the one institution to care for dependent colored children" and "that the other two Homes should turn their resources and services towards other urgent and unmet community needs."[123] To the managers of the Davis and Coleman homes, turning over their operations to the largely white managers of the HCC, with whom they had cordial but minimal contact, probably seemed out of the question. In 1929 their institutions were still more than three-quarters full, and while they struggled for resources, they were serving the difficult adolescent population for whom there were few alternatives. The HCC had struggled for decades to deal effectively with this age group, and now that it was only accepting children under the age of ten, they may not have wished to expand their scope to include these children once again.

Whether it was institutional pride, resistance to integrating the boards, or the many distractions of the difficult Depression years (the stock market crash came just months after Tyson released her report), the three orphanages remained independent. Davis operated until the late 1950s and Coleman until the mid 1940s. Despite reformers' emphasis on efficiency, decades of an arm's-length relationship between the HCC and African American institutions discouraged the consolidation.

❊   ❊   ❊

While Nellie Grant has become the modern symbol of the HCC's founding against the backdrop of racial segregation, none of the origin stories reveals her connection later in life to the institution. Nellie stayed at the orphanage for three years, leaving in 1883 when she was about ten years old. The managers did not record where she went, but as she was an orphan approaching the upper age limit of the home, they quite likely indentured her to a family to continue her education and learn domestic skills. Around the age of nineteen, Nellie married Sherman Earley and gave birth to their first daughter. Another daughter and a son followed, but within a few years the young family was in trouble. Nellie returned to the HCC in December of 1901 seeking admission for her three children, now aged nine, seven, and four. The managers accepted them, noting in their logbook, "Mother was first child in Home."[124] They also named Sherman in the admission record, indicating that he was still alive, though he may have been working away from the city or had abandoned his family.

In any case, Nellie, now approximately twenty-eight, appears to have had sole responsibility for the care of her children. By July of 1903, nineteen months after placing them, Nellie had fallen behind in her board payments, prompting the managers to declare, "Mrs Earley must either pay her children's board or take them from the Home." Nellie quickly wrote to the managers, who noted, "A letter was read from Mrs. Early saying that she had been sick and would pay her childrens boarding as soon as possible."[125] This suggests that Nellie had been unable to work due to illness and did not have the income to pay the boarding fees; Sherman was absent from this picture entirely, as the managers corresponded solely with her. A few months later, the children left the orphanage; although the managers did not record who retrieved them, it was most likely Nellie who returned for her children after nearly two full years in the institution.

Nellie's willingness to place her children in the HCC suggests a certain level of satisfaction with her own experience at the orphanage. Yet, when she placed her children in 1901, she had no other institutional options for child care, as no additional homes for African American children had opened in the twenty-one years since her own admission to the orphanage. The Nellie Grant Earley story reveals the trenchant problems faced by poor families that could repeat across generations, as instability in employment, housing, and healthcare could lead to recurring child care crises. These problems were exacerbated by racism, segregation, and inferior or absent social services and institutions. The history of the HCC's first fifty years illustrates an early attempt to address these issues: a tentative experiment in interracial cooperation that ultimately led to integration in child welfare work.

While during its first five decades the HCC did not challenge the underlying assumption that dependent children would remain racially segregated, under pressure from the state progressive reformers, individual staff members, and—crucially—the persistent efforts of African American leaders, the institution slowly strengthened its ties with the black middle class. With an increasing number of African American managers and senior staff in its ranks, the orphanage also eventually moved to integrate its clientele. The HCC officially changed its name in 1954 to its long-standing moniker, the Termon Avenue Home for Children, and in 1960 amended its charter to eliminate references to "Negro" and "colored" children. It also began meeting with the juvenile court to encourage the placement of more white children in an effort to more fully desegregate its population. In 1970 the institution merged with the Girls Service Club, a program sponsored by the Junior League for white teenaged girls dating back to the 1920s, and became the modern-day Three Rivers Youth.

CONTESTING ORPHANS

I certify that the above statement in regard to the child proposed for admission to the U. P. Orphans' Home is correct.

                                   James Caldwell

The story of my great-great grandfather, the widower James Caldwell, sparked my interest in the topic of orphanages. But when this project began, I was under the impression, based on family recollections, that Caldwell had placed his children in a Methodist orphanage. I had already decided to study the Home for Colored Children, as there was such a gap in the historiography on institutions for African American children, and when I discovered its "sister" agency, the United Presbyterian Orphan's Home, founded by the same minister, the opportunity to do a comparative study seemed irresistible. It wasn't until I had spent several months reading old documents at the Mars Home for Youth (formerly UPOH), that I discovered Caldwell had, in fact, placed his children in that orphanage. It was a deeply emotional experience, peering down at his neat signature on the admission application, where he agreed to pay fifty cents a week each for four of his children. I was looking at the moment, frozen in time, when this father gave up his children. The entire book of admission applications contained just such moments, of desperate parents seemingly "giving up" their children to the orphanage. But knowing the family history, knowing that this particular story actually ended with reunification, convinced me to look further at the ways in which poor parents used these institutions for their own purposes.

Caldwell succeeded in preserving his family, maintaining close ties to his children throughout their adult lives, but not without cost. He only managed to retrieve two of his daughters and take them back home when they aged out of the orphanage. The elder of the two, Susie, spent her teen years and young adulthood keeping house for her father and taking care of her youngest sister, Mayme, undoubtedly an enormous responsibility for such a young person. Two young sons had died in infancy, one likely while living with a wet nurse or in a baby institution, and another daughter died of epilepsy in a state-run facility. Caldwell sent two other siblings, Archie and Bertha (my great grandmother), to live on a farm in an adjoining county as teens, in what was probably an informal indentureship, arranged privately and not through the orphanage. Yet even Archie and Bertha had regular contact with their father, and their own children got to know their grandfather well. Though most of Caldwell's children remained in UPOH far longer than the average, he had not simply abandoned them there. Rather, he used the institution to meet his own child care needs and ultimately preserved some sense of family unity. To this day, his grandchildren, now in their eighties and nineties, hold an annual Caldwell reunion with up to four generations in attendance.

Stakeholders and Negotiation

James Caldwell's experience highlights the way in which orphanages served as "community institutions," serving the needs of the local people who used them.[1] Yet institutional child care was contested terrain. Both UPOH and the HCC illustrate the ways in which many different stakeholders negotiated the development of child care institutions, each with sometimes competing agendas and expectations. For example, to the managers, who were largely middle-class white women, the institutions provided a meaningful channel for their energies outside their own homes. Their orphanage work gave them a good deal of power as they participated in the business world, conducted real estate and investment transactions, and dealt with multiple government agencies, all within the acceptable bounds of middle-class maternalism. Their volunteer work fulfilled a sense of Christian duty in providing charity to the poor, which as a performative ritual was meant to bring them closer to the unwashed masses, yet simultaneously served to underscore and prop up class differences. Similarly, the managers displayed motives of social control, wishing to not only assist poor children, but to reform poor families themselves. These managing women were the most powerful stakeholders in the orphanages, but they were never alone; their control of the institutions was mediated by constant interaction with working-class families, reformers, staff, and the broader community.

Working parents, for instance, turned to the orphanages to meet their (usually) short-term child care needs. They recognized that they were recipients of charity, sometimes employing narratives of charitable assistance in their petitions for help, and other times "working the system" to get what they needed. Yet parents also insisted that they remain in control of their children while in the institutions and often treated their boarding payments as a fee-for-service. While they never had authority equal to that of the managers, they effectively used the institutions as temporary child care centers. Their ultimate power lay in their collective demand, or lack of demand for services, and families could "vote with their feet," by withdrawing their children, sometimes even against the wishes of the institutional managers. For example, while demand remained high for admission to both the HCC and UPOH, the Allegheny Day Nursery, run by a group of UPOH managers, was forced to close when it could not maintain sufficient enrollment. Parents also resisted indenturing their children, as the foster care system evolved in this period, preferring instead to keep their children in the orphanages where they had more contact and some measure of influence over them.

Progressive reformers, especially those at the local and state level, only slowly gained power relative to the managers in this turn-of-the-century period. Many reformers wished to deinstitutionalize children altogether, or at the very least, modernize existing institutions by introducing new scientific methods and updating facilities. They exerted increasing pressure on the orphanages by the 1920s but still lacked coercive legal muscle. At times the reformers were aided by staff members working from within the institutions themselves, and at other times staff could work at cross-purposes, resisting modernization. While orphanage staff took its first tentative steps toward professionalization in the early twentieth century, especially in the matron's position, most institution workers remained working-class women, drawn from the same communities as their clients. For many staff members, the orphanages provided crucial employment, and for a substantial number, allowed solo mothers to keep their children with them while working. Whether embracing reforms or rejecting them, staff played a critical role in carrying out the day-to-day policies of the institutions and consistently negotiated with the managers over control of their own labor, free time, and care of the children.

Finally, the managers had to contend with the broader community, from neighbors to donors to leaders of the local black community. While the orphanages may have been "community institutions," not everyone was thrilled to have them in their backyard. Neighbors complained about odors from outhouses and unruly children, and the HCC managers discovered that racial attitudes prevented them from moving into many areas. For example, in 1882, when the orphanage outgrew its first building, "they could not find a building whose owner was willing to rent it for a Home for Colored Children," and they eventually had to find a way to purchase their own property.[2] Similarly, a group of Allegheny residents organized to oppose UPOH's plan to expand its orphanage hospital. In 1896 Dr. James B. Herron donated nearby property worth $35,000 (over $900,000 in 2010 dollars) so they could build a new hospital to serve the entire community, but opponents succeeded in getting a state law passed requiring signatures from several top city officials before establishing any "hospital, cemetery or pest-house" in the district. The women of UPOH and their association, UPWANA, responded with 1,100 signatures on a petition, but the mayor still would not sign off on the project, and they took it to the courts, where they won. Under appeal from the city, they won again at the state Supreme Court level, overturning the law, but the incident provides a good example of the opposition the institutions sometimes faced within their own immediate neighborhoods.[3]

On the other hand, UPOH was tremendously successful at raising money from a national, even international, network of donors and forging a sense of community among its supporters. The donors, who included many working-class and rural families, formed strong ties to the institution through regular correspondence with the managers, articles in the church papers, and visits to the orphanage on its annual Donation Day. The very act of giving also created bonds between the many women who contributed through their participation in congregation-based Ladies Aid Societies, where they often performed communal work such as piecing quilts for the children. In contrast, race complicated the HCC's relationship with the broader community, and the organization had a much more ambivalent relationship with donors, both black and white. While bequests from several key white donors allowed the orphanage to survive difficult financial times, in its first fifty years it never achieved wide support from whites, turning instead to the state for charitable assistance. African Americans had supported the institution from its inception, yet the managers resisted forging stronger ties to black donors, even under mounting pressure from progressive reformers. By the 1920s the HCC also came under increasing pressure from Pittsburgh's black middle class to integrate its staff and board. This effort was eventually successful and went a long way toward warming the relationship between the orphanage and the broader community.

All of this give-and-take between the managers and the orphanages' other constituents meant that the managers did not have free rein in developing the institutions. They were the most powerful shapers of orphanage policy and practice, but there were limits to their authority. Through the process of negotiation and cooperation, the various orphanage stakeholders together forged an institutional response to a turn-of-the-century child care crisis.

Child Care Since 1929

By the end of the orphanages' first half-century, the gender, race, and class ideologies of child welfare were firmly entrenched, and they significantly affected the development of child care after 1929. Orphanage care for white children was premised on the breadwinner model: that white fathers ought to support their wives and children through wage labor, though not direct caretaking. White mothers' wage work, therefore, was an unfortunate, and temporary, necessity when families lost their male breadwinner. This model did not question white women's economic dependency or white men's supposed inability to provide adequate child care as single fathers. At the same time, orphanage care for African American children presumed that black women would carry the double burden of motherhood and wage labor while treating black men as absent fathers. Although poor families themselves may have disputed these characterizations—for instance, seeing women's wage work as a valuable contribution to the family and not an abdication of parenting responsibility—they nevertheless could not overturn these racial and gender ideologies at their foundation.

For over fifty years, both orphanages had focused on children in their public discourse, emphasizing the children's needs and not those of their working parents. Neither orphanage had ever articulated child care as a legitimate need, let alone a right, for wageworkers, to be paid for with public dollars. Child care thus remained closely associated with charity. While the HCC sought public funds for its home, the managers did not claim their constituents were parents entitled to state subsidies, but rather, they petitioned Pennsylvania to provide charitable relief to support dependent children. Though attitudes toward child care began to shift in the mid-twentieth century, the United States remained firmly wedded to the breadwinner model, treating the family as a highly private entity, and working parents—especially single mothers—as charitable objects.

Where other industrialized nations developed publicly supported child care systems of varying degrees over the course of the twentieth century, the United States evolved as an outlier in its fierce resistance to such an arrangement.[4] In stark contrast to nearly all of its peers, the United States continues to treat child care as a private concern and provides limited assistance only through welfare, the most highly stigmatized form of government support.

Unlike other social insurance programs, such as pensions or unemployment, which have been constructed as a right or entitlement of workers, welfare benefits remain, instead, charity for the poor. Because people of color are disproportionately represented among the poor, public assistance, and by extension, publicly funded child care, are also highly racialized.[5]

Yet, in times of national crisis, the country has briefly flirted with the idea of publicly subsidized child care. In response to the deepening depression, the federal government established an Emergency Nursery School program in 1933 that, at its height, served seventy-five thousand poor children.[6] But this program had limited reach and maintained the connection between child care and charity. New Deal programs continued this pattern, as the maternalist reformers crafting the new social welfare policies pitied single women with children but did not consider them entitled to rights-based or compensation-based programs, such as Social Security.[7] Instead, women's claims on the state were restricted to needs-based claims, and their primary aid program (Aid to Dependent Children) became highly stigmatized. What's more, the stratified welfare system, like its predecessor in the mothers' pension programs, maintained racial expectations of black women's labor, this time specifically excluding domestic workers, the occupation of the vast majority of laboring African American women.[8]

During the crisis of World War II, the 1941 Lanham Act created child care centers for women working in war-related efforts. The government eventually opened over three thousand child care centers in all but one state, but these largely closed with the end of the war.[9] However, with more married women working, and particularly as more middle-class women worked, the idea of child care as temporary, unfortunate, and charitable also began to change. Some working mothers began to assert their right to child care.[10] Attitudes were also affected by the kindergarten movement, which started in the nineteenth century for poor and immigrant families but was embraced by middle-class families for their children, and later the nursery school movement. Both movements emphasized the educational and social needs of young children, which were to be properly met outside the home under the supervision of professionals.[11] Society also became more accepting of an expanded role for government and came to view some child care as a legitimate public responsibility. At the same time, child care, especially day care, became redefined in the public's mind as a necessity for even "normal" middle-class families, whose children would also benefit from its educational and developmental emphasis.[12] While these changes did not find widespread public expression until after the postwar period, the seeds were set as early as the 1930s.

Child care received renewed attention in the 1960s, both as central to welfare reform and as a plank in the burgeoning women's rights movement. In signing the welfare law of 1962, which appropriated money for child care, President John F. Kennedy hoped to make recipients of public assistance self-sufficient. But efforts to reform welfare met with political resistance to the changing racial composition of the welfare rolls. Discrimination had effectively excluded many African Americans from receiving assistance, but as the civil rights movement progressed, this too, began to change, and the Aid to Families with Dependent Children (AFDC) program came under new attack. When AFDC recipients had been primarily white, the program went unchallenged, but as African Americans began to benefit in larger numbers, politicians, especially from the South, objected to paying black women to not work. This view drew on a long history of white assumptions about race and labor, that African American women should work and that the government should not pay them to be "idle."[13] At the same time, as part of President Lyndon Johnson's War on Poverty, the government introduced the Head Start program, aimed at meeting the health and educational needs of three- to five-year-olds, which remains to this day the only federally supported, nationwide child care program. Yet because people of color are disproportionately overrepresented among the poor, this sole form of nationalized child care remains racially segregated.[14]

Some women's groups, such as the National Organization for Women (NOW) and the National Council of Jewish Women (NCJW), pushed for better access to child care as a prerequisite for women's equality. Labor unions in the 1960s were also strong supporters of child care. But organized interests failed to overcome opposition to an ambitious, universal child care bill: in 1971, despite having passed the House and Senate, President Richard Nixon vetoed the Mondale-Brademas Bill, also known as the Act for Better Child Care, the only legislation that has ever proposed a nationally supported child care system.[15] Conservatives mounted fierce opposition to publicly funded child care throughout the 1970s and '80s, against the backdrop of a rapidly increasing proportion of working mothers. By the turn of the twenty-first century, more than three-quarters of women with school-aged children were in the labor force, and well over half with children under age three were working.[16]

Yet the United States has consistently rejected the notion of public responsibility for children, preferring instead to keep child care a private matter. In the past thirty years, the country has refused to sign three major international human rights conventions that emphasize the obligation of governments to support families with child care provisions.[17] From an international perspective, scholars have assigned the United States a failing score on nearly every measure of child and family well-being.[18] Since 1971, each time the federal government has considered child care, it has been tied to welfare legislation, keeping public monies closely affiliated with charity for the poor. Most recently, President Bill Clinton's sweeping welfare "reform" of 1996 dramatically increased demand for child care by coercing poor mothers into the labor market under threat of sanction and withdrawal of benefits, without adequately increasing corresponding funding for child care services.[19]

Ironically, in the wake of the 1996 reform, Pittsburgh stood at the center of a bold attempt to provide comprehensive child care across a wide geographic region. Had it succeeded, the ambitious plan would have been the first countywide system in the country. Launched by the United Way of Allegheny County (the successor organization to the Community Chest that the HCC had joined in 1929), the Early Childhood Initiative aimed to provide care to over 7,000 children in eighty low-income neighborhoods from 1996 to 2001. The organizers hoped to sustain the program by getting the state to commit funding, but this failed to materialize, and the per-child cost of the program far exceeded expectations. The United Way anticipated spending $4,000 to $5,000 per child, but was overwhelmed with parents' demand for full-day care, as opposed to the part-day slots organizers thought they would fill, and was burdened with the high cost of starting many new centers from scratch. At its peak, the program only served 690 children, at an average cost of $13,612 each, and it was scaled back to a demonstration project, turned over to the University of Pittsburgh to administer, and eventually discontinued.[20]

The failure of the Early Childhood Initiative reflects the way in which child care continues to be contested ground with competing agendas: the state was interested in welfare reform and getting parents into wage work, while the program administrators hoped to reform child care by focusing on quality. The community organizations recruited to provide the care wished to serve different populations—some only wanted to serve four-year-olds, for instance—and resented what they perceived as onerous reporting requirements and the many layers of administrative control. Meanwhile, parents themselves preferred to use the organizations for their own purposes, opting for full-day slots over part-day slots, and choosing the newest centers. Ultimately, in a move reminiscent of UPOH's unsuccessful Allegheny Day Nursery, the program failed to get enough parents interested, and their lack of demand for the new service shut it down.

The Orphanages since 1929

Both the Home for Colored Children and the United Presbyterian Orphans Home are still in existence today, serving families in crisis throughout southwestern Pennsylvania. Through the course of the twentieth century, the HCC and UPOH saw their populations change, as the new welfare system permitted more poor parents to keep their children at home and the emerging foster care system gradually reduced demand for institutional placements for some children. Like many other orphanages, these two institutions shifted focus: from dependency to delinquency; from children of largely "normal" families to "at-risk" youth from "broken" homes; from younger children to teens; from large institutional settings to smaller, group homes; and from a housing and educational model to a "treatment" model.[21]

In 1951 the HCC officially changed its name to the Termon Avenue Home for Children, and in 1960 it amended its charter to eliminate references to "Negro" and "colored" children. It merged in 1970 with the Girls Service Club, a program for "wayward" girls founded by the Junior League of Pittsburgh in 1924, forming Three Rivers Youth. The organization now runs five residential group homes, along with shelters, outreach centers, and family counseling services. Similarly, in 1990 UPOH changed its name to the Mars Home for Youth; its administrative offices are in the same mansion the institution has occupied since its move to Butler County in 1929, and it operates five residential group homes, an alternative school, and in-home services.

These child care institutions have successfully adapted to changing times and continue to serve important populations in the community, yet paradoxically, the child care needs they were founded to serve over 125 years ago remain, and at critical levels. Too few families have access to quality, affordable child care, and a modern child care crisis exists for the more than 15 million poor children who must compete for inadequate resources.[22] Nearly half the states have long waiting lists for publicly subsidized child care slots, and only one in seven income-eligible children ever receives assistance. Head Start reaches only half of all income-eligible four-year-olds nationwide, and most programs do not provide wraparound care (for the before- and after-school hours) for working parents. In addition, state child care subsidies often require a copayment, of up to several hundred dollars a month, making affordable child care a distant reality for many working parents.[23]

Furthermore, with no federal oversight of child care, supervision of care has been left to the states, which have frequently proven reluctant to enact or enforce even the most meager of standards, leaving vast numbers of children in highly unregulated care.[24] And because families often seek care near where they live, persistent residential segregation leads to de facto child care segregation in modern centers. Thus, a decade into the twenty-first century, child care remains largely segregated, with African American families overrepresented among the poor, who are so often dependent on unregulated care, provided by untrained and underpaid staff working in inferior facilities.

In addition, child care is still seen as inextricably linked to women's wage labor, a problem of working mothers, not working fathers; a problem of private choices and not of inadequate postindustrial wages. Parents are left to cobble together coverage: a quarter of working mothers with pre–school aged children rely on multiple arrangements, from relatives to institutions to juggling their own part-time or shift work to meet their child care needs. Thirty percent of children are being cared for by their grandparents, while another 43 percent of children are in child care centers, preschools, or family daycare centers.[25] Even the U.S. Census Bureau, in compiling these statistics, looked at the child care arrangements of pre–school aged children with working mothers, but did not ask the question about those with working fathers. Some men, especially among younger generations, have increasingly called for fathers' participation in child rearing, yet women continue to carry the disproportionate burden of care duties, both for children and for elders.[26] As such, child care inevitably remains a "women's issue," yet this very designation devalues the problem and continues to exclude men from the expectations—and very real benefits—of caring for children.

Today our child care system offers a hodgepodge of often less-than-adequate choices and vast inequities, with public funding tied to welfare and access to quality, affordable child care a mere pipedream for millions of families. Poor families, in particular, find themselves not far from the conditions of the 1880s, with few choices, long waiting lists, sometimes frightening conditions for their children, largely segregated care, and little public funding, requiring applicants to traverse a maddening maze of requirements to prove they are worthy charitable objects. It is time to address this legacy of gender, race, and class inequity built into our modern child care system. Doing so will tackle, head on, many of the unequal relationships of power and the trenchant disparities that threaten our nation's most valuable resource: its children.

APPENDIX A

Data Sets and
Statistical Methodology

Using original admissions and dismissal records from both orphanages, I created a relational database allowing me to capture over fifty variables for each child. I coded 1,597 children: 1,007 from the Home for Colored Children (HCC) and 590 from the United Presbyterian Orphan's Home (UPOH). Since no child's record contained data in every possible field, I performed most calculations on a subset of the larger database. The "n" is given for each table or figure.

Because the database is relational, I was able to preserve the relationships among children, parents, and sibling groups, permitting me to track family units over time. All children were assigned a unique case number, referenced in the footnotes throughout this study, and given substitute names to preserve anonymity. In parentheses following each case, the first number refers to the page number in the admission logbook (for UPOH) or line number in the admission register (for HCC) and the second to any cross-references in narrative histories. Example: Case #778 (88/42).

Like many institutions around the nation in this period, orphanages moved toward more bureaucratic and standardized entrance requirements in response to various reform efforts. This was certainly true at UPOH, which used preprinted, standardized application forms from its very first year and added a second set of forms for parents to fill out around 1910 that asked for additional health information. To create the UPOH data set, I used these application forms cross-referenced with logbooks kept by the admissions committee of the Board of Managers containing brief narrative "histories" for each child. I recorded every child for the first ten years (1878–88); beginning with the 1889 admission year, I switched to a one-in-four sample, coding every fourth family that applied for admission to the orphanage, permitting me to track sibling groups. Children were grouped into family units based on notes in the admission records, narrative histories, and references in the meeting minutes; children were considered "siblings" if they had the same last name and were placed in the orphanage consecutively on the same date, even if no parent information was recorded in the admission register. When examining UPOH over time, I normalize the post-1889 data.

It appears the HCC did not use standardized application forms in this period: though it is possible they have been lost, criticism leveled at this institution from child care reformers on this point of record keeping indicates they likely did not. For instance, in 1915 an investigator reported, "The records concerning the children of this institution consist only of two small books. . . . Meager data, with regard to the age, religion and parentage of the children, marks the outside limit to the knowledge which the management of this institution has concerning its wards" (Oseroff, "Report of the Allegheny County Committee Public Charities Association," 39). However, using an admission and dismissal ledger book, I was able to collect *all* the HCC records from its inception in 1880 through 1929. The sheer size of the HCC dataset (1,007 records) provides the first detailed look at institutional child care for African American children in the United States.

Biographical Comparison of HCC and UPOH Founding Managers

These were the original, or charter, members of the managing boards, who founded the orphanages in 1878 and 1880. A substantial majority of each founding board was identified through multiple sources, including U.S. federal census schedules (Allegheny and Pittsburgh, 1870, 1880, 1900, 1910, and 1920), social and business directories, meeting minutes, letters, and other orphanage documents. As a necessarily rough barometer of class, the occupations of heads-of-households (husbands or fathers) were used to assign the women to four categories: entrepreneurs (merchant, dealer, contractor); white-collar professionals (teacher, salesman, insurance agent, postmaster); skilled labor (headwaiter, porter, carpenter, glass presser, painter, cooper, roller, tinsmith); and unskilled labor (janitor, elevator operator). Members of the clergy, who would have been "white-collar professionals" for the purposes of class analysis, were also tracked. The UPOH column does not total to 100 percent, because one husband's occupation was not known.

African American and women's historians have rightly pointed out the difficulty in using men's employment as a sole determinant of class: where possible, class distinctions were corroborated with other evidence, such as ownership of real estate, location and size of homes, presence and number of live-in servants, and occupations of adult children still living at home. Many of these founding managers served for decades and brought in daughters to join the work, thus this demographic profile changed little over the course of the institutions' first fifty years.

Table A.1

	HCC	UPOH
Total number founding managers	39	17
Number identified with sources	28 (72%)	15 (88%)
Age		
Age range	26–70	23–69
Median age	40	40
Race		
White	92%	100%
Black	8%	0%
Place of birth		
Pennsylvania	71%	60%
North (OH, MA, IN)	7%	20%
South (KS, KY, VA, NC)	14%	0%
Foreign born (England, Scotland, Ireland)	7%	20%
Marital status		
Married	79%	80%
Widowed	4%	13%
Single	18%	7%
Children		
Percent with children at home	71%	73%
Median number	3	4
Age range of children	1–26	4m–28
Husband/father occupation		
Entrepreneur	29%	47%
Clergy	21%	20%
White collar professional	21%	0%
Skilled labor	14%	27%
Unskilled labor	4%	0%
Others in home		
Relatives	29%	7%
Boarders	4%	7%
Boarding with others	4%	7%
Live-in domestic servants	57%	67%

Birthplace of HCC Parents

In 1901 HCC managers began asking parents where they had been born, reflecting a growing concern with increased African American migration to the city of Pittsburgh. A statistical analysis of HCC admission logs from 1901 through 1929 shows that the orphanage served a significant number of northern-born families, but the bulk of the clientele had migrated from the Upper South, especially from the state of Virginia. There was no appreciable difference between men's and women's migration patterns, so the numbers here reflect total parents from each region.

Table A.2

	Total	Percent
North		
Indiana	1	0.3
Maine	1	0.3
New York	1	0.3
Ohio	16	4.0
Pennsylvania (other than Pittsburgh)	44	11.1
Pittsburgh	53	13.3
Subtotal	116	29.1
Upper South		
Washington, D.C.	12	3.0
Kentucky	8	2.0
Maryland	16	4.0
Virginia	143	35.9
West Virginia	21	5.3
Subtotal	200	50.3
South		
Alabama	13	3.3
Georgia	10	2.5
Louisiana	1	0.3
Mississippi	2	0.5
North Carolina	25	6.3
South Carolina	13	3.3
Tennessee	8	2.0
Texas	3	0.8
Subtotal	75	18.8
Other		
Canada	3	0.8
West Indies/Jamaica	4	1.0
Subtotal	7	1.8
Total	398	100

NOTES

Introduction. Constructing Orphans

1. Rose, *A Mother's Job*, 53.

2. Lattimore, "Pittsburgh as a Foster Mother," 339. For further comparison of day nurseries and orphanages, see chapter 3.

3. Lubove, *The Professional Altruist*; Platt, Rothman, *The Child Savers; The Discovery of the Asylum*.

4. Schlossman, *Love and the American Delinquent*; Ashby, *Saving the Waifs*; Katz, *In the Shadow of the Poorhouse*.

5. Zmora, *Orphanages Reconsidered*; Dulberger, *"Mother Donit fore the Best"*; Contosta, *Philadelphia's Progressive Orphanage*.

6. Gordon, *Heroes of Their Own Lives*; Kunzel, *Fallen Women, Problem Girls*; and Odem, *Delinquent Daughters*. For this view of orphanages, R. Friedman, *These Are Our Children*; see Cmiel, *A Home of Another Kind*; Hacsi, *Second Home*; Murdoch, *Imagined Orphans*.

7. Goodwin, *Gender and the Politics of Welfare Reform*; Skocpol, *Protecting Soldiers and Mothers*; Michel, *Children's Interests/Mothers' Rights*. Mink, *The Wages of Motherhood*.

8. Gordon, *Women, the State, and Welfare*; Muncy, *Creating a Female Dominion in American Reform*; Koven and Michel, *Mothers of a New World*; Ladd-Taylor, *Mother-Work*; Freedman, *Maternal Justice*.

9. Gordon, *Pitied But Not Entitled*; Kleinberg, *Widows and Orphans First*.

10. A number of historians have suggested that orphanages served a child care function, but they have not investigated the institutions from that position. For instance, Murdoch, *Imagined Orphans*; Hacsi, *Second Home*; Dulberger, *"Mother Donit fore the Best"*.

11. Steinfels, *Who's Minding the Children?*; Youcha, *Minding the Children*.

12. Rose, *A Mother's Job*; Michel, *Children's Interests/Mothers' Rights*.

13. No book-length historical analysis of African American child care has ap-

peared since Billingsley and Giovanni, *Children of the Storm.* Two shorter, more recent investigations are Harris, "Charity Workers and Black Activism," in *In the Shadow of Slavery;* and Morton, "Institutionalizing Inequalities."

14. Notable exceptions in the small historiography of fatherhood are Johansen, *Family Men;* LaRossa, *The Modernization of Fatherhood;* Frank, *Life with Father.*

15. For instance, S. J. Kleinberg acknowledges the large number of widowers who used orphanages but is primarily interested in the "widows and orphans" of her title (*Widows and Orphans First*). Linda Gordon's excellent analysis of the gendered underpinnings of the welfare system looks at single mothers (*Pitied But Not Entitled*). Others have focused on young mothers as objects of social reform, zeroing in on delinquency and unwed maternity (Broder, *Tramps, Unfit Mothers, and Neglected Children;* Kunzel, *Fallen Women, Problem Girls*).

16. The two orphanages opened in Allegheny City, annexed by Pittsburgh in 1907 and now known as the Northside neighborhood. Throughout this study, I use "Pittsburgh" to mean both cities, unless otherwise noted.

17. Lubove, "Pittsburgh and the Uses of Social Welfare History," 297.

18. *The Pittsburgh Survey,* 6 vols. (New York: Russell Sage Foundation, 1909–14).

19. Kleinberg, *Shadow of the Mills,* 27–39.

20. Kleinberg, *Widows and Orphans First,* 51–52.

21. Ibid. Kleinberg compared Pittsburgh to Fall River, Mass., and Baltimore.

22. On the connection between institutions and later social welfare policy, see especially Gordon, *Pitied But Not Entitled;* and Ladd-Taylor, *Mother-Work.*

23. *n*=2,016 cases. Children's Commission of Pennsylvania, *The Legal Foundations of the Jurisdiction,* 93.

24. Ibid., 88.

25. Historians have documented the way that other social problems such as domestic violence have been "discovered," and rediscovered, over time; see, e.g., Gordon, *Heroes of Their Own Lives;* E. Pleck, *Domestic Tyranny.*

Chapter 1. Institutionalizing Orphans

1. "45th Annual Report United Presbyterian Women's Association of North American," 1923, United Presbyterian Women's Association of North America collection (hereafter UPWANA), Mars Home for Youth, Mars, Pa. (hereafter MHY).

2. Ibid., 50–51.

3. "18th Annual Report United Presbyterian Women's Association," 1896, 3, UPWANA, MHY.

4. "29th Annual Report United Presbyterian Women's Association," 1907, 32, UPWANA, MHY. A note on names: when known, I use a woman's full name; otherwise, I use the married form of her husband's name (the social convention followed by most, though not all, women in this period).

5. *Pittsburg Dispatch,* January 30, 1916, clipping in Three Rivers Youth collec-

tion (hereafter TRY), Library and Archives Division, Historical Society of Western Pennsylvania, Senator John Heinz History Center, Pittsburgh (hereafter HSWP).

6. Ginzberg, *Women and the Work of Benevolence;* Hewitt, *Women's Activism and Social Change.*

7. "Board Visitors' Reports to Board, 1881–7," April–May 1883, 67, TRY, HSWP.

8. McCarthy, *Lady Bountiful Revisited.*

9. "U.P. Orphan's Home Song," 1898–1900, United Presbyterian Orphan's Home collection (hereafter UPOH), MHY.

10. $n=5/28$ of the HCC board and $n=4/15$ of the UPOH board were married to men performing either skilled or unskilled labor. Three of the thirty-nine HCC founding managers were African American.

11. The bulk of the recent orphanage historiography has directly challenged the social control theory, though without examining the class composition of institutional boards. For classic social control theory, see Lubove, *The Professional Altruist;* Rothman, *The Discovery of the Asylum;* Platt, *The Child Savers.*

12. DeVault, *Sons and Daughters of Labor.*

13. On the use of "status" in describing intraracial relationships among African Americans, see, for instance, Harris, *In the Shadow of Slavery;* Shaw, *What a Woman Ought to Be and to Do.*

14. See chapter 6 for more complete biographies of the African American women of the HCC board.

15. Rose, *A Mother's Job,* 26–27.

16. Boylan, *The Origins of Women's Activism.*

17. "19th Annual Report United Presbyterian Women's Association," 1897, 68, UPWANA, MHY.

18. A. Scott, *Natural Allies.*

19. On the Social Gospel movement in Pittsburgh, see Pritchard, "The Soul of the City," 344. For the role of the Social Gospel movement in the YWCA, see Weisenfeld, *African American Women and Christian Activism,* 32.

20. Historians of African American women's social reform work have been particularly articulate on this point. See Higginbotham, *Righteous Discontent,* Shaw, *What a Woman Ought to Be and to Do.*

21. Incorporation papers reprinted in Women's Christian Association (hereafter WCA), "Twenty-Third Annual Report of the Women's Christian Association of Pittsburgh and Allegheny, Pa," 1892, WCA annual reports (1877–79), Annual Reports collection, HSWP.

22. Ibid.

23. On efforts to control working-class women's sexuality, see Odem, *Delinquent Daughters;* Kunzel, *Fallen Women, Problem Girls;* Hicks, "'In Danger of Becoming Morally Depraved.'"

24. WCA 2nd, 3rd, 7th, and 8th annual reports summarized in newspaper clippings in Mary Hogg Brunot, "Mary Hogg Brunot Scrapbook," 1868, Papers of the

Hogg Family, 1785–1914, HSWP. A number of these institutions are still in existence today, including the Aged Protestant Women's Home (now Holmes House), and the YWCA of East Liberty (now the YWCA of Greater Pittsburgh).

25. Epstein, *The Politics of Domesticity*; Bordin, *Woman and Temperance*. On the WCTU in Pittsburgh, see Lobes, "'Hearts All Aflame.'"

26. Sims, *The Natural History of a Social Institution*; Young Women's Christian Association, "YWCA Pittsburgh, 1875–1950: A Story of Pittsburgh as Recorded by the Young Women's Christian Association," 1950, Young Women's Christian Association of Greater Pittsburgh Records, 1875–1988, HSWP; Mjagkij and Spratt, *Men and Women Adrift*.

27. Pritchard, "The Soul of the City," 333; Presbyterian Historical Society, "A Brief History of the Presbyterian Church."

28. W. H. Vincent, "The United Presbyterian Women's Association of North America, A Retrospect," 1946, UPWANA, MHY.

29. "Charter of the United Presbyterian Women's Association of North America and By-Laws of Association, Board of Directors, Orphan's Home, Columbia Hospital, Home for the Aged," 1910, UPWANA, MHY.

30. The Home for Aged People (now part of Presbyterian Senior Care) opened in Wilkinsburg where they later moved the hospital, renaming it Columbia Hospital (now part of the Forbes Health System).

31. United Presbyterian Women's Association of North America, "Charter of the United Presbyterian Women's Association of North America," 1910, UPWANA, MHY.

32. Sims, *The Natural History of a Social Institution,* 8; WCA, "11th Annual Report of the Women's Christian Association of Pittsburgh and Allegheny with Proceedings of Conference," 1879, WCA Annual Reports, HSWP.

33. The historiography of Ladies Aid Societies is quite thin, limited to articles in regional and church-based journals. For example, Blair, "Women Have a Legacy of Selfless Service"; Williamson, "'Doing What Had to Be Done.'"

34. Anna M. Cowan, "Letter to UPOH," 1885, UPOH, MHY.

35. Elvira Dunlap, "Letter to UPOH," 1893, UPOH, MHY.

36. Mary C. Lytle, "Letter to UPOH," 1882, UPOH, MHY (emphasis in original).

37. Mrs. S. E. McCormick, "Letter to UPOH," 1896, UPOH, MHY.

38. For an autobiographical narrative of Ladies Aid Society work in Pittsburgh and the aspect of its sociability, see "Jesus Freaks ca 1929–30" and "Mama: Roberta Caldwell Snyder," in Geisler, "Getting to Know Grandma."

39. Sims, *The Natural History of a Social Institution*.

40. See chapter 6 for discussion of the HCC's fundraising and relationship to the black community.

41. Fraser and Gordon, "A Genealogy of 'Dependency.'"

42. Ibid., 318.

43. "12th Annual Report of the Women's United Presbyterian Association," 1890, UPWANA, MHY.

44. Julia F. Blair, "Twenty Third Annual Report," 1904, TRY, HSWP.

45. White House Conference on the Care of Dependent Children, "Proceedings of the Conference," 8.

46. Ibid., 83. President Roosevelt invited two Pittsburgh representatives: Mrs. Hattie E. Sowers, President of the Children's Aid Society of Western Pennsylvania, and Charles F. Weller, Secretary of the Associated Charities of Pittsburgh. For a summary of national child welfare conferences, see Child Welfare League of America, "The History of White House Conferences on Children and Youth."

47. Dunham and Tyson, "Child Care in Pittsburgh," 20. On the U.S. Children's Bureau, see Lindenmeyer, *"A Right to Childhood"*; Costin, *Two Sisters for Social Justice*.

48. Cott, *The Grounding of Modern Feminism.*

49. "Minutes of the Board, 1912–16," May 1915, 176, UPOH, MHY.

50. The terms "feminism" and "maternalism" are somewhat muddled in the historiography, in part due to an earlier term "social feminism," coined in 1971, sometimes used interchangeably with "maternalism." Historians in the 1980s and early 1990s began discussing the "maternalist" origins of the welfare state, complicating the traditional narrative of U.S. social welfare, but at times also further entangling feminism, maternalism, and social reform.

51. The literature on maternalism and social welfare is still growing; for its roots, see Gordon, *Women, the State, and Welfare*; Gordon, *Pitied But Not Entitled*; Skocpol, *Protecting Soldiers and Mothers*; Boris, *Home to Work*; Muncy, *Creating a Female Dominion in American Reform.*

52. WCA, "11th Annual Report," 1879.

53. Elizabeth J. Clapp splits maternalists into "traditional maternalists" and "professional maternalists," echoing the divide Molly Ladd-Taylor sees between nineteenth-century "sentimental maternalists" and twentieth-century "progressive maternalists" (Clapp, *Mothers of All Children*; Ladd-Taylor, "Toward Defining Maternalism in U.S. History").

54. Ladd-Taylor, *Mother-Work.*

55. Goodwin, *Gender and the Politics of Welfare Reform.*

56. "Minutes of the Board, 1920–25," February 1922, 72, UPOH, MHY.

57. Ladd-Taylor, "Toward Defining Maternalism in U.S. History"; Shaw, "Black Club Women and the Creation of the National Association of Colored Women."

58. Shaw, *What a Woman Ought to Be and to Do.*

59. Ginzberg, *Women and the Work of Benevolence.*

60. Clapp, *Mothers of All Children.*

61. "Board Minutes, 1921–31," February 1931, 249, TRY, HSWP.

62. Kunzel, *Fallen Women*; Antler, *The Educated Woman and Professionalization.*

63. Preface to "39th Annual Report United Presbyterian Women's Association," 1917, UPWANA, MHY. For another example, see "47th Annual Report United Presbyterian Women's Association," 1925, 55, UPWANA, MHY.

64. Muncy, *Creating a Female Dominion in American Reform.*

65. Ginzberg, *Women and the Work of Benevolence.*

66. In 1885–86, the HCC received a $5,000 appropriation (worth over $117,000 in 2009 dollars) from the Pennsylvania legislature. See R. M. Snodgrass, "State Appropriation," 1885, TRY, HSWP.

67. "29th Annual Report United Presbyterian Women's Association," 1907, 31, UPWANA, MHY.

68. Mrs. George W. Ligo, "Letter from Board to Pittsburgh Child Welfare Study," 1930, TRY, HSWP.

69. UPOH reincorporated in 1996 as the Mars Home for Youth, and the managing board split into two entities, a board of directors and a separate foundation, both still led entirely by women. Mars Home for Youth, "Mars Home for Youth 125th Anniversary, 1878–2003," 2003, UPOH, MHY.

70. Mitchell, Albert, and Glasco, *From Colored Orphans to Youth Development,* 31, 59.

71. See chapter 6 for a discussion of Garrett and the Glascos.

72. Brown, "Maggie Lena Walker and the Independent Order of St. Luke"; Terborg-Penn, *African American Women in the Struggle for the Vote.*

73. On women's wages and family wages, see Kessler-Harris, *A Woman's Wage.*

74. Cases #898 (52/210), #899 (52/210). See appendix A for case number codes.

75. "Indenture to UPOH," 1880, UPOH, MHY.

76. "Indenture from Poor Board to UPOH," 1883, UPOH, MHY.

77. Vincent, "The United Presbyterian Women's Association of North America." See also, "35th Annual Report United Presbyterian Women's Association of North America," 1913, 101, UPWANA, MHY.

78. "41st Annual Report United Presbyterian Women's Association," 1919, 123, UPWANA, MHY.

79. "Minutes of the Allegheny Day Nursery, 1890–1893," October 19, 1891, 44, Allegheny Day Nursery collection, MHY.

80. Ibid., April 14, 1890, 17.

81. Harris, "Charity Workers and Black Activism," in *In the Shadow of Slavery,* 161.

82. A. Smith, "Study of Girls in Pittsburgh," 83.

83. W. H. Vincent, "Sixty Years of Service, 1878–1938," 1938, UPWANA, MHY; Vincent, "The United Presbyterian Women's Association of North America"; Mars Home for Youth, "Mars Home for Youth 125th Anniversary, 1878–2003." Precise dates of Mary's board service have been lost, but UPWANA's 1896 report calls her their "second President," and a letter from a Pittsburgh attorney dated 1882 addresses her as President (William P. Hunker, "Letter to UPOH," 1882, UPOH, MHY). She may have stepped down from her UPWANA post by 1883, when later sources date the presidency of her successor, Elizabeth Campbell, but she was still at her post at the HCC in 1884.

84. Alexander Geary Shafer, "Letter," 1851, in Shafer Family Collection, ancestry .com.

85. Genealogy compiled from Mary Hay Shafer family tree, ancestry.com.

86. The HCC also lists a Mrs. A. C. Patterson as a board member by 1884, but it is not clear if this is the same person.

87. Mrs. A. B. Tilford, "Letter to UPOH," 1885, UPOH, MHY. Her exact date of death is also unknown; by 1885 when this letter was written she was most certainly dead.

CHAPTER 2. RAISING ORPHANS

1. Sparks, *Capital Intentions*.

2. Biography of Isabella Nelson Longmore compiled from 1860 and 1870 census, and John Longmore Thompson, "Longmore Bible," 1952, UPWANA, MHY. The founding story claims Longmore had five children, but the 1870 census—taken in June, ten months after her husband's August 1869 death—lists only four. It is possible, of course, that Longmore gave birth to a fifth child, fathered by another man, after June 1870, but it is unlikely she remarried, as her name was still Longmore at the time of her death in 1877.

3. In 1880 thirteen-year-old Jennie Longmore was living with a couple and their son in Beaver, Pennsylvania. She was listed in the census as "at home"—in contrast to the "farm laborer" who also lived in the household—suggesting that she was in a permanent placement, not an indentured position. At the same time, James Longmore Jr. was nineteen, married, still living in Allegheny, and working as a telegraph operator. I was unable to locate Jessie (then age fifteen) or John (age eleven).

4. For another typical retelling of the story, see Mars Home for Youth, "Mars Home for Youth 125th Anniversary, 1878–2003," 2003, UPOH, MHY.

5. Analysis of eighty-one child welfare institutions active during the fifty-year period of this study (including almshouses and county homes, placement agencies, private institutions for dependent children, and homes for "delinquent" and "defective" children). See Slingerland, *Child Welfare Work in Pennsylvania;* Carnegie Library of Pittsburgh (hereafter CLP), "From Almshouse to Asylum: Orphans in Allegheny County (A Directory of Orphanages for Allegheny County, Pennsylvania)," Orphanage Directory for Allegheny County.

6. Lattimore, "Pittsburgh as a Foster Mother."

7. Kleinberg, *Shadow of the Mills*, 302.

8. Glasco, "Double Burden"; B. Hunter, "The Public Education of Blacks," 21–22.

9. Michel, *Children's Interests/Mothers' Rights;* Rose, *A Mother's Job.*

10. Lattimore, "Pittsburgh as a Foster Mother," 339; Dunham and Tyson, "Child Care in Pittsburgh," 19.

11. "Minutes of the Allegheny Day Nursery, 1890–1893," September 29, 1892, Allegheny Day Nursery collection, MHY.

12. P.L. 111, June 13, 1883; Liveright, *Poor Relief Administration in Pennsylvania,* 172; Pennsylvania Department of Welfare, "History of Child Care in Pennsylvania."

13. Slingerland, *Child Welfare Work in Pennsylvania*, 45.

14. House of the Good Shepherd in Allegheny (1872) was a large Catholic institution, while the Women's Association Christian Home was a much smaller, nonsectarian home serving only white women.

15. Case #1042 (58/312).

16. Slingerland, *Child Welfare Work in Pennsylvania*, 6.

17. St. Paul's Orphan Asylum (1840), St. Joseph's Orphan Asylum (1848, capacity 325), and St. Michael's Orphan Asylum (1873, capacity 14); Orphan's Home and Farm School (1854, capacity 100), Episcopal Church Home (1859, capacity 105), and St. Paul's Orphans' Home (of the Reformed Church) (1867, capacity 88).

18. Protestant Orphan Asylum (1832, capacity 200), Home for the Friendless (1861, capacity 175), and the Improvement Children's Home (1877, capacity 35) sponsored by the Pittsburgh Association for the Improvement of the Poor. On the first two, see J. Smith, "Child Care, Institutions, and the Best Interest of the Child."

19. Shelter for Colored Orphans (1822) run by the Quakers for girls only, and the Home for Destitute Colored Children (1855).

20. Hacsi, *Second Home*, 35–36.

21. "Minutes of the Board, 1912–16," December 1913, February 1914, 72, 84, UPOH, MHY; "Minutes of the Board, 1913–16," December 1913, 31, UPWANA, MHY.

22. Salem, *To Better Our World*. See chapter 6 for further discussion of the Coleman and Davis Homes and their relationship to the HCC.

23. Hacsi, *Second Home*; Zmora, *Orphanages Reconsidered*.

24. R. Friedman, *These Are Our Children*; Polster, *Inside Looking Out*.

25. Bodnar, Simon, and Weber, *Lives of Their Own*, 78.

26. Trotter, *River Jordan*, 78, 111; Dickerson, "The Black Church in Industrializing Western Pennsylvania."

27. *n*=264. "11th Annual Report of the Women's United Presbyterian Association and Orphans' Home. And First of the Memorial Hospital.," 1889, 21, UPWANA, MHY. These numbers were typical of other years.

28. Cases #92, #93, #94.

29. "Board Minutes, 1900–1911," November 1900, TRY, HSWP.

30. Mrs. A—W—, "Letter to UPOH," 1883, UPOH, MHY.

31. A—D—, "Last Will and Testament," 1916, UPOH, MHY. Cases #1135 (174/62), #1136 (174/62), #1137 (174/62).

32. "Minutes of the Board, 1905–8)," December 1907, 164, UPOH, MHY, 1905–8.

33. Bodnar, Simon, and Weber, *Lives of Their Own*, 24, 198.

34. Cases #794 (99/51), #795 (99/51), #795 (99/51), #797 (99/51).

35. "29th Annual Report United Presbyterian Women's Association," 1907, UPWANA, MHY.

36. "Minutes of the Board, 1899–1902," February 1900, 21, UPOH, MHY.

37. Oseroff, "Report of the Allegheny County Committee Public Charities Association," 40–41, 45, 48.

38. Murdoch, *Imagined Orphans;* Broder, *Tramps, Unfit Mothers, and Neglected Children.*

39. "20th Annual Report United Presbyterian Women's Association," 1898, UP-WANA, MHY. Case #91.

40. Hacsi, *Second Home.*

41. Statistical analysis of HCC and UPOH admissions logs and children's case histories, where the status of at least one parent is known; HCC *n*=672, UPOH *n*=578

42. Julia F. Blair, "Twenty Second Annual Report," 1903, TRY, HSWP.

43. "Minutes of the Board, 1908–12," December 1911, 237, UPOH, MHY.

44. Kleinberg, *Shadow of the Mills;* Kleinberg, *Widows and Orphans First.*

45. "17th Annual Report United Presbyterian Women's Association," 1895, 31, UPWANA, MHY.

46. Out of 536 UPOH parents for whom there is some identifying information, 226 (42 percent) contained occupational data. (The HCC did not regularly collect occupational data on parents.) "Manual labor" for women includes domestic worker, nurse, and laundress; for men, it includes general laborer, farmhand, and coal miner. "Semiskilled and skilled labor" for women includes dressmaker, seamstress, potter, baker, silk inspector, and matron; for men, it includes steamfitter, bricklayer, and carpenter. "White collar" for women includes store clerk, stenographer, and telephone operator; for men, it includes statistician, clerk, newspaper reporter, and insurance salesman.

47. My summary of "vertical occupational structure" analysis performed by Bodnar, Simon, and Weber (*Lives of Their Own,* 64.)

48. Trotter, *River Jordan,* 65.

49. Ibid., 100.

50. Ibid.

51. Kleinberg, *Shadow of the Mills,* 27–39; Greenwald, "Women and Class in Pittsburgh," 34.

52. *n*=61 of the 106 UPOH women with occupational data.

53. Greenwald, "Women and Class in Pittsburgh," 37–39. See also, Kessler-Harris. *Out to Work.*

54. Rose, *A Mother's Job,* 222.

55. Cases #879 (4/168), #880 (4/168). For other examples, see Cases #884 (20/182), #1047 (70/1), #1048 (70/1), #1049 (70/1).

56. Trotter, *River Jordan,* 29. Pittsburgh's employment options for African American women reflected national patterns; see T. Hunter, *To 'Joy My Freedom;* Clark-Lewis, *Living In, Living Out.*

57. Trotter, *River Jordan,* 26, 65. Quote from Kleinberg, *Widows and Orphans First,* 21.

58. Kleinberg, *Widows and Orphans First,* 30.

59. "Board Minutes, 1900–1911," December 1909, 322, TRY, HSWP. Case #1142 (636).

60. UPOH Cases #820 (32/97), #821 (32/97).

61. UPOH Cases #500 (56, 104/28), #501 (56, 104/28), #502 (56/22).

62. "14th Annual Report of the Women's United Presbyterian Association," 1892, UPWANA, MHY.

63. Case #164 (15/10). See also Cases #825 (44/106), #826 (44/106).

64. "Minutes of the Board, 1905–8," December 1907, 164, UPOH, MHY.

65. Cases #837– #840 (64/123).

66. Calculations based only on the widows and widowers for whom there is both a date of spousal death and child's admission. "Widows" includes a small number of abandoned women with a date of desertion.

67. Lattimore, "Pittsburgh as a Foster Mother."

68. Cases #1100 (29/31, 65), #1101 (30/31, 65).

69. Case #779 (89/43).

70. Cases # 634 (441), #635 (442), #636 (443), #637 (444), #638 (445), #683 (490).

71. June 1906 letter from UPWANA inserted in "Minutes of the Board, 1905–8," 51, UPOH, MHY.

72. "12th Annual Report of the Women's United Presbyterian Association," UPWANA, MHY.

73. Igra, *Wives without Husbands.*

74. Cases #1047 (70/1), #1048 (70/1), #1049 (70/1).

75. Cases #879 (4/168), #880 (4/168). For more examples, see Cases #739 (548), #747 (556).

76. Case #913 (72/226).

77. May, *Great Expectations.*

78. In *Pitied But Not Entitled,* Gordon discusses the way in which female reformers searched for ever-more-blameless clients, shifting their symbolic victim from the deserted wife to the widowed mother to the children themselves.

79. "Minutes of the Board, 1920–25," July 1922, 96, UPOH, MHY.

80. "Minutes of the Board, 1908–12," March 1909, 33, UPOH, MHY.

81. Cases # 777 (88/42), #778 (88/42).

82. "Minutes of the Board, 1896–99," October 1897, April 1899, UPOH, MHY. See also "Minutes of the Board, 1899–1902," January 1901, 86, UPOH, MHY; "Minutes of the Board, 1902–5," November 1905, 4, UPOH, MHY; "Minutes of the Board, 1916–20," April 1917, 32, UPOH, MHY.

83. W. W. Grier, "Letter to UPOH," 1886, UPOH, MHY (emphasis in original).

84. Cases #762 (79/39), #783 (92/44), #784 (92/44).

85. Slingerland, *Child Welfare Work in Pennsylvania,* 241.

86. Faires, "Immigrants and Industry."

87. "25th Annual Report United Presbyterian Women's Association," 1903, 113, UPWANA, MHY.

88. Of ninety-one parents for whom nationality was recorded (between 1912 and 1929 in the sample), twenty-four were foreign born.

89. 1907 survey of Pittsburgh orphanages cited in Lattimore, "Pittsburgh as a Foster Mother," 339.

90. Faires, "Immigrants and Industry"; Bodnar, Simon, and Weber, *Lives of Their Own*, 41; Bodnar, *The Transplanted*.

91. Trotter, *River Jordan;* Gottlieb, "Migration and Jobs"; Gottlieb, *Making Their Own Way;* Trotter, "Reflections on the Great Migration to Western Pennsylvania."

92. Figures include the city of Allegheny. Trotter, *River Jordan,* 66, 97.

93. Ibid., 27.

94. Slingerland, *Child Welfare Work in Pennsylvania,* 285.

95. 1907–8 report reprinted in Dinwiddie and Crowell, "The Housing of Pittsburgh's Workers." See also Tarr, *Devastation and Renewal*.

96. "14th Annual Report of the Women's United Presbyterian Association," UPWANA, MHY.

97. Cases #918 (84/236), #919 (84/236), #920 (84/236).

98. Cases #215 (/22). See also Cases #1114 (102/46), #1042 (58/312).

99. Cases #165 (16), #166 (16/10).

100. Cases #929 (108/257), #930 (108/257), #931 (108/257).

101. "Board Visitors' Reports to Board, 1881–87," November 1881, TRY, HSWP; Cases #31 (31), #32 (32).

102. Case #1033 (34/303).

103. Cases #925 (100/249), #926 (100/249), #927 (100/249).

104. Hacsi, *Second Home,* 129.

105. HCC children averaged 843 days (or 2 years, 3 months, and 23 days), while UPOH children averaged 507 days (1 year, 4 months, and 22 days).

106. Mean length of stay calculated per admission, rather than per child, since some children had more than one stay in the orphanage: 708 HCC and 436 UPOH admissions records had corresponding dismissal records (*n*=1,144 stays) to permit analysis. All dates converted to total number of days.

107. Hacsi, *Second Home,* 129.

108. Dulberger calls the Albany, New York, orphanage she studied a "poor man's boarding school" (*"Mother Donit fore the Best,"* 11). Zmora makes a similar observation about the three Baltimore orphanages she analyzes (*Orphanages Reconsidered,* 69).

109. "Minutes of the Board, 1916–1920," May 1917, 34, UPOH, MHY.

110. "13th Annual Report of the Women's United Presbyterian Association," UPWANA, MHY.

111. Holt, *The Orphan Trains;* Gordon, *The Great Arizona Orphan Abduction*.

112. "Minutes of the Board, 1896–99," May 1897, 32, UPOH, MHY. See also June 1897, 38, for another typical example.

113. "Minutes of the Board, 1899–1902," October 1901, 142, UPOH, MHY. See also "Minutes of the Board, 1912–16," February 1913, 21, UPOH, MHY.

114. B. Hunter, "The Public Education of Blacks in the City of Pittsburgh," 21.

115. "Minutes of the Board, 1920–25," April 1923, 129, UPOH, MHY. Cases #1393 (83/98), #1394 (84/98).

116. Ibid., April 1922, 82. Cases #1366 (/75), #1367 (/75), #1368 (/75).

117. Ibid., July 1922, 96.

118. W—T—, "Letter to UPOH," 1892, UPOH, MHY; Cases #827 (48/110), #828 (48/110), #829 (48/110).

119. Nationally, most orphanages would not accept children under the age of three or four. Hacsi, *Second Home,* 150.

120. "18th Annual Report United Presbyterian Women's Association," 1896, 31, UPWANA, MHY; "Minutes of the Board, 1896–99," December 1897, 67, UPOH, MHY.

121. Rose, *A Mother's Job,* 53.

122. The median calculated using total admissions (which includes the 6 percent of children who had multiple admissions) of those with both birth date and admission date ($n=1,437$).

123. $n=1,213$ dismissals

124. "Board Visitors' Reports to Board," November 1881, TRY, HSWP; Cases #31 (31), #32 (32).

125. "Minutes of the Board, 1912–16," February 1916, 226, UPOH, MHY.

126. Bodnar, Simon, and Weber, *Lives of Their Own,* 92.

127. Kleinberg, *Widows and Orphans First,* 51.

128. Lillian Marshall Brown, "Twenty Fifth Annual Report," 1906, TRY, HSWP.

129. "Minutes of the Board, 1908–12," February 1909, 26, UPOH, MHY.

130. "Board Minutes, 1921–1931," December 1928, 169, October 1929, 92, TRY, HSWP.

131. "Histories, 1878–1905," 96, UPOH, MHY.

132. "11th Annual Report of the Women's United Presbyterian Association and Orphans' Home. And First of the Memorial Hospital," UPWANA, MHY.

133. Hacsi, *Second Home,* 138.

134. $n=1,597$ children.

135. Glasco, "Optimism, Dilemmas, and Progress," 217.

136. "Minutes of the Board, 1902–05," September 1903, 60, UPOH, MHY. Cases #1005 (132/274), #1006 (132/274).

137. UPOH Cases #889 (32, 64/194), #890 (32, 64/194), #891 (32, 64/194). The Western Pennsylvania Humane Society, founded in Pittsburgh in 1874, placed abused, neglected, and destitute children with relatives, in institutions, and in private homes.

138. Family retrieved 57 percent of HCC and 54 percent of UPOH children on their second and subsequent stays.

139. UPOH $n=60/590$; HCC $n=36/1,007$.

140. $n=77/96$ children with multiple stays. Seventeen percent stayed three times ($n=16/96$), only 2 percent stayed four times ($n=2/96$), and one child stayed five times. There was one African American sibling group who had three stays.

141. The average length of first stay for HCC children with multiple stays was 1,044 days (2 years, 10 months) versus 482 days (1 year, 3 months) for UPOH children.

142. HCC children averaged 632 days (1 year, 8 months) versus 319 days (10 months) for UPOH children.

143. Cases #505 (60), #510 (60), #511 (60).

144. "Minutes of the Board, 1920–25," March 1925, 238, UPOH, MHY. "Minutes of the Board, 1925–30," July 1926, 46, UPOH, MHY.

145. Thompson, "Longmore Bible." The "Longmore Bible" may not have belonged to Isabella: though it has an inscription from her grandson, John Longmore Thompson, dated 1952 when he donated the book to the home indicating that it was hers, the bible also contains a plate stating, "Presented to Jessie Thompson by John G. Thompson 1885." This suggests the bible may have been a gift from John Thompson to his wife, Jessie, who was likely Isabella's eldest daughter; she would have been twenty in 1885, and it is possible John presented the book as a wedding gift or upon the birth of a child.

146. "12th Annual Report of the Women's United Presbyterian Association," 10, UPWANA, MHY.

147. Cases #1 (1), #2 (2), #3 (3), #4 (4).

CHAPTER 3. BOARDING ORPHANS

1. Lillian Marshall Brown, "Twenty Fifth Annual Report," 1906, TRY, HSWP.

2. "13th Annual Report of the Women's United Presbyterian Association," 1891, 10, UPWANA, MHY; "20th Annual Report United Presbyterian Women's Association," 1898, 18, UPWANA, MHY.

3. WCA, "Twenty-Third Annual Report," 1892, Annual Reports collection, HSWP.

4. n=615

5. n=869 HCC records without placement data; 553 (64 percent) had at least one living parent.

6. Cases #827 (48/110), #828 (48/110), #829 (48/110).

7. Odem, *Delinquent Daughters*; Hicks, "'In Danger of Becoming Morally Depraved.'"

8. Children's Commission of Pennsylvania, *The Legal Foundations of the Jurisdiction, Powers, Organization and Procedure*, 98.

9. "Board Minutes, 1900–1911," May 1907, 220, TRY, HSWP. See also "Board Minutes, 1900–1911," October 1906, 195, TRY, HSWP.

10. Children's Commission of Pennsylvania, *The Legal Foundations of the Jurisdiction, Powers, Organization and Procedure*, 95.

11. "Constitution and By-Laws of the Home for Colored Children," 1881, TRY, HSWP. UPOH records, n=388 / 654.

12. WCA, "11th Annual Report of the Women's Christian Association of Pittsburgh and Allegheny with Proceedings of Conference," 1879, WCA Annual Reports, HSWP.

13. WCA, "Twenty-Third Annual Report," 1892, Annual Reports, HSWP.

14. L—J. D—, "Letter to UPOH," 1880, UPOH, MHY.

15. "Board Minutes, 1900–1911," February 1903, 67, TRY, HSWP. Cases #602 (409), #603 (410), #604 (411).

16. "Minutes of the Board, 1899–1902," January 1901, 86, UPOH, MHY,.

17. J. A. D—, "Letter to UPOH," 1894, UPOH, MHY.

18. Lattimore, "Pittsburgh as a Foster Mother."

19. Analysis of income for 1881 and 1882 general operating budgets. Emily Hunnings, "Treasurer's Book Colored Orphan Asylum," 1880–83, TRY, HSWP.

20. "13th Annual Report of the Women's United Presbyterian Association," UPWANA, MHY.

21. Case #156 (9/7).

22. Cases #209 (36/21), #210 (36/21), #211 (36/21). For a typical case at the HCC, see Case #713 (520).

23. "Board Minutes, 1900–1911," September 1908, 271, TRY, HSWP.

24. Bodnar, Simon, and Weber, *Lives of Their Own*, 102; Trotter, *River Jordan*, 100.

25. "Minutes of the Board, 1899–1902," September 1901, 131, UPOH, MHY. See also "Minutes of the Board 1896–99," September 1898, 121, UPOH, MHY. "Minutes of the Board, 1920–25," October 1923, 154, UPOH, MHY.

26. "Minutes of the Board, 1916–20," November 1917, 68, UPOH, MHY.

27. Ibid., October 1919, 201.

28. "Minutes of the Board, 1905–8," March 1908, 184, UPOH, MHY; "Minutes of the Board, 1912–16," March 1915, 164, UPOH, MHY.

29. "Minutes of the Board, 1899–1902," March 1902, 181, UPOH, MHY.

30. "Minutes of the Board, 1902–5," October 1903, 68, UPOH, MHY.

31. "Minutes of the Board, 1896–99," 103 UPOH, MHY; "Minutes of the Board, 1902–5," 75, UPOH, MHY. "Minutes of the Board, 1916–1920," January 1917, 15, UPOH, MHY.

32. "Board Minutes, 1900–1911," February 1902, 101, TRY, HSWP.

33. "Minutes of the Board, 1925–30," October 1926, 57, UPOH, MHY.

34. Case #1585 (1103). For similar examples, see "Board Minutes, 1921–31," February 1929, 172, TRY, HSWP; "Board Minutes, 1900–1911," July 1900, TRY, HSWP.

35. "Minutes of the Board, 1912–15," March 1915, 163, UPOH, MHY.

36. "Board Minutes, 1900–1911," August 1900, TRY, MHY.

37. "12th Annual Report of the Women's United Presbyterian Association," 1890, 16, UPWANA, MHY.

38. "Minutes of the Board, 1920–25," August 1923–January 1924, UPOH, MHY.

39. Ibid., May–June 1921, 35, 40.

40. "Board Visitors' Reports to Board," 1881–87, TRY, HSWP.

41. G—M—, "Letter to UPOH," 1894, UPOH, MHY.

42. "Minutes of the Board, 1896–99," November 1898, 131, UPOH, MHY.

43. On working-class use of clothing to challenge middle-class assumptions of class status, see Enstad, *Ladies of Labor, Girls of Adventure*.

44. Hacsi, *Second Home*, 154.

45. "16th Annual Report United Presbyterian Women's Association," 1894, 14, UPWANA, MHY.

46. "Board Minutes, 1900–1911," 1902, 42, TRY, HSWP.

47. Mrs. George W. Ligo, "Letter from Board to Pittsburgh Child Welfare Study," 1930, TRY, HSWP.

48. Murdoch, *Imagined Orphans*.

49. Rose, *A Mother's Job*, 61.

50. "Board Visitors' Reports to Board," June–July 1882, TRY, HSWP.

51. "39th Annual Report United Presbyterian Women's Association," 1917, 109, UPWANA, MHY.

52. "39th Annual Report United Presbyterian Women's Association," 109, UPWANA, MHY; "41st Annual Report United Presbyterian Women's Association," 1919, 124, UPWANA, MHY.

53. "25th Annual Report United Presbyterian Women's Association," 1903, 95, UPWANA, MHY.

54. "Board Minutes, 1900–1911, February 1907, 208, TRY, HSWP.

55. "Minutes of the Board, 1896–99," April 1897, 27, UPOH, MHY.

56. "Board Minutes, 1921–1931," May–June 1924, 83, TRY, HSWP. Cases #1313 (922), #1314 (923), #1315 (924).

57. "Minutes of the Board, 1902–5," June 1904, 119, UPOH, MHY. See also "Minutes of the Board, 1896–99," March 1897, 23, UPOH, MHY. "Minutes of the Board, 1899–1902," February 1900, April 1901, 21, 105, UPOH, MHY.

58. "Minutes of the Board, 1902–5," December 1903, 93, UPOH, MHY.

59. "Minutes of the Board, 1912–16," February 1914, 83, UPOH, MHY. See also "Minutes of the Board, 1905–8," September 1908, 223, UPOH, MHY; "Minutes of the Board, 1912–16," May 1915, 171, UPOH, MHY.

60. Katz, "The History of an Impudent Poor Woman," 228.

61. "Minutes of the Board, 1902–5," December 1904, 155, UPOH, MHY.

62. Ibid., March 1905, 174.

63. Ibid., October 1903, 69. See also "Minutes of the Board, 1902–5," March 1905, 174, UPOH, MHY; "Minutes of the Board, 1905–8," November 1907, 161, UPOH, MHY. On women's use of deception in dealing with day nurseries, see Rose, *A Mother's Job*, 64.

64. "Board Minutes, 1900–1911," June 1910, 342, TRY, HSWP.

65. "Minutes of the Board, 1905–8," February 1906, 21, UPOH, MHY.

66. Kunzel, *Fallen Women, Problem Girls*.

67. Gordon, *Heroes of Their Own Lives*, 90–91; Hacsi, *Second Home*, 108.

68. "Board Minutes, 1900–1911," March, May, June 1903, 70, TRY, HSWP; Cases #650 (457), #651 (458), #652 (459).

69. "Board Minutes, 1900–1911," May 1905, 140, TRY, HSWP.

70. "Minutes of the Board (UPOH)," September 1908, 223.

71. For a parallel on women seeking assistance from domestic abuse agencies, see Gordon, *Heroes of Their Own Lives*, 295.

72. Dulberger, *"Mother Donit fore the Best."*

73. "Minutes of the Board, 1920–25," February 1924, July 1925, 182, 258, UPOH, MHY.

74. "Minutes of the Board, 1899–1902," March 1902, 181, UPOH, MHY.

75. Ibid., February 1901, 92. Cases #922 (92/243), #923 (92/243).

76. "Board Minutes, 1900–1911," February 1903, 67, TRY, HSWP. Cases #602 (409), #603 (410), #604 (411).

77. "Minutes of the Board, 1905–8," April 1907, 120, UPOH, MHY.

78. W—T—, "Letter to UPOH," 1892, UPOH, MHY.

79. For typical example, see "Board Minutes, 1900–1911," October 1910, 363, TRY, HSWP.

80. Ibid.

81. "35th Annual Report United Presbyterian Women's Association of North America," 1913, 102, UPWANA, MHY.

82. "Minutes of the Board, 1920–25," August 1921, 48, UPOH, MHY.

83. "Minutes of the Board, 1899–1902," May 1900, 37, UPOH, MHY.

84. United Presbyterian Orphan's Home Rules, typed sheet inserted in "Minutes of the Board, 1925–30," UPOH, MHY.

85. Ibid., July 1929, 209.

86. "Board Minutes, 1900–1911," November 1901, 34, TRY, HSWP.

87. "35th Annual Report United Presbyterian Women's Association of North America," 102, UPWANA, MHY.

88. "Board Minutes, 1921–1931," May 1924, 83, TRY, HSWP.

89. Ibid., March 1926, 120.

90. "Minutes of the Board, 1896–99," January, February 1899, 144, 50, UPOH, MHY.

91. "Minutes of the Board, 1905–8," March 1908, 186, UPOH, MHY.

92. "Board Minutes, 1900–1911," July 1902, 50, TRY, HSWP.

93. "Minutes of the Board, 1912–16," September 1915, 196, UPOH, MHY.

94. Ibid., October 1915, 200.

95. "Minutes of the Board, 1902–5," September 1904, 134, UPOH, MHY.

96. Ibid.

97. "Minutes of the Board, 1925–30," July 1930, 277, UPOH, MHY.

98. "Minutes of the Board, 1920–25," September 1921, 51, UPOH, MHY. See also "Minutes of the Board, 1899–1902," December 1900, 80, UPOH, MHY.

99. "Minutes of the Board, 1916–1920," May 1919, 177, UPOH, MHY.

100. "Minutes of the Board, 1902–5," November 1903, 78, UPOH, MHY.

101. "Minutes of the Board, 1912–16," June 1915, 179, UPOH, MHY.

102. "Minutes of the Board, 1916–1920," December 1919, May 1920, 221, 49, UPOH, MHY.

103. Glasco, "Optimism, Dilemmas, and Progress," 21.

104. "Board Visitors' Reports to Board," March–April 1885, 107, TRY, HSWP. Case #264 (123). For another example, see "Minutes of the Board, 1899–1902," April 1901, 105, UPOH, MHY.

105. "Board Minutes, 1921–1931," March 1922, 23, TRY, HSWP.

106. "Minutes of the Board, 1899–1902," March 1901, 99, UPOH, MHY. Case #917 (80/233).

107. "Minutes of the Board, 1902–5," August 1903, 55, UPOH, MHY.

108. "Minutes of the Board, 1899–1902," July 1901, 125, UPOH, MHY.

109. Ibid.

110. "Minutes of the Board, 1916–1920," September 1918, 119, UPOH, MHY.

111. "Board Minutes, 1921–1931," February 1929, 172, TRY, HSWP. Cases #1584 (1102), #1585 (1103).

112. Ibid., November 1924, 99. Cases #1523 (1040), #1524 (1041).

113. "Minutes of the Board, 1912–16," October 1914, 130, UPOH, MHY.

114. Ibid., November 1914, 140.

115. "Board Minutes, 1921–1931," June 1922, 29, TRY, HSWP.

116. "Minutes of the Board, 1925–30," December 1927, 125, UPOH, MHY.

117. Todar, "Todar's Online Textbook of Bacteriology."

118. Based on records where retrieving party could be determined: HCC $n=543$, UPOH $n=451$.

119. "Minutes of the Board, 1912–16," December 1914, 146, UPOH, MHY; "Minutes of the Board, 1896–99," May 1900, 37, UPOH, MHY.

120. "Board Minutes, 1900–1911," July 1900, TRY, HSWP. Case #571 (374).

121. "Minutes of the Board, 1899–1902," February 1900, 21, UPOH, MHY.

122. "Minutes of the Board, 1902–5," February 1904, 99, UPOH, MHY.

123. Ibid., March 1904, 104.

124. Ibid.

125. "Minutes of the Board, 1905–8," April 1907, 123, UPOH, MHY.

126. Ibid., May 1907, 124.

127. "Minutes of the Board, 1925–30," December 1928, 177, UPOH, MHY. Nine Allegheny City women founded the Curtis Home in 1894 to care for unwed mothers and their newborns; by 1923, it had shifted to caring for girls aged four to sixteen.

128. Ibid., April 1929, 193.

129. Ibid., May 1930, 264.

130. "Minutes of the Board, 1912–16," June 1914, 113, UPOH, MHY.

131. "Minutes of the Board, 1899–1902," June 1902, 206, UPOH, MHY. See also "Minutes of the Board, 1920–25," February 1924, 182, UPOH, MHY.

132. "Minutes of the Board, 1925–30," October 1927, 110, UPOH, MHY.

133. "Board Minutes, 1900–1911," March 1911, 382, TRY, HSWP. Case #754 (563).

134. Askeland, "Informal Adoption, Apprentices, and Indentured Children," 8.

135. Holt, *The Orphan Trains*; Gordon, *The Great Arizona Orphan Abduction*.

136. Holt, "Adoption Reform, Orphan Trains, and Child-Saving."

137. William P. Hunker, "Letter to UPOH," 1882, UPOH, MHY; "Indenture from Poor Board to UPOH," 1883, UPOH, MHY.

138. "Constitution and By-Laws of the Home for Colored Children," TRY, HSWP.

139. William Wilson, letter in minute book, "Minutes of the Board, 1920–25," October 1923, 159, UPOH, MHY.

140. See for instance, UPOH Cases #162 (13/9), #433 (293), #881 (8); HCC Case #1476 (1005).

141. Askeland, "Informal Adoption, Apprentices, and Indentured Children," 8.

142. Tiffin, *In Whose Best Interest?*; J. Smith, "Child Care, Institutions, and the Best Interest of the Child."

143. Holt, "Adoption Reform, Orphan Trains, and Child-Saving"; Modell, *A Sealed and Secret Kinship*.

144. Hacsi, *Second Home*, 137.

145. P.L. 961, May 11, 1927; Strauss and Rome, *The Child and the Law in Pennsylvania*, 102; Liveright, *Poor Relief Administration in Pennsylvania*, 172.

146. Thurston, *The Dependent Child*, 237.

147. Liveright, *Poor Relief Administration in Pennsylvania*; Creagh, "Science, Social Work, and Bureaucracy," 34.

148. Oseroff, "Report of the Allegheny County Committee Public Charities Association," 8. See also Slingerland, *Child Welfare Work in Pennsylvania*.

149. $n=184/1,597$ children (HCC $n=813$, UPOH $n=593$ total dismissals).

150. "43rd Annual Report United Presbyterian Women's Association," 1921, 122, UPWANA, MHY.

151. 23 percent of those children placed out or adopted were full orphans ($n=39/172$); the rest had single parents, an incompetent parent, or parents whose status was simply not recorded.

152. William P. Hunker, "Letter to UPOH," 1883, UPOH, MHY.

153. "32nd Annual Report United Presbyterian Women's Association of North America," 1910, 92, UPWANA, MHY.

154. Michel, *Children's Interests/Mothers' Rights*, 45.

155. "Minutes of the Board, 1905–8," May 1906, 44, UPOH, MHY.

156. D—, "Letter to UPOH," UPOH, MHY.

157. Case #122.

158. Creagh, "Science, Social Work, and Bureaucracy," 36.

159. "Minutes of the Board, 1896–99," November 1896, 3, UPOH, MHY.

160. Zipf, "Reconstructing 'Free Woman'"; R. Scott, "The Battle over the Child."

161. Harris, "Charity Workers and Black Activism," in *In the Shadow of Slavery*, 167. My summary of her indenture figures: $n=347/1,257$ children indentured (pp. 163–65).

162. "Board Minutes, 1900–1911," March 1906, 167, TRY, HSWP.

163. "Requirements Governing Applicants for Children Placed in Private Homes," 1920+, TRY, HSWP.

164. UPOH Case #169 (18/10). See also "Minutes of the Board, 1905–8," May 1906, 44, UPOH, MHY.

165. Mrs. S. H—, "Letter to UPOH," 1888, UPOH, MHY.

166. "Minutes of the Board, 1896–99)," June–October 1897, 38, 42, 48, 54, UPOH, MHY.

167. Ibid., October 1899, 184.

168. "Board Minutes, 1900–1911," October 1901, 32, TRY, HSWP. Case #439 (299).

169. J—E. and M—A. R—, "Letter to UPOH," 1892, UPOH, MHY. Case #790 (95/47).

170. For another example, see "Minutes of the Board, 1902–5," September 1904, 135, UPOH, MHY.

171. Ibid., October 1905, 215.

172. "Minutes of the Board, 1905–8," May 1906, 44, UPOH, MHY. Case #781 (91/44).

173. "Board Minutes, 1900–1911," November 1904, 125, TRY, HSWP.

174. "Minutes of the Board, 1902–5," January, March 1904, 97, 102, UPOH, MHY.

175. "Minutes of the Board, 1899–1902," August–September 1902, 215, 17, UPOH, MHY. Case #868 (/95). For another example, see "Minutes of the Board, 1902–5," November 1904, 146, UPOH, MHY.

176. "Minutes of the Board, 1899–1902," November 1901–April 1902, 151, 62, 74, 90, UPOH, MHY.

177. "Board Minutes, 1921–1931," September 1923, 62, TRY, HSWP. Case #1183 (681).

178. "Minutes of the Board, 1912–1916," May–June 1915, 176, 79, UPOH, MHY; "Minutes of the Board, 1916–1920," June 1918–June 1920, 104, 84, 95, 255, UPOH, MHY. Case #890 (32, 64/194). For another example, see "Board Minutes, 1900–1911," November 1904, 125, TRY, HSWP.

179. "Minutes of the Board, 1905–8," November 1905, 5, UPOH, MHY. For other examples, see "Minutes of the Board, 1896–99," May 1897, 32, UPOH, MHY. "28th Annual Report of the United Presbyterian Women's Association of North America," 1906, 113, UPWANA, MHY.

180. "Minutes of the Board, 1899–1902," April 1902, 190, UPOH, MHY.

181. "Minutes of the Board, 1912–16," April 1916, 238, UPOH, MHY. Cases #886 (28/190), #887 (28/190), #888 (28/190).

182. "Minutes of the Board, 1896–99," September 1897–October 1898, 48, 54, 71, 77, 121, UPOH, MHY. Cases #872 (120/157), #873 (120/157).

183. "Minutes of the Board, 1905–8," August 1907, 144, UPOH, MHY.

184. Case #790 (95/47).

185. For examples of children running away from the HCC, see "Board Visitors' Reports to Board," May 1882, TRY, HSWP; "Board Minutes, 1900–1911," July 1906, August 1910, 186, 356, TRY, HSWP. At UPOH, see "Minutes of the Board,

1899–1902," April 1901, 105, UPOH, MHY; "Minutes of the Board, 1902–5," July 1903, 50, UPOH, MHY.

186. "Minutes of the Board, 1905–8," November 1906–August 1907, 88, 136, 42, UPOH, MHY. Case #886 (28/190). For another UPOH example, see "Minutes of the Board, 1912–16," May–June 1916, 247, 48, UPOH, MHY. Case #1109 (66/40/62).

187. "Board Minutes, 1900–1911," October 1906–January 1907, 195, TRY, HSWP. Case #582 (385). For examples of teens running away from indentures arranged through a New York orphanage, see Dulberger, *"Mother Donit fore the Best."*

188. "The United Presbyterian Women's Association of North America, 80 Years of Service," 1958, UPWANA, MHY.

189. HCC 1948–49 Annual Report, TRY, HSWP. For a similar orphanage transition, see Cmiel, *A Home of Another Kind.*

Chapter 4. Fathering Orphans

1. "Histories, 1878–1905," 96, UPOH, MHY. Additional family history from Geisler, "Getting to Know Grandma"; Agnes F. MachDonald, "Letter to manager," 1894, UPOH, MHY.

2. "14th Annual Report of the Women's United Presbyterian Association," 1892, 35, UPWANA, MHY.

3. 41 percent of UPOH children had solo fathers, plus 5 percent with both parents living, which makes the total 46 percent (see figure 2.4).

4. Kleinberg, *Widows and Orphans First,* 27, 179n49.

5. Lattimore, "Pittsburgh as a Foster Mother," 378–80. The 1907 survey found 156 children institutionalized because their mother had died versus 123 whose father had died.

6. Cmiel, *A Home of Another Kind,* 17; Kleinberg, *Widows and Orphans First,* 177n31.

7. Stearns, *Be a Man!;* Rotundo, *American Manhood.*

8. Cott, *The Bonds of Womanhood.*

9. Demos, "The Changing Faces of Fatherhood"; J. Pleck, "American Fathering in Historical Perspective."

10. Rotundo, "American Fatherhood"; Griswold, *Fatherhood in America.*

11. Lupton and Barclay, *Constructing Fatherhood;* Coltrane, *Family Man.*

12. Stearns, "Fatherhood in Historical Perspective"; Parke and Stearns, "Fathers and Child Rearing."

13. Kerber, "Separate Spheres, Female Worlds, Woman's Place"; Cott, "On Men's History and Women's History."

14. LaRossa, *The Modernization of Fatherhood;* Frank, *Life with Father;* Johansen, *Family Men.*

15. Frank, *Life with Father,* 5; Zelizer, *Pricing the Priceless Child.*

16. Case #924 (96/246).

17. Case #1033 (34/303).

18. Includes only children where the managers noted at least one parent was "living." $n=245$ with living mother; $n=230$ with living father.

19. "Minutes of the Board, 1920–25," March 1924, 187, UPOH, MHY.

20. "18th Annual Report United Presbyterian Women's Association," 1896, 31, UPWANA, MHY.

21. "Minutes of the Board, 1902–5," February 1903, 23, UPOH, MHY.

22. Overview of widowers from Kleinberg's analysis of the census data from three cities (Pittsburgh, Baltimore, and Fall River, Mass.) in 1880, 1900, and 1920. Kleinberg, *Widows and Orphans First,* 25–26.

23. 1910 and 1920 census records, Allegheny County, Pennsylvania; Geisler, "Getting to Know Grandma."

24. Cases #1067 (106/16), #1068 (106/16).

25. Cases #836 (64/123), #837 (64/123), #838 (64/123), #839 (64/123), #840 (64/123).

26. Average=496 days; $n=162$. See also table 2.2.

27. "14th Annual Report of the Women's United Presbyterian Association," 28, UPWANA, MHY (emphasis in original).

28. Ella D. Hamilton, "Letter to UPOH," 1882, UPOH, MHY.

29. Cases #844 (76/133), #845 (76/133).

30. Dulberger, *"Mother Donit fore the Best."*

31. Cases #827 (48/110), #828 (48/110), #829 (48/110).

32. W—T—, "Letter to UPOH," 1892, UPOH, MHY.

33. Ibid.

34. "Minutes of the Board, 1899–1902," May 1900, 37, UPOH, MHY; "Minutes of the Board, 1925–30," July 1930, 277, UPOH, MHY.

35. "Minutes of the Board, 1916–1920," March 1919, 158, UPOH, MHY.

36. $n=169$ widows, 185 widowers. See table 4.4.

37. "Minutes of the Board, 1899–1902," December 1901, 162, UPOH, MHY. Cases #925 (100/249), #926 (100/249), #927 (100/249).

38. "Minutes of the Board, 1902–5," June 1904, 119, UPOH, MHY.

39. "Minutes of the Board, 1916–1920," June 1917, 42, UPOH, MHY.

40. For an analysis of widows' wage strategies in Pittsburgh, see Kleinberg, *Widows and Orphans First.*

41. Most solo parents had lost a spouse to death, but the category also includes spouses who had deserted, divorced, separated, or were incompetent.

42. "Minutes of the Board, 1916–1920," April–May 1917, 28, 33, UPOH, MHY. Case #1136 (138, 120/53/60).

43. Cases #145, #146.

44. Case #1111 (92/45). A few months later, the managers dismissed Coulter's two other children when he failed to pay their board. For another example, see Case #1125 (138, 122/53/60).

45. $n=24/215$ UPOH children placed by fathers vs. $n=15/241$ placed by mothers.

46. Kleinberg, *Widows and Orphans First.*

47. Elman and London, "Sociohistorical and Demographic Perspectives on Remarriage in 1910," 202.

48. Case #1019 (5/285).

49. Kleinberg examined the 1885–86 and 1900 marriage dockets (*Shadow of the Mills*, 259).

50. Michel, *Children's Interests/Mothers' Rights*, 325n143; Gordon, *Pitied But Not Entitled*, 19.

51. Kleinberg, *Widows and Orphans First*, 23.

52. $n=36/215$ UPOH widowers' children returned to their fathers after a remarriage vs. $n=6/162$ widow's children returned to their mothers after a remarriage.

53. $n=36/150$ (24 percent) UPOH widowers' children who returned to their fathers for any reason.

54. $n=13$ UPOH fathers who remarried (for whom there is complete data). The median was twenty-four months; the shortest span was six months; the longest was sixty months (or five years). There was not enough comparable data to analyze UPOH widows.

55. The classic is the "Moynihan Report," which reflected the work of E. Franklin Frazier, who interpreted the black family as the broken legacy of slavery: Moynihan, "The Negro Family."

56. Genovese, *Roll, Jordon, Roll*; Blassingame, *The Slave Community*; Gutman, *The Black Family in Slavery and Freedom*.

57. White, *Ar'nt' I a Woman?*; J. Jones, *Labor of Love, Labor of Sorrow*; Stevenson, *Life in Black and White*.

58. E. Pleck, *Black Migration and Poverty*.

59. Schwalm, *A Hard Fight for We*; Morgan, *Laboring Women*.

60. Edwards, *Gendered Strife and Confusion*.

61. Willie and Reddick, *A New Look at Black Families*; Hamer, *What It Means to Be Daddy*.

62. Jewell, *Survival of the African American Family*.

63. Tolnay, *The Bottom Rung*; E. Pleck, *Black Migration and Poverty*.

64. Roberts, "The Absent Black Father"; Connor and White, "Fatherhood in Contemporary Black America."

65. Cases #1 (1), #2 (2), #3 (3), #4 (4). Biographical details from the 1880 U.S. Census of Allegheny City: this was the only name match in the city, though it is possible, of course, that Highland was living elsewhere. Nonetheless, these biographical details would have been quite typical for a man using the HCC at this time.

66. "Board Minutes, 1900–1911," December 1902, 63, TRY, HSWP. Cases #634 (441), #635 (442), #636 (443), #637 (444), #638 (445), #683 (490).

67. Ibid., March 1903, 70.

68. Cases #1202 (709), #1203 (710).

69. Cases #1476 (1005), #1477 (1006). See also Cases #1530 (1047), #1564 (1081).

70. Sudarkasa, "African American Female-Headed Households," 174.

71. Gutman, *The Black Family in Slavery and Freedom;* Franklin, "African American Families," 5.

72. There may even have been a "southern advantage" for migrants who tended to maintain family and marital stability; see Tolnay, "The Great Migration and Changes to the Northern Black Family."

73. Cases #1543 (1060), #1544 (1061), #1545 (1062), #1547 (1064). For similar examples, see Cases #21 (21), #22 (22), and #44 (44); also, see "Board Minutes, 1900–1911," August 1900, TRY, HSWP.

74. "Board Minutes, 1900–1911," February 1903, 67, TRY, HSWP.

75. *n*=313/1,007 children (31 percent).

76. Ellen C. Potter, M.D., "Letter from Dept. of Welfare to Mrs. Robert Monroe," 1924, TRY, HSWP.

77. Schwalm, *A Hard Fight for We;* Hine, "Black Migration to the Urban Midwest."

78. Shaw, *What a Woman Ought to Be and to Do;* Clark-Lewis, *Living In, Living Out.*

79. Cases #1601 (1119), #1602 (1120). For other examples of fathers who moved while their children were in the orphanage, see Cases #757 (566), #936 (574), #937 (575).

80. "Board Minutes, 1900–1911," February 1903, 67, TRY, HSWP.

81. "Board Minutes, 1921–1931," May 1924, 83, TRY, HSWP. Cases #1313 (922), #1314 (923), #1315 (924).

82. "Board Visitors' Reports to Board, 1881–7," November 1881, TRY, HSWP.

83. "Board Minutes, 1900–1911," August 1910, 356, TRY, HSWP. See same page for another example of parent requesting help with transportation.

84. Lillian Marshall Brown, "Twenty Fifth Annual Report," 1906, TRY, HSWP.

85. "Board Minutes, 1900–1911," January 1903, 65, TRY, HSWP. Case #622 (429). For another example, see "Board Visitors' Reports to Board," July 1883, TRY, HSWP.

86. "Board Minutes, 1900–1911," September–October 1902, 56, TRY, HSWP. Case #429 (289).

87. Zipf, "Reconstructing 'Free Woman'"; R. Scott, "The Battle over the Child."

88. Cases #1454 (983), #1455 (984), #1456 (985).

89. Elman and London, "Sociohistorical and Demographic Perspectives on Remarriage in 1910," 210.

90. Cases #665 (472), #666 (473), #667 (474).

91. Geisler, "Getting to Know Grandma," July 22, 2006.

CHAPTER 5. REFORMING ORPHANS

1. "History Termon Avenue Home for Children," 1931+, TRY, HSWP; "Termon Ave. Home for Colored Children Serving a Great Need," *Pittsburgh Courier,* January 18, 1941.

2. General Poor Relief Act, 111, June 13, 1883.

3. Liveright, *Poor Relief Administration in Pennsylvania,* 172.

4. Slingerland, *Child Welfare Work in Pennsylvania,* 45; Pennsylvania Department of Welfare, "History of Child Care in Pennsylvania," 1.

5. Liveright, Poor Relief Administration in Pennsylvania, 172.

6. Rafter, *Partial Justice;* Getis, *The Juvenile Court and the Progressives;* Tiffin, *In Whose Best Interest?*

7. Kunzel, *Fallen Women, Problem Girls;* Ladd-Taylor, *Mother-Work.*

8. Mitchell, Albert, and Glasco, *From Colored Orphans to Youth Development,* 20.

9. Muncy, *Creating a Female Dominion in American Reform.* Specifically in child welfare reform, see Lindenmeyer, *"A Right to Childhood";* Costin, *Two Sisters for Social Justice.*

10. Slingerland, *Child Placing in Families,* 36.

11. Butler, *Women and the Trades;* Lattimore, "Pittsburgh as a Foster Mother"; Byington, *Homestead;* Eastman, *Work-Accidents and the Law.* For historical analysis of the survey, see Greenwald and Anderson, *Pittsburgh Surveyed.*

12. Slingerland, *Child Welfare Work in Pennsylvania.*

13. On the topic of African American children, for instance, see Morrison, "Study of One Hundred Forty-One Dependent Negro Children"; Covington, "Occupational Choices in Relation to Economic Opportunities of Negro Youth in Pittsburgh"; Yarbrough, "The Educational Status of Negro Public School Children."

14. Oseroff, "Report of the Allegheny County Committee Public Charities Association."

15. At the HCC, see "Board Minutes, 1900–1911," December 1908, March and May 1909, June 1910, TRY, HSWP; and "Board Minutes, 1921–1931," October 1922, and August 1927, TRY, HSWP. At UPOH, see "Minutes of the Board, 1916–1920," January 1918, UPOH, MHY.

16. For a discussion of the HCC's fundraising and interaction with the Welfare Fund, see chapter 6.

17. P.L. 90, April 24, 1869. Liveright, *Poor Relief Administration in Pennsylvania.*

18. "Board Visitors' Reports to Board, 1881–87," November 1887, 124, TRY, HSWP.

19. "Minutes of the Board, 1920–25," March 1924, 189, UPOH, MHY.

20. Strauss and Rome, *The Child and the Law in Pennsylvania;* Liveright, *Poor Relief Administration in Pennsylvania.*

21. Moss, "Ellen C. Potter, M.D., F.A.C.P.," 355. For Potter's writing, see especially *Annals of the American Academy of Political and Social Science* and the *Journal of Criminal Law and Criminology.*

22. Ellen C. Potter, M.D., "Letter to Board from State Secretary of Welfare," 1923, TRY, HSWP.

23. Ellen C. Potter, M.D., "Letter from Dept. of Welfare to Mrs. Robert Monroe," 1924, TRY, HSWP

24. "Minutes of the Board, 1920–25," November 1924, 99, UPOH, MHY.

25. "Board Minutes, 1900–1911," February 1904, 101, TRY, HSWP.

26. "Board Minutes, 1900–1911," July 1902, 50, TRY, HSWP.

27. "Board Minutes, 1921–31," November 1923, 66, TRY, HSWP.

28. "Board Minutes, 1921–31," April 1924, 79, TRY, HSWP.

29. Mrs. George W. Ligo, "Letter from Board to Pittsburgh Child Welfare Study," 1930, TRY, HSWP.

30. "Minutes of the Board, 1920–25," May 1925, 246, UPOH, MHY.

31. "Minutes of the Board, 1925–30," May 1927, 93, UPOH, MHY.

32. "Minutes of the Board, 1920–25," May 1922, 90, UPOH, MHY.

33. "Board Minutes, 1900–1911," January 1904, 98, TRY, HSWP.

34. J. M. Baldy, "Letter to Board from State Commissioner of Public Welfare," 1922, TRY, HSWP.

35. "Board Minutes, 1921–31," March–April 1924, 75, TRY, HSWP.

36. Cavalla, *Muscles and Morals;* Riess, *City Games.*

37. On playgrounds at the HCC, see "Board Minutes, 1900–1911," July 1909, May 1910, 303, 38, TRY, HSWP; "Board Minutes, 1921–31," May 1929, 178, TRY, HSWP. At UPOH, see "Minutes of the Board, 1908–12," May 1911, 197, UPOH, MHY; "Minutes of the Board, 1912–16," October 1914, 130, UPOH, MHY.

38. Oseroff, "Report of the Allegheny County Committee Public Charities Association," 7.

39. Slingerland, *Child Welfare Work in Pennsylvania,* 134.

40. Ibid., 20–21.

41. Ibid., 139.

42. Baldy, "Letter to Board from State Commissioner of Public Welfare," 1922, TRY, HSWP.

43. Potter, "Letter to Board from State Secretary of Welfare," 1923, TRY, HSWP.

44. "Board Minutes, 1921–31," October 1924, 97, TRY, HSWP.

45. Ibid., December 1928, 169.

46. Cases #1592 (1110), #1593 (1111).

47. "Board Minutes, 1921–31," October 1924, 97, TRY, HSWP. Case #1525 (1042).

48. Oseroff, "Report of the Allegheny County Committee Public Charities Association," 8.

49. Slingerland, *Child Welfare Work in Pennsylvania,* 128.

50. Analysis of U.S. Census report, 1923, Children under Institutional Care, table 2, pp. 18–19, in Thurston, *The Dependent Child,* 237.

51. Dunham and Tyson, "Child Care in Pittsburgh," 22.

52. Ligo, "Letter from Board to Pittsburgh Child Welfare Study," 1930, TRY, HSWP.

53. "20th Annual Report United Presbyterian Women's Association," 1898, 18, UPWANA, MHY.

54. "24th Annual Report United Presbyterian Women's Association," 1902, 45, UPWANA, MHY.

55. "26th Annual Report United Presbyterian Women's Association," 1904, 105, UPWANA, MHY. Starting that year, H. J. Heinz served on the UPWANA advisory board.

56. W. H. Vincent, "Sixty Years of Service, 1878–1938," 1938, UPWANA, MHY.

57. A few historians have examined the top administrator, whether superintendent or matron, in some depth. Notably, Freedman, *Maternal Justice*; Dulberger, *"Mother Donit fore the Best."*

58. Hacsi, *Second Home,* 87–88.

59. Rose found day nursery staff ratios in Philadelphia of 4/100 and 3/50. Rose, *A Mother's Job,* 56.

60. Child to staff ratios based on 1880, 1900, 1910, 1920, and 1930 census data.

61. Slingerland, *Child Welfare Work in Pennsylvania,* 242–43.

62. "Board Minutes, 1900–1911," October 1902, 58, TRY, HSWP.

63. Hacsi, *Second Home,* 87. For the history of the professionalization of social work, see Kunzel, *Fallen Women, Problem Girls.* For social work in Pittsburgh, see Lobes, "'Hearts All Aflame.'"

64. Kleinberg, *Widows and Orphans First.*

65. Rose, *A Mother's Job,* 59.

66. Staff biographies compiled from census records, admissions logs, children's histories, and meeting minutes. Quotation noted in "Histories," 1878–1905, UPOH, MHY; Rose Case #'s 95, 96, 97; Reid Case #'s 98, 99, 100.

67. "Board Minutes, 1900–1911," January 1908, 242, TRY, HSWP.

68. "Minutes of the Board, 1896–99," September 1898, 113, UPOH, MHY.

69. "Board Minutes, 1921–1931," August 1924, 92, TRY, HSWP.

70. T. Hunter, *To 'Joy My Freedom,* 28–29, 58–61; On the strategy of quitting, also see Clark-Lewis, *Living In, Living Out.*

71. "Minutes of the Board, 1896–99," November 1896–May 1897, UPOH, MHY.

72. "19th Annual Report United Presbyterian Women's Association," 1897, 50, UPWANA, MHY.

73. "Board Visitors' Reports to Board," March 1885, 99, TRY, HSWP.

74. "24th Annual Report United Presbyterian Women's Association," 45, UP-WANA, MHY.

75. At the HCC, seven out of fifteen matrons remained a year or less, and at UPOH, six out of thirteen during the period of this study.

76. "Board Minutes, 1900–1911," October 1902, 58, TRY, HSWP.

77. "Minutes of the Board, 1902–5," March 1903, 32, UPOH, MHY.

78. "Board Minutes, 1900–1911," March and April 1907, 211, TRY, HSWP.

79. Ibid., July 1908, 265.

80. "Minutes of the Board, 1905–8," February 1907, 106–12, UPOH, MHY.

81. UPOH Rules, loose sheet in minute book, "Minutes of the Board, 1925–30," UPOH, MHY.

82. "Board Minutes, 1921–31," January 1924, TRY, HSWP.

83. Slingerland, *Child Welfare Work in Pennsylvania,* 243.

84. "Board Minutes, 1900–1911," February, March 1903, 67, TRY, HSWP.

85. Ibid., July 1903, 84.

86. "Minutes of the Board, 1905–8," February 1907, 106–12, UPOH, MHY.

87. "Board Minutes, 1921–31," October 1929, TRY, HSWP.

88. "Minutes of the Board, 1902–5," May 1905, 189, UPOH, MHY.

89. "Minutes of the Board, 1896–99," May 1897–November 1898, UPOH, MHY.

90. "Minutes of the Board, '905–8," February 1907, 106–12, UPOH, MHY.

91. T. Hunter, *To 'Joy My Freedom*, 61, 225–27.

92. "Board Minutes, 1921–31," March–November 1924, 75–94, TRY, HSWP.

93. Ibid., September–October 1924, 94.

94. All quotes from letters of November 22 and 26, and December 15, 1897. A. M. Gebhart, "Letter to UPOH," 1897, UPOH, MHY.

95. Stanley, "The Labor Question and the Sale of Self," in *From Bondage to Contract*; Roediger, *The Wages of Whiteness*.

96. "Board Minutes, 1900–1911," February 1910, TRY, HSWP.

97. "Minutes of the Board, 1916–20," April 1919, 169, UPOH, MHY.

98. "Minutes of the Board, 1905–8," February 1907, 106–12, UPOH, MHY.

99. "Board Minutes, 1900–1911," July 1910, 351, TRY, HSWP.

100. Oseroff, "Report of the Allegheny County Committee Public Charities Association," 40.

101. "Report to the State Board of Public Charities," 1916, TRY, HSWP.

102. "Board Minutes, 1900–1911," March 1907, 211, TRY, HSWP.

103. On the HCC staff transition after the mid-twentieth century, see Mitchell, Albert, and Glasco, *From Colored Orphans to Youth Development*. In the postwar period, see Fousekis, "Fighting for Our Children."

104. "26th Annual Report United Presbyterian Women's Association," UPWANA, MHY.

105. "Board Minutes, 1921–31," December 1929, 197, TRY, HSWP.

106. Ibid., typed reports in back of minute book.

107. "Board Minutes, 1900–1911," August 1908, 269, TRY, HSWP.

108. In 1948 HCC hired Ruth M. Bonsteel as director. With a background in settlement house work, she brought in caseworkers, further professionalizing the staff. For more on later staff changes at the HCC, see Mitchell, Albert, and Glasco, *From Colored Orphans to Youth Development*.

109. Lillian Marshall Brown, "Twenty Fifth Annual Report," 1906, TRY, HSWP.

Chapter 6. Segregating Orphans

1. Lillian Marshall Brown, "Twenty Fifth Annual Report," 1906, TRY, HSWP. Cases #1 (1), 2 (2), 3 (3), 4 (4).

2. The HCC admission book records her age as seven, then someone has written in above "6 or 7." Examples of those using the much younger age include "Fiftieth Anniversary of the Home for Colored Children N.S. Pittsburgh, PA," 1931, TRY,

HSWP, and "Termon Ave. Home for Colored Children Serving a Great Need," *Pittsburgh Courier*, January 18, 1941.

3. "Brief History and Interim Report of the Termon Avenue Home for Children," 1964, TRY, HSWP.

4. The Sixty-Day Law was passed in 1883, while the HCC was founded in 1880 (General Poor Relief Act, 111, [June 13]). For HCC founding stories, see "Fiftieth Anniversary of the Home for Colored Children N.S. Pittsburgh, PA.," "History Termon Avenue Home for Children," 1931+, and "Termon Ave. Home for Colored Children Serving a Great Need," TRY, HSWP. One source names the poorhouse as the "Almshouse of Allegheny," which was no doubt the Allegheny City Home. Neighboring Pittsburgh had its own poorhouse, the City Home, and the county ran the Allegheny County Home, also known as Woodville.

5. "Fiftieth Anniversary of the Home for Colored Children N.S. Pittsburgh, PA.," "Termon Ave. Home for Colored Children Serving a Great Need," TRY, HSWP.

6. Dyer, "Black History Month."

7. "Fiftieth Anniversary of the Home for Colored Children N.S. Pittsburgh, PA," TRY, HSWP.

8. Three Rivers Youth, "History."

9. Julia F. Blair, "Third Annual Report of Home for Colored Children," 1884, TRY, HSWP.

10. Trotter, *River Jordan*, 66, 97; Weber, "Residential and Occupational Patterns of Ethnic Minorities," 319; Gottlieb, *Making Their Own Way*, 65.

11. Faulkner, *Women's Radical Reconstruction*.

12. Blair, "Third Annual Report of Home for Colored Children," TRY, HSWP.

13. Harris, "Charity Workers and Black Activism," in *In the Shadow of Slavery*, 168.

14. Jacobson, *Whiteness of a Different Color*.

15. "Board Minutes, 1900–1911," July 1902, 50, TRY, HSWP.

16. Case #558 (361).

17. "Board Minutes, 1921–31," September 1923, TRY, HSWP. Cases #1202 (709), #1203 (710).

18. Haskell Indian National University, "School History."

19. Gordon, *The Great Arizona Orphan Abduction*.

20. Williams, *Self-taught*; Anderson, *The Education of Blacks in the South*.

21. "Board Visitors' Reports to Board, 1881–87," TRY, HSWP.

22. Anne S. Phillips, "Thirtieth Annual Report," 1911, TRY, HSWP.

23. B. Hunter, "The Public Education of Blacks in the City of Pittsburgh," 21; Gutkind, "Desegregation of Pittsburgh Public Schools."

24. Hacsi, "Education and Building Character," in *Second Home*; Cmiel, *A Home of Another Kind*.

25. "Board Visitors' Reports to Board," April 26–May 5, 1881, TRY, HSWP.

26. Ibid., February 15, 1882.

27. Lillian Marshall Brown, "Twenty Sixth Annual Report," 1907, TRY, HSWP.

28. Ellen C. Potter, M.D., "Letter from Dept. of Welfare to Mrs. Robert Monroe," 1924, TRY, HSWP.

29. "Constitution and By-Laws of the Home for Colored Children," 1881, TRY, HSWP.

30. "Fiftieth Anniversary of the Home for Colored Children N.S. Pittsburgh, PA," TRY, HSWP.

31. Anderson, *The Education of Blacks in the South,* 80.

32. Ibid., 92.

33. Geneva College, "Mission Statement." Case #955 (592).

34. Lincoln University, "About Lincoln University."

35. "Board Minutes, 1900–1911," April 5, 1904, 105, TRY, HSWP. Case #275 (134).

36. Ibid., December 4, 1900. Case #433 (293).

37. Ibid., August 6, 1901. Case #462 (322).

38. Ibid., February 1910. Case #693 (500).

39. WCA, "Twenty-Third Annual Report," Annual Reports, HSWP.

40. Julia F. Blair, "Twenty Second Annual Report," 1903, TRY, HSWP; "Board Minutes, 1900–1911," TRY, HSWP.

41. "Board Minutes, 1900–1911," December 1904, 127, TRY, HSWP.

42. Ibid., June 1908.

43. Ibid., December 4, 1900; Blair, "Twenty Second Annual Report," TRY, HSWP.

44. For this debate at another black orphanage, see Harris, "Charity Workers and Black Activism," in *In the Shadow of Slavery.* See also Denton, *Booker T. Washington and the Adult Education Movement*; Provenzo, *Du Bois on Education.*

45. "Board Minutes, 1900–1911," February 5, 1901, TRY, HSWP.

46. Presentation to the Parents' National Educational Union (PNEU), England, reprinted in Russell, "On Some Aspects of Slojd."

47. Salomon, *The Theory of Educational Sloyd,* 6–7.

48. J. M. Baldy, "Letter to Board from State Commissioner of Public Welfare," 1922, TRY, HSWP.

49. "History Termon Avenue Home for Children," TRY, HSWP.

50. "Board Minutes, 1921–1931," August and September, 1921, TRY, HSWP.

51. Biographies compiled from census records (1870, 1880, 1900, 1910, 1920, and 1930) as well as meeting minutes, newspaper clippings, and other archival materials.

52. See for instance Grossman, *Land of Hope.*

53. Bodnar, Simon, and Weber, *Lives of Their Own,* 178.

54. Ibid., 177.

55. Gottlieb, *Making Their Own Way;* Trotter, "Reflections on the Great Migration to Western Pennsylvania."

56. Mitchell, Albert, and Glasco, *From Colored Orphans to Youth Development,* 14, 20.

57. See ibid., 26, for the HCC board constitution of the mid- to late twentieth century.

58. For examples of black-managed institutions outside of Pittsburgh, see Byars, "Lexington's Colored Orphan Industrial Home"; Bartlett and McClellan, "The Final Ministry of Amanda Berry Smith."

59. Belfour, "Charles Avery, Early Pittsburgh Philanthropist"; Carnegie Library of Pittsburgh, "North Side: Charles Avery." For examples of white-managed institutions outside of Pittsburgh, see Mabee, "Charity in Travail"; Harris, "Charity Workers and Black Activism," in *In the Shadow of Slavery*; Jenkins, "Almira S. Steele and the Steele Home for Needy Children."

60. In 1969 the state demolished the three-story red brick building that housed Avery College to build Interstate 279 North. On Avery College as a child care institution, see Slingerland, *Child Welfare Work in Pennsylvania*, 190.

61. Emily Hunnings, "Treasurer's Book Colored Orphan Asylum, 1880–83," TRY, HSWP.

62. "Board Minutes, 1900–1911," February 1905, 132, TRY, HSWP.

63. Tucker's article was later reprinted in the *Pittsburgh Survey*. For an analysis, see Glasco, "Optimism, Dilemmas, and Progress," 211.

64. "Baptist and Methodist Ministers Laud Courier's Unemployment Program," *Pittsburgh Courier*, December 1, 1923.

65. O'Donnell, "The Care of Dependent African-American Children in Chicago."

66. Weisenfeld, *African American Women and Christian Activism*, 13.

67. Ibid., 35–36.

68. Ibid., 159.

69. "Board Minutes, 1921–1931," August 1921, 9, TRY, HSWP.

70. Weisenfeld, *African American Women and Christian Activism*, 33.

71. On black women in the national movement, see ibid.; see also A. Jones, "Struggle among Saints."

72. That year, the WCA gave the HCC $500 "for the special account"; see "Board Minutes, 1921–1931," May/June 1921, 3, TRY, HSWP.

73. Spratt, "To Be Separate or One"; Sims, *The Natural History of a Social Institution*

74. Young Women's Christian Association, "YWCA Pittsburgh, 1875–1950: A Story of Pittsburgh as Recorded by the Young Women's Christian Association," 1950, Appendix, Young Women's Christian Association of Greater Pittsburgh Records, 1875–1988, HSWP.

75. "Board Visitors' Reports to Board," March 1882, TRY, HSWP.

76. Harris, "Charity Workers and Black Activism," in *In the Shadow of Slavery*.

77. October 1924 letter from Mrs. Hall quoted in "Board Minutes, 1921–1931," 97, TRY, HSWP.

78. "Managers and Funding," in Hacsi, *Second Home*.

79. Wilbur F. Maxwell, "Letter to Board from the Welfare Fund of Pittsburgh," 1930, TRY, HSWP; United Way of Allegheny County, "Timeline."

80. "Board Minutes, 19210193," August 1929, TRY, HSWP.

81. Maxwell, "Letter to Board from the Welfare Fund of Pittsburgh," TRY, HSWP.

82. 451 out of 614 children admitted from 1901 to 1929, or 73 percent, had records containing information on parents' place of birth. See appendix C.

83. Gottlieb, *Making Their Own Way*, 66.

84. "Board Minutes, 1921–1931," November 1924, 99, TRY, HSWP.

85. Potter, "Letter from Dept. of Welfare to Mrs. Robert Monroe," TRY, HSWP.

86. Typed summary of Tyson's report included in "Board Minutes, 1921–1931," February 1931, TRY, HSWP.

87. "Constitution and By-Laws of the Home for Colored Children," TRY, HSWP.

88. "Board Minutes, 1921–1931," November 1929, 195, TRY, HSWP.

89. Ibid., December 1929, 201.

90. Mrs. George W. Ligo, "Letter from Board to Pittsburgh Child Welfare Study," 1930, TRY, HSWP.

91. "Children's Home 'Cruelties' Exposed," *Pittsburgh Courier*, June 3, 1933.

92. "Termon Ave. Home for Colored Children Serving a Great Need," TRY, HSWP.

93. Dr. Henry M. Garrett, "Letter to Board from Dr. Garrett," 1919, TRY, HSWP.

94. "Board Minutes, 1921–1931," February 1926, 199, TRY, HSWP.

95. Glasco, "Taking Care of Business."

96. Founded in 1907, the *Pittsburgh Courier* gained a national readership after 1910; see Nelson, "Publisher Robert Lee Vann." The Pittsburgh city edition of the paper was used for this analysis, to ascertain levels of local support.

97. Blair, "Twenty Second Annual Report." The four churches were Bethel (Wylie Ave.) AME, the Warren ME, the John Wesley AMEY, and Grace Presbyterian Church.

98. Ellen C. Potter, M.D., "Letter to Board from State Secretary of Welfare," 1923, TRY, HSWP.

99. "Board Minutes, 1921–1931," November 1924, 99, TRY, HSWP.

100. Ibid.

101. Ibid., January 1923, 43.

102. Ibid., January 1924, 70.

103. Ibid., September 1921, 11.

104. Ibid., February 1923, 45.

105. Mitchell, Albert, and Glasco, *From Colored Orphans to Youth Development*.

106. "Board Minutes, 192–1931," April 1930, TRY, HSWP. While it is tempting to read into the frequent misspelling of the Glasco's name, the recording secretaries of both institutions often misspelled other board members' names—black and white.

107. Ibid., December 1929, 197.

108. Dessa M. James, "1922 Annual Report," 1922, TRY, HSWP.

109. Jeannette C. Kennedy, "Letter to State Board of Public Charities from Home," 1917, TRY, HSWP; Robert M. McWade, "Letter to Board from Aetna Insurance," 1918, TRY, HSWP.

110. Letter from Elizabeth T. Shipley in "Board Minutes, 1921–1931," June 1931, TRY, HSWP.

111. Blair, "Twenty Second Annual Report," TRY, HSWP.

112. Slingerland, *Child Welfare Work in Pennsylvania.*

113. "Coming Events," *Pittsburgh Courier,* June 14, 1912.

114. Oseroff, "Report of the Allegheny County Committee Public Charities Association," 42.

115. Ibid., 46.

116. Based on an exhaustive search of the paper from 1911 to 1929 and a survey of articles from the 1930s and '40s.

117. "Community Mourns Loss of Prominent Citizen," *Pittsburgh Courier,* August 25, 1928.

118. "Baptist and Methodist Ministers Laud Courier's Unemployment Program," *Pittsburgh Courier,* December 1, 1923.

119. "Report on Conference of Homes for Colored Children," 1927, TRY, HSWP.

120. "Board Minutes, 1921–1931," June 1928, 156, TRY, HSWP.

121. Ibid., May 1929, 178.

122. Ibid., June 1929, 180.

123. Ibid., summary of report in February 1931 minutes.

124. Cases #618 (425), #619 (426), #620 (427).

125. "Board Minutes, 1900–1911," July–August, 1903, 84, TRY, HSWP.

Conclusion. Contesting Orphans

1. This is Hacsi's term for orphanages; Hacsi, *Second Home.*

2. "Fiftieth Anniversary of the Home for Colored Children N.S. Pittsburgh, PA," 1931, TRY, HSWP.

3. The association eventually built Columbia Hospital in Wilkinsburg, just outside city limits. "19th Annual Report United Presbyterian Women's Association," 1897, UPWANA, MHY.

4. Folbre and Bittman, *Family Time;* Michel and Mahon, *Child Care Policy at the Crossroads.*

5. There is a growing body of literature on the race, class, and gender implications of U.S. social welfare development; one classic is Gordon, *Pitied But Not Entitled.*

6. Stoltzfus, *Citizen, Mother, Worker,* 9.

7. Ladd-Taylor, *Mother-Work.*

8. Gordon, *Pitied But Not Entitled.*

9. Cohen, *Championing Child Care;* Stoltzfus, *Citizen, Mother, Worker,* 10. Only New York kept its program going until 1948, and California eventually rolled its centers into a statewide program.

10. Rose, *A Mother's Job,* 181.

11. Beatty, *Preschool Education in America.*

12. Rose, *A Mother's Job,* 125.

13. Levy and Michel, "More Can Be Less," 242.

14. Polakow, *Who Cares for Our Children?* 8.

15. Cohen, *Championing Child Care,* 22–53.

16. Figures for 2004. Polakow, *Who Cares for Our Children?* 9.

17. These include the Convention on the Elimination of All Forms of Discrimination against Women (CEDAW), adopted in 1979 by the United Nations, ratified by 169 countries, and called the "international bill of rights for women"; the Convention of the Rights of the Child (CRC), ratified by 191 countries; and the International Covenant on Economic, Social, and Cultural Rights (ICESCR), ratified by 145 countries. Polakow, *Who Cares for Our Children?* 162–63.

18. Ibid., 163.

19. Cohen, *Championing Child Care*, 91–134.

20. Gill, Dembosky, and Caulkins, *A "Noble Bet" in Early Care and Education.*

21. For an analysis of this transition at a similar institution during the twentieth century, see Cmiel, *A Home of Another Kind.*

22. U.S. Bureau of the Census, "Income, Poverty, and Health Insurance Coverage."

23. Polakow, *Who Cares for Our Children?* 10–11.

24. Ibid., 169–74.

25. Laughlin, *Who's Minding the Kids?*

26. Folbre and Bittman, *Family Time.*

BIBLIOGRAPHY

Archival Collections

Library and Archives Division, Historical Society of Western Pennsylvania (HSWP), Senator John Heinz History Center: Pittsburgh, Pennsylvania

- Home for Colored Children (HCC) records, Three Rivers Youth (TRY) collection
- Mary Hogg Brunot records, Papers of the Hogg Family, 1785–1914, collection
- Women's Christian Association (WCA) annual reports (1877–1879), Annual Reports collection
- YWCA records, Young Women's Christian Association of Greater Pittsburgh Records, 1875–1988 collection

Mars Home for Youth (MHY): Mars, Pennsylvania

- Allegheny Day Nursery collection
- United Presbyterian Orphan's Home (UPOH) collection
- United Presbyterian Women's Association of North America (UPWANA) collection

Carnegie Library of Pittsburgh (CLP): Pittsburgh, Pennsylvania

- Biography Card Catalog, reference index: Pennsylvania Room
- Charles Avery records, digital collection (www.clpgh.org/exhibit .neighborhoods/northside/nor_n110.html)
- "Historic Women of Pennsylvania and Prominent Women of Contemporary Pittsburgh," 1932–1942, reference index: Pennsylvania Room
- 1904 Social Register of Pittsburgh: Pennsylvania Room
- Orphanage Directory for Allegheny County, digital collection (http://www.clpgh .org./locations/pennsylvania/orphanages/dir.html)
- Women's Christian Association (WCA) annual reports (1875–1876) in Institutional Records collection: Pennsylvania Room
- YWCA files in Institutional Records collection: Pennsylvania Room

Historic Pittsburgh digital library (digital.library.pitt.edu/pittsburgh)

- G. M. Hopkins Company Maps, Maps collection

Ancestry.com (wwww.ancestry.com)

- Mary S. Fulton records, Shafer Family collection
- United States Census records (1850–1930), U.S. Census collection

Published Primary Sources

Butler, Elizabeth Beardlsey. *Women and the Trades, Pittsburgh, 1907–1908.* 6 vols. Vol. 1, *Pittsburgh Survey.* New York: Russell Sage Foundation, 1909.

Byington, Margaret F. *Homestead: The Households of a Mill Town.* 6 vols. Vol. 2, *Pittsburgh Survey.* New York: Russell Sage Foundation, 1910.

Children's Commission of Pennsylvania. *The Legal Foundations of the Jurisdiction, Powers, Organization and Procedure of the Courts of the Pennsylvania in Their Handling of Cases of Juvenile Offenders and of Dependent and Neglected Children.* Philadelphia: Children's Commission of Pennsylvania, 1926.

Covington, Floyd C. "Occupational Choices in Relation to Economic Opportunities of Negro Youth in Pittsburgh." Master's thesis, University of Pittsburgh, 1928.

Dinwiddie, Emily Wayland, and F. Elisabeth Crowell. "The Housing of Pittsburgh's Workers." In *The Pittsburgh District: The Civic Frontage,* edited by Paul Underwood Kellog, 87–123. New York: Russell Sage Foundation, 1914.

Dunham, Arthur, and Helen Glenn Tyson. "Child Care in Pittsburgh: The Pittsburgh Child Welfare Study, Report No. 1—Summary." Pittsburgh: Pittsburgh Federation of Social Agencies, 1930.

Eastman, Crystal. *Work-Accidents and the Law.* 6 vols. Vol. 3, *Pittsburgh Survey.* New York: Russell Sage Foundation, 1910.

Geisler, Gertrude. "Getting to Know Grandma." http://www.andrew.cmu.edu/user/ramey/GettingToKnowGrandma/Contents.htm.

Lattimore, Florence. "Pittsburgh as a Foster Mother." In *The Pittsburgh District: The Civic Frontage,* edited by Paul U. Kellog, 337–452. New York: Russell Sage Foundation, 1914.

Laughlin, Lynda. *Who's Minding the Kids? Child Care Arrangements: Spring 2005 and Summer 2006.* Current Population Reports, P70-121. U.S. Census Bureau, Washington, D.C., 2010.

Liveright, Alice F. *Poor Relief Administration in Pennsylvania.* Harrisburg, Pa.: State Department of Welfare, 1934.

Morrison, Anna Canady. "Study of One Hundred Forty-One Dependent Negro Children Placed in Boarding Homes by the Juvenile Court of Allegheny County." Master's thesis, University of Pittsburgh, 1925.

Moss, Margaret Steel. "Ellen C. Potter, M.D., F.A.C.P." *Public Administration Review* 1, no. 4 (1941): 351–62.

Oseroff A.M., Abraham. "Report of the Allegheny County Committee Public Charities Association of Pennsylvania on Subsidized Institutions for the Care of Dependent, Delinquent, and Crippled Children." Public Charities Association of Pennsylvania, 1915.

Pennsylvania Department of Welfare, Rural Child Welfare Unit. "History of Child Care in Pennsylvania." 1940.

The Pittsburgh Courier, City Edition. Pittsburgh. Consulted 1912–41.

Russell, C. "On Some Aspects of Slojd." *Parents Review* 4 (1893/94): 321–33.

Salomon, Otto A. *The Theory of Educational Sloyd.* Boston: Silver, Burdett and Company, 1900.

Slingerland, William H. *Child Placing in Families: A Manual for Students and Social Workers.* New York: Russell Sage Foundation, 1919.

———. *Child Welfare Work in Pennsylvania: A Cooperative Study of Child-Helping Agencies and Institutions.* New York: Russell Sage Foundation, Department of Child Helping, 1915.

Smith, Anne Rylance. "Study of Girls in Pittsburgh." Pittsburgh: Central YWCA of Pittsburgh, 1925.

Strauss, Lillian L., and Edwin P. Rome. *The Child and the Law in Pennsylvania.* Philadelphia: Public Charities Association of Pennsylvania, 1943.

Thurston, Henry W. *The Dependent Child: A Story of Changing Aims and Methods in the Care of Dependent Children.* New York: Columbia University Press, 1930.

U.S. Bureau of the Census. "Income, Poverty, and Health Insurance Coverage in the United States: 2009." Report P60, n.238, table B-2, pp. 62–67.

White House Conference on the Care of Dependent Children. "Proceedings of the Conference on the Care of Dependent Children." Washington, D.C., 1909.

Yarbrough, Dean Scruggs. "The Educational Status of Negro Public School Children as Reflecting Economic and Social Problems." Master's thesis, University of Pittsburgh, 1926.

Secondary Sources

Anderson, James D. *The Education of Blacks in the South, 1860–1935.* Chapel Hill: University of North Carolina, 1988.

Antler, Joyce. *The Educated Woman and Professionalization: The Struggle for a New Feminine Identity, 1890–1920.* New York: Garland, 1987.

Ashby, LeRoy. *Endangered Children: Dependency, Neglect, and Abuse in American History.* New York: Twayne Publishers, 1997.

———. *Saving the Waifs: Reformers and Dependent Children, 1890–1917.* Philadelphia: Temple University Press, 1984.

Askeland, Lori. "Informal Adoption, Apprentices, and Indentured Children in the Colonial Era and the New Republic, 1605–1850." In *Children and Youth in Adoption, Orphanages, and Foster Care: A Historical Handbook and Guide,* edited by Lori Askeland, 3–16. Westport, Conn.: Greenwood Press, 2006.

Bartlett, David C., and Larry A. McClellan. "The Final Ministry of Amanda Berry Smith: An Orphanage in Harvey, Illinois, 1895–1918." *Illinois Heritage* 1, no. 2 (1998): 20–25.

Beatty, Barbara. *Preschool Education in America: The Culture of Young Children from the Colonial Era to the Present*. New Haven: Yale University Press, 1995.

Belfour, Stanton. "Charles Avery, Early Pittsburgh Philanthropist." *Western Pennsylvania Historical Magazine* 43 (March 1960): 19–22.

Bellingham, Bruce William. "Little Wanderers: A Sociohistorical Study of Nineteenth Century Origins of Child Fostering and Adoption Reform Based on Early Records of the New York Aid Society." PhD diss., University of Pennsylvania, 1984.

Billingsley, Andrew, and Jeanne M. Giovanni. *Children of the Storm: Black Children and American Child Welfare*. New York: Harcourt, 1972.

Blair, Jennifer. "Women Have a Legacy of Selfless Service." *Alabama Baptist Historian* 37, no. 2 (2001): 78–81.

Blassingame, John W. *The Slave Community: Plantation Life in the Antebellum South*. New York: Oxford University Press, 1972.

Bodnar, John. *The Transplanted: A History of Immigrants in Urban America*. Bloomington, IN, 1985.

Bodnar, John, Roger D. Simon, and Michael P. Weber. *Lives of Their Own: Blacks, Italians, and Poles in Pittsburgh, 1910–1960*. Urbana: University of Illinois Press, 1982.

Bordin, Ruth. *Woman and Temperance: The Quest for Power and Liberty, 1873–1900*. 2nd ed. Philadelphia: Temple University Press, 1981.

Boris, Eileen. *Home to Work: Motherhood and the Politics of Industrial Homework in the United States*. Cambridge: Cambridge University Press, 1994.

Boylan, Anne M. *The Origins of Women's Activism: New York and Boston, 1797–1840*. Chapel Hill: University of North Carolina Press, 2002.

Broder, Sherri. *Tramps, Unfit Mothers, and Neglected Children: Negotiating the Family in Nineteenth-Century Philadelphia*. Philadelphia: University of Pennsylvania Press, 2002.

Brown, Elsa Barkley. "Maggie Lena Walker and the Independent Order of St. Luke." *Signs* 14, no. 3 (1989): 610–33.

Brunger, Ronald A. "The Ladies Aid Societies in Michigan Methodism." *Methodist History* 5, no. 2 (1967): 31.

Byars, Lauretta F. "Lexington's Colored Orphan Industrial Home, 1892–1913." *Register of the Kentucky Historical Society* 89, no. 2 (1991): 147.

Carnegie Library of Pittsburgh, Neighborhoods Exhibit. "North Side: Charles Avery." http://www.clpgh.org/exhibit.neighborhoods/northside/nor_n110.html.

Carp, E. Wayne. "Orphanages: The Strengths and Weaknesses of a Macroscopic View." *Reviews in American History* 27, no. 1 (1999): 105–11.

Cavalla, Dominick. *Muscles and Morals: Organized Playgrounds and Urban Reform, 1880–1920*. Philadelphia: University of Pennsylvania Press, 1981.

Child Welfare League of America. "The History of White House Conferences on Children and Youth." Arlington, Va., 2008.

Ciani, Kyle E. "Childcare in Paradise: The Boundaries of Reform in San Diego, 1850s–1940s." Forthcoming, manuscript in possession of author, 2009.

Clapp, Elizabeth J. *Mothers of All Children: Women Reformers and the Rise of Juvenile Courts in Progressive Era America*. University Park: Pennsylvania State University Press, 1998.

Clark-Lewis, Elizabeth. *Living In, Living Out: African American Domestics and the Great Migration*. New York: Kodansha America, Inc., 1996.

Clement, Priscilla Ferguson. "Children and Charity: Orphanages in New Orleans, 1817–1914." *Louisiana History* 27, no. 4 (1986): 337–51.

Cmiel, Kenneth. *A Home of Another Kind: One Chicago Orphanage and the Tangle of Child Welfare*. Chicago: University of Chicago Press, 1995.

Coburn, Carol K. "Ethnicity, Religion, and Gender: The Women of Block, Kansas, 1868–1940." *Great Plains Quarterly* 8, no. 4 (1988): 222.

Cohen, Sally S. *Championing Child Care*. New York: Columbia University Press, 2001.

Coltrane, Scott. *Family Man: Fatherhood, Housework, and Gender Equity*. New York: Oxford University Press, 1996.

Connor, Michael E., and Joseph L. White. "Fatherhood in Contemporary Black America: Invisible but Present." In *Black Fathers: An Invisible Presence in America*, edited by Michael E. Connor and Joseph L. White, 3–16. Mahwah, N.J.: Lawrence Erlbaum Associates, 2006.

Contosta, David R. *Philadelphia's Progressive Orphanage: The Carson Valley School*. University Park: Pennsylvania State University Press, 1997.

Costin, Lela B. *Two Sisters for Social Justice: A Biography of Grace and Edith Abbott*. Urbana: University of Illinois Press, 1983.

Cott, Nancy F. *The Bonds of Womanhood: "Woman's Sphere" in New England, 1780–1835*. New Haven: Yale University Press, 1977.

———. *The Grounding of Modern Feminism*. New Haven: Yale University Press, 1987.

———. "On Men's History and Women's History." In *Meanings for Manhood: Constructions of Masculinity in Victorian America*, edited by Mark C. Carnes and Clyde Griffen, 205–12. Chicago: University of Chicago Press, 1990.

Creagh, Dianne. "Science, Social Work, and Bureaucracy: Cautious Developments in Adoption and Foster Care, 1930–1969." In *Children and Youth in Adoption, Orphanages, and Foster Care: A Historical Handbook and Guide*, edited by Lori Askeland, 31–44. Westport, Conn.: Greenwood Press, 2006.

Crenson, Matthew A. *Building the Invisible Orphanage: A Prehistory of the American Welfare System*. Cambridge, Mass.: Harvard University Press, 1998.

Demos, John. "The Changing Faces of Fatherhood." In *Father and Child: Developmental and Clinical Perspectives*, edited by Stanley H. Cath, Alan R. Gurwitt, and John Munder Ross, 425–45. Boston: Little, Brown, 1982.

Denton, Virginia Lantz. *Booker T. Washington and the Adult Education Movement*. Gainesville: University Press of Florida, 1993.

DeVault, Ileen A. *Sons and Daughters of Labor: Class and Clerical Work in Turn-of-the-Century Pittsburgh*. Ithaca: Cornell University Press, 1990.

Dickerson, Dennis C. "The Black Church in Industrializing Western Pennsylvania, 1870–1950." In *African Americans in Pennsylvania: Shifting Historical Perspectives*, edited by Joe Wiliam Trotter and Eric Ledell Smith, 388–402. University Park: Pennsylvania State University Press, 1997.

Donovan, Mary Sudman. "Zealous Evangelists: The Woman's Auxiliary to the Board of Missions." *Historical Magazine of the Protestant Episcopal Church* 51, no. 4 (1982): 371.

Downs, Susan Whitelaw, and Michael W. Sherraden. "The Orphan Asylum in the Nineteenth Century." *Social Service Review* 57 (June 1983): 272–90.

Dulberger, Judith A. *"Mother Donit fore the Best": Correspondence of a Nineteenth-Century Orphan Asylum*. Syracuse: Syracuse University Press, 1996.

Dunaway, Wilma A. *The African-American Family in Slavery and Emancipation*. Cambridge: Cambridge University Press, 2003.

Dyer, Ervin. "Black History Month: City's Well-Off Assisted Black Orphans in 1880." *Pittsburgh Post-Gazette*, February 1, 2006.

Edwards, Laura. *Gendered Strife and Confusion: The Political Culture of Reconstruction*. Urbana: University of Illinois Press, 1997.

Elman, Cheryl, and Andrew S. London. "Sociohistorical and Demographic Perspectives on Remarriage in 1910." *Social Science History* 26 (2002): 199–241.

Enstad, Nan. *Ladies of Labor, Girls of Adventure: Working Women, Popular Culture, and Labor Politics at the Turn of the Twentieth Century*. New York: Columbia University Press, 1999.

Epstein, Barbara Lee. *The Politics of Domesticity: Women, Evangelism, and Temperance in Nineteenth-Century America*. Middletown: Wesleyan University Press, 1981.

Faires, Nora. "Immigrants and Industry: Peopling the 'Iron City.'" In *City at the Point: Essays on the Social History of Pittsburgh*, edited by Samuel P. Hayes, 5–31. Pittsburgh: University of Pittsburgh Press, 1989.

Faulkner, Carol. *Women's Radical Reconstruction: The Freedmen's Aid Movement*. Philadelphia: University of Pennsylvania Press, 2004.

Folbre, Nancy, and Michael Bittman, eds. *Family Time: The Social Organization of Care*. London: Routledge, 2004.

Fousekis, Natalie. "Fighting for Our Children: Women's Activism and the Battle for Child Care in California, 1940–1965." PhD diss., University of North Carolina, 2000.

Frank, Stephen M. *Life with Father: Parenthood and Masculinity in the Nineteenth-Century American North*. Edited by Joan E. Cashin and Ronald G. Walters. Baltimore: Johns Hopkins University Press, 1998.

Frankel, Noralee, and Nancy S. Dye. *Gender, Class, Race and Reform in the Progressive Era*. Lexington: University Press of Kentucky, 1991.

Franklin, John Hope. "African American Families: A Historical Note." In *Black Families*, edited by Harriette Pipes McAdoo, 3–6. 4th ed. Thousand Oaks, Calif.: Sage Publications, 2007.

Fraser, Nancy, and Linda Gordon. "A Genealogy of 'Dependency': Tracing a Key-word of the U.S. Welfare State." *Signs* 19, no. 2 (1994): 309–36.

Freedman, Estelle B. *Maternal Justice: Miriam Van Waters and the Female Reform Tradition.* Chicago: University of Chicago Press, 1996.

Friedman, Reena Sigman. *These Are Our Children: Jewish Orphanages in the United States, 1880–1925.* Hanover: Brandeis University Press, 1994.

Friedman, S. Morgan. "The Inflation Calculator." http://www.westegg.com/inflation/.

Geer, Emily Apt. "Lucy W. Hays and the Woman's Home Missionary Society." *Hayes Historical Journal* 4, no. 4 (1984): 5.

Geneva College. "Mission Statement." Beaver Falls, Pa. http://www.geneva.edu/object/aboutgeneva_mission.html.

Genovese, Eugene D. *Roll, Jordon, Roll: The World the Slaves Made.* New York: Pantheon Books, 1974.

Getis, Victoria. *The Juvenile Court and the Progressives.* Urbana: University of Illinois Press, 2000.

Gill, Brian P., Jacob W. Dembosky, and Jonathan P. Caulkins. *A "Noble Bet" in Early Care and Education: Lessons from One Community's Experience.* Santa Monica, Calif.: RAND, 2002.

Ginzberg, Lori. *Women and the Work of Benevolence: Morality, Politics, and Class in the Nineteenth-Century United States.* New Haven: Yale University Press, 1990.

Glasco, Laurence. "Double Burden: The Black Experience in Pittsburgh." In *City at the Point: Essays on the Social History of Pittsburgh*, edited by Samuel P. Hays, 69–109. Pittsburgh: University of Pittsburgh Press, 1989.

———. "Optimism, Dilemmas, and Progress: The Pittsburgh Survey and Black Americans." In *Pittsburgh Surveyed: Social Science and Social Reform in the Early Twentieth Century*, edited by Maurine W. Greenwald and Margo Anderson, 205–20. Pittsburgh: University of Pittsburgh Press, 1996.

———. "Taking Care of Business: The Black Entrepreneurial Elite in Turn-of-the-Century Pittsburgh." *Pittsburgh History* 78, no. 4 (1995–96): 177–82.

Goodwin, Joanne L. *Gender and the Politics of Welfare Reform: Mothers' Pensions in Chicago, 1911–1929.* Chicago: University of Chicago Press, 1997.

Gordon, Linda. "Black and White Visions of Welfare: Women's Welfare Activism, 1890–1935." *Journal of American History* 78 (September 1991): 559–90.

———. *The Great Arizona Orphan Abduction.* Cambridge, Mass.: Harvard University Press, 1999.

———. *Heroes of Their Own Lives: The Politics and History of Family Violence, Boston 1880–1960.* New York: Penguin Books, 1988.

———. *Pitied But Not Entitled: Single Mothers and the History of Welfare, 1890–1935.* New York: Simon and Schuster, 1994.

———. "Putting Children First: Women, Maternalism, and Welfare in the Early Twentieth Century." In *U.S. History as Women's History: New Feminist Essays*, edited by Linda K. Kerber, Alice Kessler-Harris, and Kathryn Kish Sklar, 63–86. Chapel Hill: University of North Carolina Press, 1995.

———. *Women, the State, and Welfare*. Madison: University of Wisconsin Press, 1990.

Gottlieb, Peter. *Making Their Own Way: Southern Blacks' Migration to Pittsburgh, 1916–1930*. Urbana: University of Illinois Press, 1987.

———. "Migration and Jobs: The New Black Workers in Pittsburgh, 1916–1930." In *African Americans in Pennsylvania: Shifting Historical Perspectives*, edited by Joe William Trotter Jr. and Eric Ledell Smith, 272–86. Harrisburg: Pennsylvania Historical and Museum Commission, 1997.

Greenwald, Maurine Weiner. "Women and Class in Pittsburgh, 1850–1920." In *City at the Point: A Social History of Pittsburgh*, edited by Samuel P. Hays, 33–67. Pittsburgh: University of Pittsburgh Press, 1989.

Greenwald, Maurine W., and Margo Anderson, eds. *Pittsburgh Surveyed: Social Science and Social Reform in the Early Twentieth Century*. Pittsburgh: University of Pittsburgh Press, 1996.

Griswold, Robert L. *Fatherhood in America: A History*. New York: BasicBooks, 1993.

Grossman, James R. *Land of Hope: Chicago, Black Southerners, and the Great Migration*. Chicago: University of Chicago Press, 1989.

Gutkind, Richard David. "Desegregation of Pittsburgh Public Schools, 1968–1980: A Study of the Superintendent and Educational Policy Dynamics." PhD diss., University of Pittsburgh, 1983.

Gutman, Herbert. *The Black Family in Slavery and Freedom, 1750–1925*. New York: Vintage Books, 1976.

Hacsi, Timothy A. *Second Home: Orphan Asylums and Poor Families in America*. Cambridge, Mass.: Harvard University Press, 1997.

Hamer, Jennifer. *What It Means to Be Daddy: Fatherhood for Black Men Living Away from Their Children*. New York: Columbia University, 2001.

Harris, Leslie M. *In the Shadow of Slavery: African Americans in New York City, 1626–1863*. Chicago: University of Chicago Press, 2003.

Haskell Indian National University. "School History." Lawrence, Kans. http://www.haskell.edu/haskell/about.asp.

Hewitt, Nancy A. *Women's Activism and Social Change: Rochester, New York 1822 1872*. Ithaca: Cornell University Press, 1984.

Hicks, Cheryl D. "'In Danger of Becoming Morally Depraved': Single Black Women, Working-Class Black Families, and New York State's Wayward Minor Laws, 1917–1928." *University of Pennsylvania Law Review* 151, no. 6 (2003): 2077–121.

Higginbotham, Evelyn Brooks. "The Metalanguage of Race." *Signs* 17, no. 2 (1992): 251–74.

———. *Righteous Discontent: The Women's Movement in the Black Baptist Church, 1880–1920*. Cambridge, Mass.: Harvard University, 1993.

Hine, Darline Clark. "Black Migration to the Urban Midwest: The Gender Dimension, 1915–1945." In *The Great Migration in Historical Perspective: New Dimensions of Race, Class, and Gender*, edited by Joe William Trotter, 127–46. Bloomington: Indiana University Press, 1991.

Holt, Marilyn Irvin. "Adoption Reform, Orphan Trains, and Child-Saving, 1851–1929." In *Children and Youth in Adoption, Orphanages, and Foster Care: A Historical Handbook and Guide*, edited by Lori Askeland, 17–30. Westport, Conn.: Greenwood Press, 2006.

———. *The Orphan Trains: Placing Out in America*. Lincoln: University of Nebraska Press, 1992.

Hunter, Barbara Jean. "The Public Education of Blacks in the City of Pittsburgh, 1920–1950: Actions and Reactions of the Black Community in Pursuit of Educational Equality." PhD diss., University of Pittsburgh, 1987.

Hunter, Tera. *To 'Joy My Freedom: Southern Black Women's Lives and Labors After the Civil War*. Cambridge, Mass.: Harvard University Press, 1997.

Igra, Anna R. *Wives without Husbands: Marriage, Desertion, and Welfare in New York, 1900–1935*. Chapel Hill: University of North Carolina Press, 2007.

Jacobson, Matthew Frye. *Whiteness of a Different Color: European Immigrants and the Alchemy of Race*. Cambridge, Mass.: Harvard University Press, 1998.

Jenkins, Gary C. "Almira S. Steele and the Steele Home for Needy Children." *Tennessee Historical Quarterly* 48, no. 1 (1989): 29–36.

Jewell, K. Sue. *Survival of the African American Family: The Institutional Impact of U.S. Social Policy*. Westport, Conn.: Praeger Publishers, 2003.

Johansen, Shawn. *Family Men: Middle-Class Fatherhood in Early Industrializing America*. New York: Routledge, 2001.

Jones, Adrienne Lash. "Struggle among Saints: African American Women and the YWCA, 1870–1920." In *Men and Women Adrift: The YMCA and the YWCA in the City*, edited by Nina Mjagkij and Margaret Spratt, 160–87. New York: New York University Press, 1997.

Jones, Jacqueline. *Labor of Love, Labor of Sorrow: Black Women, Work, and the Family from Slavery to the Present*. New York: BasicBooks, 1985.

Jones, Marshall B. "Crisis of the American Orphanage, 1931–1940." *Social Service Review* 63, no. 4 (1989): 613–29.

Katz, Michael B. "The History of an Impudent Poor Woman in New York City from 1918–1923." In *The Uses of Charity: The Poor on Relief in the Nineteenth Century Metropolis*, edited by Peter Mandler, 227–46. Philadelphia: University of Pennsylvania Press, 1990.

———. *In the Shadow of the Poorhouse: A Social History of Welfare in America*. New York: BasicBooks, 1987.

Kerber, Linda K. "Separate Spheres, Female Worlds, Woman's Place: The Rhetoric of Women's History." *Journal of American History* 75 (1988): 9–39.

Kessler-Harris, Alice. *Out to Work: A History of Wage-Earning Women in the United States*. New York: Oxford University Press, 1982.

———. *A Woman's Wage: Historical Meanings and Social Consequences*. Lexington: University Press of Kentucky, 1990.

Kleinberg, S. J. "Seeking the Meaning of Life: The Pittsburgh Survey and the Family." In *Pittsburgh Surveyed: Social Science and Social Reform in the Early Twentieth*

Century, edited by Maurine W. Greenwald and Margo Anderson, 88–105. Pittsburgh: University of Pittsburgh Press, 1996.

———. *Shadow of the Mills: Working-Class Families in Pittsburgh, 1870–1907.* Pittsburgh: University of Pittsburgh Press, 1989.

———. *Widows and Orphans First: The Family Economy and Social Welfare Policy, 1880–1939.* Urbana: University of Illinois Press, 2006.

Kornbluh, Felicia A. "The New Literature on Gender and the Welfare State: The U.S. Case." *Feminist Studies* 22, no. 1 (1996): 170–97.

Koven, Seth, and Sonya Michel, eds. *Mothers of a New World: Maternalist Politics and the Origins of Welfare States.* London: Routledge, 1993.

Kristufek, Richard. "The Immigrant and the Pittsburgh Public Schools: 1870–1940." EdD diss., University of Pittsburgh, 1975.

Kunzel, Regina G. *Fallen Women, Problem Girls: Unmarried Mothers and the Professionalization of Social Work, 1890–1945.* New Haven: Yale University Press, 1993.

Ladd-Taylor, Molly. *Mother-Work: Women, Child Welfare, and the State, 1890–1930.* Urbana: University of Illinois Press, 1994.

———. "Toward Defining Maternalism in U.S. History." *Journal of Women's History* 5, no. 2 (1993): 110–13.

LaRossa, Ralph. *The Modernization of Fatherhood: A Social and Political History.* Chicago: University of Chicago Press, 1997.

Levy, Denise Urias, and Sonya Michel. "More Can Be Less: Child Care and Welfare Reform in the United States." In *Child Care Policy at the Crossroads: Gender and Welfare State Restructuring,* edited by Sonya Michel and Rianne Mahon, 239–63. New York: Routledge, 2002.

Lincoln University. "About Lincoln University." Chester County, Pa. http://www .lincoln.edu/about.html.

Lindenmeyer, Kriste. *"A Right to Childhood": The U.S. Children's Bureau and Child Welfare.* Urbana: University of Illinois Press, 1997.

Lobes, Loretta. "'Hearts All Aflame': Women and the Development of New Forms of Social Service Organizations, 1870–1930." PhD diss., Carnegie Mellon University, 1996.

Lubove, Roy. "Pittsburgh and the Uses of Social Welfare History." In *City at the Point: Essays on the Social History of Pittsburgh,* edited by Samuel P. Hays, 295–326. Pittsburgh: University of Pittsburgh Press, 1989.

———. *The Professional Altruist: The Emergence of Social Work as a Career, 1880–1930.* Cambridge, Mass.: Harvard University Press, 1965.

Lupton, Deborah, and Lesley Barclay. *Constructing Fatherhood: Discourses and Experiences.* London: Sage Publications, 1997.

Mabee, Carlton. "Charity in Travail: Two Orphan Asylums for Blacks." *New York History* 55 (1974): 55–77.

May, Elaine Tyler. *Great Expectations: Marriage and Divorce in Post-Victorian America.* Chicago: University of Chicago Press, 1980.

McCarthy, Kathleen D., ed. *Lady Bountiful Revisited: Women, Philanthropy, and Power*. New Brunswick: Rutgers University Press, 1990.

Michel, Sonya. *Children's Interests/Mothers' Rights: The Shaping of America's Child Care Policy*. New Haven: Yale University Press, 1999.

Michel, Sonya, and Rianne Mahon, eds. *Child Care Policy at the Crossroads: Gender and Welfare State Restructuring*. New York: Routledge, 2002.

Mink, Gwendolyn. *The Wages of Motherhood: Inequality in the Welfare State, 1917–1942*. Ithaca: Cornell University Press, 1995.

Mitchell, Patricia Pugh, Margaret C. Albert, and Laurence Glasco. *From Colored Orphans to Youth Development: The 125-Year History of Three Rivers Youth, 1880–2005*. Pittsburgh: University of Pittsburgh, 2006.

Mjagkij, Nina, and Margaret Spratt, eds. *Men and Women Adrift: The YMCA and the YWCA in the City*. New York: New York University Press, 1997.

Modell, Judith S. *A Sealed and Secret Kinship: The Culture of Policies and Practices in American Adoption*. New York: Berghahn Books, 2002.

Morgan, Jennifer L. *Laboring Women: Reproduction and Gender in New World Slavery*. Philadelphia: University of Pennsylvania Press, 2004.

Morton, Marian J. "Institutionalizing Inequalities: Black Children and Child Welfare in Cleveland, 1859–1998." *Journal of Social History* 34, no. 1 (2000): 141.

Moynihan, Daniel P. "The Negro Family: The Case for National Action." Washington, D.C.: Office of Policy Planning and Research, United States Department of Labor, March 1965.

Muncy, Robyn. *Creating a Female Dominion in American Reform, 1890–1935*. Oxford: Oxford University Press, 1991.

Murdoch, Lydia. *Imagined Orphans: Poor Families, Child Welfare, and Contested Citizenship in London*. New Brunswick: Rutgers University Press, 2006.

Nelson, Stanley. "Publisher Robert Lee Vann." *The Black Press: Soldiers without Swords*. PBS. http://www.pbs.org/blackpress/news_bios/courier.html.

Odem, Mary E. *Delinquent Daughters: Protecting and Policing Adolescent Female Sexuality in the United States, 1885–1920*. Chapel Hill: University of North Carolina Press, 1995.

O'Donnell, Sandra M. "The Care of Dependent African-American Children in Chicago: The Struggle between Black Self-Help and Professionalism." *Journal of Social History* 27, no. 4 (1994): 763–76.

O'Neill, William L. *Everyone Was Brave: A History of Feminism in America*. New York: Quadrangle Books, 1971.

Parke, Ross D., and Peter Stearns. "Fathers and Child Rearing." In *Children in Time and Place: Developmental and Historical Insights*, edited by Glen H. Elder Jr. and John Modell, 147–70. Cambridge: Cambridge University Press, 1993.

Pitts, Leonard, Jr. *Becoming Dad: Black Men and the Journey to Fatherhood*. Chicago: Agate, 2006.

Platt, Anthony. *The Child Savers: The Invention of Delinquency*. Chicago: University of Chicago Press, 1974.

Pleck, Elizabeth Hafkin. *Black Migration and Poverty: Boston 1865–1900.* New York: Academic Press, 1979.

———. *Domestic Tyranny: The Making of Social Policy against Family Violence from Colonial Times to the Present.* New York: Oxford University Press, 1987.

Pleck, Joseph H. "American Fathering in Historical Perspective." In *Changing Men: New Directions on Men and Masculinity,* edited by Michael S. Kimmel, 83–97. Newbury Park, Calif.: Sage Publications, 1987.

Polakow, Valerie. *Who Cares for Our Children? The Child Care Crisis in the Other America.* New York: Teachers College Press, 2007.

Polster, Gary Edward. *Inside Looking Out: The Cleveland Jewish Orphan Asylum, 1868–1924.* Kent: Kent State University Press, 1990.

Presbyterian Historical Society. "A Brief History of the Presbyterian Church in this Country." Philadelphia. http://www.history.pcusa.org/pres_hist/briefhist.html.

Pritchard, Linda K. "The Soul of the City: A Social History of Religion in Pittsburgh." In *City at the Point: Essays on the Social History of Pittsburgh,* edited by Samuel P. Hays, 327–60. Pittsburgh: University of Pittsburgh Press, 1989.

Provenzo, Eugene F. *Du Bois on Education.* Lanham, Md.: Rowman and Littlefield, 2002.

Rafter, Nicole Hahn. *Partial Justice: Women in State Prisons, 1800–1935.* Boston: Northeastern University Press, 1985.

Regosin, Elizabeth. *Freedom's Promise: Ex-Slave Families and Citizenship in the Age of Emancipation.* Charlottesville: University Press of Virginia, 2002.

Riess, Steven A. *City Games: The Evolution of American Urban Society and the Rise of Sports.* Urbana: University of Illinois Press, 1996.

Roberts, Dorothy. "The Absent Black Father." In *Lost Fathers: The Politics of Fatherlessness in America,* edited by Cynthia R. Daniels, 145–61. New York: St. Martin's Press, 1998.

Roediger, David R. *The Wages of Whiteness: Race and the Making of the American Working Class.* Rev. ed. London: Verso, 1999.

Rose, Elizabeth. *A Mother's Job: The History of Day Care, 1890–1960.* New York: Oxford University Press, 1999.

Rothman, David J. *The Discovery of the Asylum: Social Order and Disorder in the New Republic.* Boston: Little, Brown, 1971.

Rotundo, E. Anthony. "American Fatherhood: A Historical Perspective." *American Behavioral Scientist* 29 (September/October 1985): 7–25.

———. *American Manhood: Transformations in Masculinity from the Revolution to the Modern Era.* New York: BasicBooks, 1993.

Salem, Dorothy. *To Better Our World: Black Women in Organized Reform, 1890–1920.* Black Women in United States History, edited by Darlene Clark Hine 14. New York: Carlson Publishing, Inc., 1990.

Sappol, Michael. "The Uses of Philanthropy: The Colored Orphan Asylum and Its Clients." Masters thesis, Columbia University, 1990.

Schlossman, Steven. *Love and the American Delinquent*. Chicago: University of Chicago Press, 1977.

———. *Transforming Juvenile Justice: Reform Ideals and Institutional Realities, 1825–1920*. Dekalb: Northern Illinois Press, 2005.

Schwalm, Leslie A. *A Hard Fight for We: Women's Transition from Slavery to Freedom in South Carolina*. Urbana: University of Illinois Press, 1997.

Scott, Anne Firor. *Natural Allies: Women's Associations in American History*. Urbana: University of Illinois Press, 1991.

Scott, Rebecca J. "The Battle over the Child: Child Apprenticeship and the Freedman's Bureau in North Carolina." In *Growing Up in America: Children in Historical Perspective*, edited by N. Ray Hiner and Joseph M. Hawes, 193–207. Urbana: University of Illinois Press, 1985.

Shaw, Stephanie J. "Black Club Women and the Creation of the National Association of Colored Women." *Journal of Women's History* 3 (1991): 10–25.

———. *What a Woman Ought to Be and to Do: Black Professional Women Workers during the Jim Crow Era*. Chicago: University of Chicago Press, 1996.

Sims, Mary S. *The Natural History of a Social Institution: The Young Women's Christian Association*. New York: The Woman's Press, 1936.

Sklar, Kathryn Kish. "The Historical Foundations of Women's Power in the Creation of the American Welfare State, 1830–1930." In *Mothers of a New World: Maternalist Politics and the Origins of the Welfare State*, edited by Seth Koven and Sonya Michel, 43–93. London: Routledge, 1993.

Skocpol, Theda. *Protecting Soldiers and Mothers: The Political Origins of Social Policy in the United States*. Cambridge, Mass.: Harvard University Press, 1992.

Smith, Julie L. "Child Care, Institutions, and the Best Interest of the Child: Pittsburgh's Protestant Orphan Asylum and the Home for Friendless Children, 1832–1928." PhD diss., Carnegie Mellon University, 1994.

Smoot, Pamela Annette. "Self Help and Institution Building in Pittsburgh, Pennsylvania, 1830–1945." PhD diss., Michigan State University, 1998.

Sparks, Edith. *Capital Intentions: Female Proprietors in San Francisco, 1850–1920*. Chapel Hill: University of North Carolina Press, 2006.

Spratt, Margaret. "To Be Separate or One: The Issue of Race in the History of the Pittsburgh and Cleveland YWCAs, 1920–1946." In *Men and Women Adrift: The YMCA and the YWCA in the City*, edited by Nina Mjagkij and Margaret Spratt, 188–205. New York: New York University Press, 1997.

Stanley, Amy Dru. *From Bondage to Contract: Wage Labor, Marriage, and the Market in the Age of Slave Emancipation*. Cambridge: Cambridge University Press, 1998.

Stearns, Peter. *Be a Man! Males in Modern Society*. New York: Holmes and Meier, 1979.

———. "Fatherhood in Historical Perspective: The Role of Social Change." In *Fatherhood and Families in Cultural Context*, edited by Frederick W. Bozett and Shirley M. H. Hanson, 28–52. New York: Springer, 1991.

Steinfels, Margaret O'Brien. *Who's Minding the Children?: The History and Politics of Day Care in America.* New York: Simon and Schuster, 1973.

Stevenson, Brenda E. *Life in Black and White: Family and Community in the Slave South.* New York: Oxford University Press, 1996.

Stoltzfus, Emilie. *Citizen, Mother, Worker: Debating Public Responsibility for Child Care after the Second World War.* Chapel Hill: University of North Carolina Press, 2003.

Sudarkasa, Niara. "African American Female-Headed Households: Some Neglected Dimensions." In *Black Families,* edited by Harriette Pipes McAdoo, 172–83. 4th ed. Thousand Oaks, Calif.: Sage Publications, 2007.

Tarr, Joel A. *Devastation and Renewal: An Environmental History of Pittsburgh and Its Region.* Pittsburgh: University of Pittsburgh Press, 2003.

Terborg-Penn, Rosalyn. *African American Women in the Struggle for the Vote, 1850–1920.* Bloomington: Indiana University Press, 1998.

Three Rivers Youth. "History." Pittsburgh. http://www.threeriversyouth.org.

Tiffin, Susan. *In Whose Best Interest? Child Welfare Reform in the Progressive Era,* Westport, Conn.: Greenwood Press, 1982.

Todar, Kenneth. *Todar's Online Textbook of Bacteriology.* University of Wisconsin–Madison. http://www.textbookofbacteriology.net.

Tolnay, Stewart E. *The Bottom Rung: African American Family Life on Southern Farms.* Urbana: University of Illinois Press, 1999.

———. "The Great Migration and Changes to the Northern Black Family, 1940–1990." *Social Forces* 75, no. 4 (1997): 1213–38.

Trotter, Joe William, Jr. "Reflections on the Great Migration to Western Pennsylvania." *Pittsburgh History* 78, no. 4 (1995–96): 153–57.

———. *River Jordan: African American Urban Life in the Ohio Valley.* Lexington: University Press of Kentucky, 1998.

Trotter, Joe William, Jr., and Eric Ledell Smith, eds. *African Americans in Pennsylvania: Shifting Historical Perspectives.* Harrisburg: Pennsylvania Historical and Museum Commission, 1997.

United Way of Allegheny County. "Timeline." Pittsburgh. http://www.unitedwaypittsburgh.org/AboutUs.aspx?id=172.

Weber, Michael P. "Residential and Occupational Patterns of Ethnic Minorities in Nineteenth Century Pittsburgh." *Pennsylvania History* 44 (1977): 317–34.

Weisenfeld, Judith. *African American Women and Christian Activism: New York's Black YWCA, 1905–1945.* Cambridge, Mass.: Harvard University Press, 1997.

White, Deborah Gray. *Ar'nt' I a Woman?: Female Slaves in the Plantation South.* New York: Norton, 1985.

Whiteley, Marilyn Fordig. ""Doing Just About What They Please": Ladies' Aids in Ontario Methodism." *Ontario History* 82, no. 4 (1990): 289.

Wilkinson, Patrick. "The Selfless and the Helpless: Maternalist Origins of the U.S. Welfare Policy." *Feminist Studies* 25, no. 3 (1999): 571–97.

Williams, Heather Andrea. *Self-taught: African American Education in Slavery and Freedom*. Chapel Hill: University of North Carolina, 2005.

Williamson, Erik Luther. "'Doing What Had to Be Done': Norwegian Lutheran Ladies Aid Societies of North Dakota." *North Dakota History* 57, no. 2 (1990): 2–13.

Willie, Charles Vert, and Richard J. Reddick. *A New Look at Black Families*. 5 ed. Walnut Creek, Calif.: Altamira Press, 2003.

Youcha, Geraldine. *Minding the Children: Child Care in American from Colonial Times to the Present*. New York: Scribner, 1995.

Zelizer, Viviana. *Pricing the Priceless Child: The Changing Social Value of Children*. New York: BasicBooks, 1985.

Zipf, Karin L. "Reconstructing 'Free Woman': African-American Women, Apprenticeship, and Custody Rights during Reconstruction." *Journal of Women's History* 12, no. 1 (2000): 8–31.

Zmora, Nurith. *Orphanages Reconsidered: Child Care Institutions in Progressive Era Baltimore*. Philadelphia: Temple University Press, 1994.

CREDITS

The author gratefully acknowledges the following organizations that granted permission to reproduce photographs appearing in the specified figures in the book:

Bidwell United Presbyterian Church, Pittsburgh, Pennsylvania: "HCC Board member Mary (Mattie) C. Glasco" (figure 6.1) and "Rev. Benjamin F. Glasco" (figure 6.2).

Legacy Center, Drexel University College of Medicine, p. 1476: "Dr. Ellen C. Potter" (figure 5.2).

Library and Archives Division, Senator John Heinz History Center: "HCC building, Termon Avenue" (figure 5.4).

Staff and Board of Directors of Mars Home for Youth, Mars, Pennsylvania: "UPOH photographs and illustrations, 1880–1929" (figure 5.3) and "UPOH nursery children with staff, 1922" (figure 5.5).

A portion of chapter 4 appeared previously in: Jessie B. Ramey, "'I Dream of Them Almost Every Night': Working Class Fathers and Orphanages in Pittsburgh, 1878–1929," *Journal of Family History* 37, no. 1 (January 2012).

INDEX

JESSIE B. RAMEY is an ACLS New Faculty Fellow in Women's Studies and History at the University of Pittsburgh.

THE WORKING CLASS IN AMERICAN HISTORY

Worker City, Company Town: Iron and Cotton-Worker Protest in Troy
   and Cohoes, New York, 1855–84   *Daniel J. Walkowitz*
Life, Work, and Rebellion in the Coal Fields: The Southern West Virginia
   Miners, 1880–1922   *David Alan Corbin*
Women and American Socialism, 1870–1920   *Mari Jo Buhle*
Lives of Their Own: Blacks, Italians, and Poles in Pittsburgh,
   1900–1960   *John Bodnar, Roger Simon, and Michael P. Weber*
Working-Class America: Essays on Labor, Community, and American
   Society   *Edited by Michael H. Frisch and Daniel J. Walkowitz*
Eugene V. Debs: Citizen and Socialist   *Nick Salvatore*
American Labor and Immigration History, 1877–1920s:
   Recent European Research   *Edited by Dirk Hoerder*
Workingmen's Democracy: The Knights of Labor
   and American Politics   *Leon Fink*
The Electrical Workers: A History of Labor at General Electric
   and Westinghouse, 1923–60   *Ronald W. Schatz*
The Mechanics of Baltimore: Workers and Politics in the Age
   of Revolution, 1763–1812   *Charles G. Steffen*
The Practice of Solidarity: American Hat Finishers in the
   Nineteenth Century   *David Bensman*
The Labor History Reader   *Edited by Daniel J. Leab*
Solidarity and Fragmentation: Working People and Class Consciousness
   in Detroit, 1875–1900   *Richard Oestreicher*
Counter Cultures: Saleswomen, Managers, and Customers in American
   Department Stores, 1890–1940   *Susan Porter Benson*
The New England Working Class and the New Labor History   *Edited by
   Herbert G. Gutman and Donald H. Bell*
Labor Leaders in America   *Edited by Melvyn Dubofsky and
   Warren Van Tine*
Barons of Labor: The San Francisco Building Trades and Union Power
   in the Progressive Era   *Michael Kazin*
Gender at Work: The Dynamics of Job Segregation by Sex during
   World War II   *Ruth Milkman*
Once a Cigar Maker: Men, Women, and Work Culture in American
   Cigar Factories, 1900–1919   *Patricia A. Cooper*
A Generation of Boomers: The Pattern of Railroad Labor Conflict
   in Nineteenth-Century America   *Shelton Stromquist*
Work and Community in the Jungle: Chicago's Packinghouse Workers,
   1894–1922   *James R. Barrett*
Workers, Managers, and Welfare Capitalism: The Shoeworkers and Tanners
   of Endicott Johnson, 1890–1950   *Gerald Zahavi*

The University of Illinois Press
is a founding member of the
Association of American University Presses.

Composed in 10/13 Sabon LT Std Roman
by Celia Shapland
at the University of Illinois Press
Manufactured by Thomson-Shore, Inc.

University of Illinois Press
1325 South Oak Street
Champaign, IL 61820-6903
www.press.uillinois.edu